Jah Kingdom

Jah Kingdom
Rastafarians, Tanzania, and Pan-Africanism
in the Age of Decolonization

....

MONIQUE A. BEDASSE

The University of North Carolina Press   Chapel Hill

© 2017 The University of North Carolina Press
All rights reserved
Set in Charis and Lato by Westchester Publishing Services
Manufactured in the United States of America

The University of North Carolina Press has been a member of the Green Press Initiative since 2003.

Library of Congress Cataloging-in-Publication Data
Names: Bedasse, Monique A., author.
Title: Jah kingdom : Rastafarians, Tanzania, and pan-Africanism in the age of decolonization / Monique A. Bedasse.
Description: Chapel Hill : University of North Carolina Press, [2017] | Includes bibliographical references and index.
Identifiers: LCCN 2017004066 | ISBN 9781469633589 (cloth : alk. paper) | ISBN 9781469633596 (pbk : alk. paper) | ISBN 9781469633602 (ebook)
Subjects: LCSH: Rastafarians—Tanzania. | Tanzania—History—1964- | Blacks—Migrations.
Classification: LCC DT448.2 .B43 2017 | DDC 305.6/996760967809048—dc23
LC record available at https://lccn.loc.gov/2017004066

Cover illustration: *Not Far Away* by Ras Daniel Heartman, used courtesy of Ato Roberts/Ras Daniel Heartman Estate.

Portions of this work were previously published in a different form as "To Set-Up Jah Kingdom: Joshua Mkhululi, Rastafarian Repatriation, and the Black Radical Network in Tanzania," *Journal of Africana Religions* 1, no. 3 (2013): 293–323. It is used here with the permission of Pennsylvania State University Press.

Contents

Acknowledgments, ix

Introduction, 1
Trodding Diaspora

1 Without Vision the People Perish, 20
  The Divine, Regal, and Noble Afrikan Nation

2 Tanzania, 48
  Site of Diaspora Aspiration

3 The Wages of Blackness, 78
  Rastafari and the Politics of Pan-Africanism after Flag Independence

4 Diasporic Dreams, African Nation-State Realities, 106

5 Sow in Tears, Reap in Joy, 135
  Rastafarian Repatriation and the African Liberation Struggle

6 Strange Bedfellows, 169
  Rastafari, C. L. R. James, and the "Africa" in Pan-Africanism

Epilogue, 182

Notes, 191

Bibliography, 225

Index, 245

Illustrations

Ras Daniel Heartman, Ras Ato Kidani Roberts, and Joshua Mkhululi, 124

Signature Rasta colors, 162

Trinity symbol, 163

Beyond reggae and "peace and love," 164

Nyabingi drumming, Tanzania, 165

Acknowledgments

I could not have written this book without Ras Bupe Karudi, and I must begin by thanking him for trusting me with a history he held sacred. The stack of documents he so graciously delivered to me at the University of Dar es Salaam in 2007 provided the foundation for this project. He joined the ancestors in May 2016 and will not see the published text, but it is my sincere hope that he would have recognized himself and the history he helped to make in its pages.

Joshua Mkhululi welcomed me into his home in Arusha, shared stories of his journey, and gave me important documents. I regret that he left this earth in 2009, shortly after we met. My gratitude and respect continue to outlive him.

Special thanks to Ras Ato Kidani Roberts for responding to my numerous calls and text messages whenever I needed to check random details about his experience and that of his brilliant father, the late Ras Daniel Heartman. His keen insights and assessment of the journey added rich texture to this book, and his wit made us fast friends. I also thank Iman Mani for taking the time to talk to me and for sharing details of a very personal experience.

Kisembo Karudi's thoughts pushed me into new analytical spaces and her unique perspective kept me on my toes. I am indebted to her for meeting with me and for always responding to my questions about various aspects of her life. Her razor-sharp sense of humor and warmth quickly blurred the lines between work and merriment.

My research in Tanzania would have been difficult without the many, many acts of kindness and support from two special people who have become good friends: I am indebted to Jotham "Gotta" Warioba and Wende Mponzi. At the University of Dar es Salaam, I was fortunate to have the support of Kai Aldin Mutembei and F. E. M. K. Senkoro.

I am grateful to Peter Pinda for his kind spirit and for the ease with which he spoke to me about his role in the repatriation. Thanks also to Joseph Butiku for talking to me about Nyerere, Jamaica, and pan-Africanism.

Several archivists deserve special mention. The late Louis Marriott directed me to meaningful sources at the Michael Manley Foundation and enthusiastically discussed Manley's engagement with pan-African politics. I thank Jake Homiak for his kindness, deep knowledge of Rastafari, and for helping me navigate the sources at the National Anthropological Archives of the Smithsonian Institution. Along with the staff at the Alma Jordan Library in Trinidad, I thank Johnson Lugoye, librarian at the Nyerere Foundation; Greyson Nyenga, archivist at the Tanzania National Archives; and Emma Harrison at the Black Cultural Archives in Brixton, London.

Several individuals deserve my gratitude for having agreed to talk to me and enriching the book in the process: thanks to Joseph Christie, Errol McDonald, Beverley Manley, Grace Pennicott-Smith, Robin "Jerry" Small, and the late Dudley Thompson.

I have benefited from the kindness of several scholars and friends who have gone beyond the call of duty to offer me substantive feedback. Michael Gomez has taught us how to study Africa and its diaspora in tandem. He has set a standard to which I can only aspire. I thank him for his awe-inspiring work, and for his kindness—he offered game-changing suggestions and encouragement for which I am eternally grateful. I have come to depend on Jonathan Fenderson's fierce intellect, profound grasp of my interventions, and unfiltered feedback. Minkah Makalani and I have had wonderful conversations about black internationalism and C. L. R. James. His fertile mind helped me to hone my ideas. Nathan Connolly's penetrating questions, encouragement, and candor served the book at a crucial point in its gestation. With record speed, Michael Witter read the entire manuscript and asked astute questions that could only come from his impressive mind. Jahlani Niaah offered critical comments and suggestions that pushed me to refine certain arguments. My dear friend and fellow Tanzanianist Alia Paroo encouraged me along the way and asked sharp questions that helped shape the final version of my introduction. Thanks also to Michael Barnett, Jim Brennan, Maurice Hobson, Priya Lal, and Jeffrey Ogbar for generative exchanges and other forms of support.

This book has been with me at several institutions, and I am thankful for the support of individuals at each. In large measure, the Africana Studies and Research Center at Cornell University shaped me as a scholar; from there I thank N'Dri Thérèse Assié-Lumumba, Ayele Bekerie, Abdul Nanji, Locksley Edmondson, and James Turner.

At the University of Miami, Edmund Abaka was always certain of my potential. I thank him for his confidence in me and his unwavering support over the years. Donald Spivey has always been in my corner and has been a trusted mentor and friend. Kate Ramsey's sharp intellect made this book better. Thanks also to Malcolm Frierson, Lenny del Granado, Mary Lindemann, Michael Miller, Guido Ruggiero, Channelle Rose, and Diane Spivey.

At Connecticut College, faculty support facilitated research trips to Tanzania, Jamaica, and Trinidad. I am also grateful for the support I received from Dave Canton, Ann Marie Davis, Mark Forster, Jennifer Fredericks, Leo Garofalo, Cherise Harris, Aida Heredia, Nancy Lewandowski, Jen Manion, Fred Paxton, Sarah Queen, Rosemarie Roberts, Cathy Stock, Lisa Wilson, and Abigail Van Slyck. From my time at Conn I have gained two beautiful friendships that transcend the professional realm: in immeasurable ways, Jim Downs has been a real friend and an avid supporter of my scholarship, and Nathalie Etoke has encouraged me at every step of the way.

At Washington University in St. Louis, I have benefited tremendously from the brilliance of Jean Allman and Tim Parsons. Jean read the entire manuscript, and her feedback was a gift. Tim has shown real enthusiasm for my project since I arrived as a postdoctoral fellow in 2013, and I thank him for his comments on chapters and for his unwavering support. Wilmetta Diallo, Samba Diallo, and Mungai Mutonya are exceptional scholars and wonderful human beings who make the halls of the Department of African and African American Studies a warm and intellectually stimulating place. I am indebted to Lori Watt for reading parts of the manuscript, for her wonderful suggestions, and for her warmth when I joined the Department of History. Adrienne Davis and Gerald Early have welcomed me to Wash U with alacrity, and I deeply appreciate the multiple forms of support I have received from both. For memorable acts of kindness, I also wish to thank John Baugh, Rudolph Clay, Peter Kastor, Sonia Lee, Bill Maxwell, Jeffrey McCune, Sowande Mustakeem, Shanti Parikh, Trevor-Joy Sangrey, Janary Stanton, Anika Walke, Rebecca Wanzo, and Rafia Zafar.

Ameenah Shakir has been with me through every stage of this book, and on several occasions I relied upon her unmatched intellect to remind me of its core arguments. Of greater importance, however, is the fact that she has been a true and incomparable friend to me through all of life's challenges since we met in 2003. I am lucky to have close friends who have been in my circle for decades. They have cheered me along and have provided a respite from writing at essential moments: thanks to Ayanna Durant, Michelle Forbes, Simone Gentles, Dominique Hines, Kelly Lue, Stacy Montwell, Tracie Scott-Thompson, and Lumumba Shabazz.

When I was thirteen years old my mother randomly declared to someone that I would spend my life in a university. With uncanny confidence, she spoke my professional life into being. This was not the only thing she "knew" about me, and her knowing has made me fearless. Her love is my anchor. She also makes for a really good research assistant, responding to calls from Connecticut, Miami, St. Louis, and Tanzania to track down people and to collect documents from archives. She also acted as chauffeur on my research trips to Jamaica. To have a mother like mine, as well as my dear Auntie Ruthie, can only be described as an abundance of riches. Ruthie is thirty years older than I am, but is still the coolest and funniest girlfriend in my contact list; ours is a special bond I treasure. My siblings Timmy Bedasse, Abi Hoilett, and Hannah Hoilett-Frierson, and my sister-in-law Shahini Bedasse, have offered various forms of encouragement. I will never forget the love and support from my cousin Milton Samuels and my uncle Robert Bedasse. My Samuda family has provided support over the years: very special thanks to Jen, Lloyd, Michael, and Peta-Gaye. Jen was a mother to me and her recent departure from this world has left a void like no other. I was fortunate to be the recipient of her unconditional love. For taking me to the archives in Jamaica and for general exuberance in response to the book, I thank my father, Howard "Spred" Bedasse. My stepfather Rupert Hoilett has engaged me in multiple conversations about the work and has contributed immensely to my thinking about Rastafari.

Like no one else, Lerone Martin understands that support comes in many forms. The kindest human being, he happily performed too many of the mundane tasks from which every author seeks to be rescued. His penchant for short sentences that pack a punch also helped me as I polished the book.

Brandon Proia is a generous human being and effective editor who worked to make this process a smooth one for me. It was a pleasure to work with him. I also thank my production editor, Annette Calzone, for her kindness, patience, and efficiency.

· · · · · ·

I had initially planned to write a book about the pan-African connections forged when the freedom fighters of the liberation movements sought refuge in Tanzania after it became the headquarters of the liberation committee of the Organization of African Unity in 1963. But that was not to be. On my first trip to Tanzania I met Tanzanians who made me know that there was indeed a history of Rastafarian repatriation to be written. A Tanzanian Rastafarian woman suggested that I talk to Ras Bupe Karudi, and my first meeting with him set me on a different path, though still one that turned on pan-African linkages. Though I am no longer committed to some of the cosmological stances of Rastafari, I have come to understand that this project chose me.

My Rastafarian parents were members of the Twelve Tribes of Israel. At the beginning of every year, my stepfather declared that we only had "one year left in Babylon." We did not repatriate to Africa, but my childhood allowed me to immediately gain the trust that guaranteed my access to fiercely protected Rastafarian archives. It also showed me how pan-African networks take shape and endure. When I struggled to find contact information for Jamaican Rastafarians in Tanzania, a phone call to my mother in Jamaica easily solved that problem, even when she did not personally know those whom I sought to find. I am indebted to this network from which I gained not only understanding but also primary documents. Along with my parents, this network includes Sangi Davis, Angela "Bunny" Heron, Taitu Heron, and many others.

Reflecting their unwavering engagement with epistemological questions, Rastafarians often assert that "the half has never been told." I do not propose to have rectified that here, but at the very least I offer that which they have long deserved: a serious engagement with their efforts to "set up Jah Kingdom" in Africa.

Jah Kingdom

Introduction
Trodding Diaspora

∙∙

Kisembo Karudi was born in Kingston, Jamaica, during the 1950s, that final decade before the island made the transition from British colony to independent nation-state. The last of six girls raised by her mother, Kisembo spent the early 1970s putting her high school diploma to good use working in a bank, and worshiping in a Methodist church shortly after dawn each Sunday. Her life was by no means intolerable, but she was unable to shake the feeling that she was somehow spiritually adrift—that, in her own words, "something was missing." That changed in 1974 when she met the love of her life, Ras Bupe Karudi, and he introduced her to Jah, the black god of Rastafarians.[1] Like many other Afro-Jamaicans who had found a powerful sense of self in the Rastafarian movement since the 1930s, Kisembo and Ras Bupe, whom she married in 1979, claimed to have "became conscious" through Rastafari. From then on, their lives were governed by the principles of a worldview that rooted them in an African identity. They rejected Jamaican identity (Jamaica was "Babylon") and nurtured the desire to physically repatriate to Africa ("Zion"). They were Africans wandering in the diaspora. By 1978 they were ready to leave Babylon once and for all. They knew that "Africa was the place for all Rastafarians."[2]

Founded by the descendants of enslaved Africans in Jamaica in the early 1930s, the Rastafarian movement declared that Ras Tafari Makonnen, Emperor of Ethiopia, was divine.[3] He was crowned His Imperial Majesty Emperor Haile Selassie I of Ethiopia on November 2, 1930, and Rastafarians proclaimed him to be the 225th descendent of King Menelik I of Ethiopia. Referring to him as Jah, this theological claim was based on a long history of biblical and secular Ethiopianism both in and outside of Jamaica.[4] Within the context of enslavement and colonialism, Rastafarians in Jamaica understood their state of being as one of exile that was marked by alienation and oppression. Their desire to return to Zion (Africa) spiritually, psychologically, intellectually, and physically signified their resistance to what they believed to be oppressive circumstances and their determination to reclaim an African identity. For Rastafarians, the move from Babylon was not migration; it was repatriation. This desire to repatriate, as opposed to migrate, meant they would not be visitors to or in Africa. Africa was their homeland, to which they planned to return. I use the word "repatriation" throughout the book to reinforce Rastafarians' use of it as an epistemological claim that their source of identity construction was in Africa and not on New World plantations. "Repatriation" captures the Rastafarians' worldview from their perspective. It is key to grasping their unshakable understanding of Africa as the homeland to which they hoped to return.

Rastafarian repatriation to Africa has left a powerful international footprint. Most studies of the Rastafarian movement's growth in a global context, however, have privileged its transmission through cultural markers such as reggae music and art.[5] The highly recognizable Rasta iconography has long been associated with the process by which this once marginal movement transitioned into the mainstream, as well as the ways in which international consumers of such iconography have adapted Rastafari to different local circumstances. *Jah Kingdom* instead emphasizes an interior history of Rastafari that sees its evolution from within, and not from the perspectives of those who have adapted the movement's cultural symbols to different local circumstances. Along with Kisembo and Ras Bupe, the Rastafarian men and women who sought to "set up Jah Kingdom" in Africa placed Rastafari at the very center of pan-African discourse and practice. To them pan-Africanism meant that all black people came from Africa, and they saw themselves as a part of a global liberation struggle that linked them to Africans on the continent and across the diaspora. As their experience makes clear, repatriation, and not popular culture, constituted the most meaningful vehicle of Rastafari's international growth. From this angle, what was most significant about Rastafari was not the impact of the cultural representations with which it is most often associated but its continued efforts to translate its philosophies into action in Africa and the involvement of its members with a vast and varied (black) international network of scholars, politicians, laypeople, and activists who shared a belief in the liberatory potential of repatriation to Africa. *Jah Kingdom* foregrounds Rastafari's continued connection to the black radical and pan-African politics that gave life to the idea of repatriation.

Tanzania availed itself as Zion. A beacon of post-independence pan-African activity, Tanzania enters this history of Rastafarian repatriation and redirects a historiography that has long focused on Ethiopia as *the* promised land for Rastafarians.[6] This is as illuminating for the history of Tanzania as it is for the history of Rastafari. More than just the African scene for the Rastafarian engagement with Africa, Tanzanian state actors and citizens constitute continental Africans who, like Rastafarians, were committed to formulating "diaspora" as a concept, process, and mode of identification.

Trodding Diaspora

Rastafari's complex and multifaceted contribution to the moment of decolonization is best captured by the term "trodding diaspora." Rastafarians use "trod" to refer to journey or travel. A mainstay of the Rastafarian lexicon, it functions both on a physical and a spiritual/mystical level simultaneously. As a framework for this study, trodding diaspora encompasses four critical points. First, it privileges movement; to "trod" is to move within, between, and beyond the boundaries of any particular nation-state. Second, it recognizes how Rastafarians understood Africa to be the root of diaspora. But rather than a root waiting to be merely framed, claimed, or rejected, it talks back to diaspora and helps to shape it. Third, trodding diaspora insists that we map the distance between an imagined Africa and the physical journey to discover complex African realities. Finally, in recognizing Rastafari's physical trod to Africa as one that created a transnational archival trail, I use the term "trodding diaspora" to argue for an approach to postindependence histories of Africa and the Caribbean that is necessarily multisited and incorporates and transcends conventional archives. In other words, trodding diaspora constitutes the particularities and challenges of writing diaspora.

Through trodding diaspora, *Jah Kingdom* focuses on movement first and foremost. National boundaries collapse in the face of Rastafari's insistence on the transnational connection among Africans in Africa and across the diaspora. But Rastafarians also moved in and out of multiple black spaces, making transcultural links, constituting difference, and refocusing Rastafari's diversity in the process. On their way to Africa, the Rastafarians of *Jah Kingdom* moved within the Western world, helping to make, while also expanding their understanding of, the nuances within global blackness. In the words of one prominent Rastafarian elder who had traveled throughout the Caribbean and North America and to London, "as nomads of the Rasta faith, [we] must win freedom . . . and trod all over earth and learn the ways, cultures and traditions of many people."[7] But for Rastafarians these sojourns all ended in one place: home, in Africa. Their transnationalism coexisted with their investment in the idea of Africa as the root of diaspora and the only place they could achieve freedom.[8]

With respect to the second point of trodding diaspora, this history is grounded in the Rastafarian conceptualization of "diaspora," which stresses a singular framework of African origin.[9] Those steeped in cultural studies and postmodernist frameworks have emphatically rejected discourses of "origins," "homeland," or "roots."[10] Such theorists accuse "roots" discourses of an essentialism that stems from the fanciful imaginings of diasporic Africans clinging to a simplistic identity based on racial purity.[11] This idea has been propelled forward by the assumption that engagement with such frameworks is devoted to an uncritical rendering of seamless unity. This scholarly trend is connected to the propensity to separate the study of the African diaspora from the study of Africa.[12] At the core of the erasure of Africa lies the prevailing idea of the continent as static and outside the purview of history. The refusal to engage Africa is also based on the erroneous notion that romanticized ideas of it stem solely from the experiences of New World slavery to which continental Africans cannot relate. Besides the fact that transatlantic slavery is indeed relevant to continental African history, this fails to see the ways in which slavery and colonialism were part and parcel of a globalizing system of European oppression that affected both Africa and its diaspora.[13] Furthermore, as is the case with the Rastafarian movement, the diasporic redemption of Africa has been engaged with remembering the anti-Africa discourses of both slavery *and* colonialism. It is the case that being on the continent excluded Africans from the "poetics and politics of exilic longing."[14] But the psychic assault on African humanity perpetrated by colonialism as a knowledge regime compelled some continental Africans to reclaim and reconstruct Africa in service of their anticolonial politics, as did their diasporic counterparts.

The process by which Rastafarians actualized the goal of repatriation demands serious exploration of how their dreams translated into a lived reality. Indeed, my exploration of the ways in which Rastafarian ideals sometimes clashed with local realities in Tanzania demonstrates that the engagement with origins discourses does not automatically elide nuance. But Rastafarian repatriation to Africa is relevant to modern African history in another way: it is necessary to ponder how continental Africans processed, used, appropriated, related to and rejected diasporic presentations of Africa in the postindependence period. Beyond the stories of diasporic Africans who are disabused of such longings for a homeland when they discover their inapplicability in modern Africa,[15] there are also stories of how continental and diasporic Africans, despite local differences, imagined the world anew through pan-African politics and tried to build it. Of utmost importance is the interaction between these Rastafarians on the trod and the local Tanzanians who embraced Rastafari as a serious philosophy. As those who "trod diaspora," the Rastafarians set in motion social processes far beyond the initial goals of the repatriation when the local movement broke off into sects, with one even declaring its independence from the Jamaican Rastafarians, insisting that Rastafari had its roots in East Africa.

Tanzania was fertile ground. When Rastafarian repatriation began there in 1976, Tanzania had emerged as an independent African nation that inspired diasporic Africans with both its rhetoric and its actions.[16] Tanzania gained independence from Britain in 1961 and Julius Nyerere, its first president and most influential leader, emerged as a philosopher who believed in the power of ideas as a crucial component of decolonization.[17] By 1968 Tanzania had gained the reputation across the African diaspora as an African state determined to chart its own course based on the concept of *ujamaa* (African socialism). Reference to a diasporic perception of Tanzania fails to adequately address a multiplicity of viewpoints among different observers within the diaspora. Still, a generally positive response to Tanzania, pregnant with optimism, was pervasive. The state's declaration of nonalignment in the midst of Cold War tensions and its support of African liberation movements as the headquarters of the Liberation Committee of the Organization of African Unity appealed to progressive black people globally.[18] Many nurtured the perception that Tanzania represented an "adamant position against white supremacy everywhere and especially in Southern Africa."[19] As the black power movement came into full swing in the United States, many of its advocates saw Tanzania as an ideologically progressive African state and acknowledged its role as a base for the liberation movements of southern Africa.

Jah Kingdom considers more than just the geographical backdrop for the repatriation. It explores the views of international trodding from the perspectives of Tanzania and its people. Scholars of the North American variant of the black power movement have made great strides in recognizing the undeniable impact of Tanzania and of Nyerere on black power advocates.[20] *Jah Kingdom* builds on this work, but also diverges from it by venturing beyond North American archival and analytical contexts for the black American engagement with Tanzania. Dar es Salaam was a generative hub of pan-African activity deserving of the attention given to cities of the Global North that have contributed to the evolution of pan-African linkages, such as London and Paris. Through the theoretical imperative of trodding diaspora, it becomes clear that Tanzania and Tanzanian actors contributed to the making of pan-Africanism far beyond the well-known history of how diasporic Africans attempted to reconnect with a somewhat quixotic Africa through Tanzania's particular expressions of nationalism.

The space between transnational connections and ever-evolving local realities meant that the diasporic notion of Tanzania was sometimes frozen in time or slow to recognize any disconnect between state policies and how they actually played out on the ground. The state had been plagued by several paradoxes.[21] Villagization had been voluntary between 1967 and 1972, but after 1973 it became a mandatory initiative under Operation Vijiji.[22] Furthermore, the state seriously curtailed the power of workers by banning independent unions and exercising control over the media. In addition, despite the assertion of self-reliance, the state depended heavily on Western foreign aid. Any idea of Tanzania (and of Nyerere) that placed emphasis on the way in which the state represented itself tended to flatten the processes by which state officials arrived at consensus and ignored the reality of dissent and negotiation that yielded the end result. It is useful to think of Tanzania "not as a unified entity and cohesive actor but as a divided terrain of contestation."[23] History attests to the fact that within the Tanzanian state were several competing Tanzanias at any given moment.

Though it can be problematic, the power of the spiritual/mystical (imaginary) Africa remains important. Thus, as its third key intervention, trodding diaspora takes seriously the context for the construction of a romanticized Africa, recognizing its transformative power even as an idea. It also goes further to follow the transformation of the imaginary Africa by way of travel to particular sites in Africa. In many of the documents penned by Rastafarians, they have replaced the *c* in the word "Africa" with a *k*. This use of "Afrika" was common in black nationalist circles during the 1980s, and many perceived the use of the *k* as a means of connecting to linguistic spelling standards in ancient African languages. It was also vaguely associated with subversive politics. In quoting from these Rastafarian documents, I have retained their spelling, which functions as a representation of the particular ways in which Rastafarians invented Africa.[24] The trod was essentially a diaspora experience that read Africa as "Afrika" until they repatriated and the experience shifted their reading to accommodate continental realities.

Through the framework of "trodding diaspora" *Jah Kingdom* also engages questions of the archive. To center the trod as travel is to recognize that Rastafarians embody the archive. Scholars have documented the difficulty involved with gaining access to Rastafarian knowledge. Rastafarians typically engage in secrecy and are unapologetically selective when deciding which researchers they will trust with such knowledge.[25] Their sustained struggle against imposed, erroneous, and unsanctioned definition results in an unwillingness to pander to the methodological processes of scholars, whom Rastafarians often subject to a rigorous and demanding series of "tests" to determine motive. They have self-consciously identified and named the colonial/written archives as "imperial" and thus unreliable in the reconstruction of Rasta histories. As such, their emphasis on orality represents a choice to seek an autonomous intellectual space.[26] Rastafari's rebellion against Babylon included a rebellion against its archive.

If knowledge of Rastafari is contained within Rastafarian bodies, their bodies traveled as archives, and the transnational human networks they created as a result of travel form a crucial component of the research process for this history. Other scholars have remarked upon the clash between nation-state and diaspora,[27] but "trodding diaspora" calls attention to how this clash relates to the methodological imperatives of writing diaspora. To follow the Rastafarian network of evidence is also an effort to unearth the global histories created by black radicals, and it changes the way we imagine and construct Rasta histories. Not only was Rastafari a hindrance to the consolidation of the Jamaican nation-state, but it also destabilized the autonomy of the national archive.[28] The fragments of this history were spread across different geographical boundaries and languages as Rastafarians trod within and outside Babylon.

I could not have written this history without the trust of Ras Bupe Karudi and Joshua Mkhululi, the Rastafarians who emerged as the leaders of the repatriation.[29] Along with interviews, these men also supplied me with previously unharvested written documents. To be sure, the personal writings of each Rastafarian represent certain analytic tensions that characterize Rastafari as a whole. As a decentralized movement that celebrates both individual subjectivity and community (captured in the Rastafarian notion of "I-n-I"), these documents reveal both the idiosyncrasies of each author and the unifying assumptions that are foundational to the movement at large. Rastafarians' conflicting responses to the realities of life in Tanzania also yield important lessons about the role of personalities in Rastafari leadership. The voices of these two men are supplemented by the oral testimonies of other Rastafarians who heeded their calls to put Tanzania's offer of permanent residency and land to good use.

Notwithstanding the continued relevance of oral sources, indispensable deposits of written data provide meaningful source materials to reconstruct Rasta histories. Written sources (often colonial, and thus deserving of sustained scrutiny) have documented Rastafari since its emergence, and international trods have led to the formation of organizations that, through newsletters, personal correspondence, and organizational papers have documented their engagement with issues such as unification, repatriation to Africa, globalization, and women's rights within Rastafari.[30] These papers offer critical details about their multidimensional journey.

My search for documents began in Dar es Salaam, Tanzania, where the Rastafarians allowed me into the inner world of a pilgrimage that began on Jamaican soil. But theirs was a journey that involved a much wider black international network, and it became clear that I would have to embark on a transnational search to locate snippets of the repatriation—often in unexpected places. In following their lead, my project expanded and came to depend on a wide range of primary documents from Jamaica, Tanzania, England, Trinidad, and the United States. Along with the documents detailing correspondence between Rastafarians and nonstate actors across the black world, these include state documents and cables from Tanzania, the British archives and the U.S. Department of State. This means that though I privilege the interpretation offered by Rastafarian oral and written sources, I also incorporate the offerings housed in more conventional archives. In the end, my archival sojourn reinforces the view that national archives are far from complete in uncovering histories of pan-African linkages and that we benefit greatly from following the far-reaching circuits of the Rastafarians themselves.

Among the materials I received from the Rastafarians are numerous state documents that reveal their interactions with Tanzanian officials. They are not in the Tanzania National Archive (TNA), but are in my possession. The collections at the TNA include records from the postindependence period, and several historians have mined them with success, even as some documents have yet to be filed in a standardized way. Admittedly, the state documents I use are probably still classified "active" and remain in local offices or agencies. The library and resource center at the Mwalimu Nyerere Foundation proved extremely useful, as the speeches and other documents (from the 1960s through 1990s) that I found there provided me with evidence of Nyerere's interactions with the Caribbean and with pan-African politics in general. Historian Leander Schneider has written, though, of the likelihood that some of the documents from the postindependence period in Tanzania may be irretrievably lost.[31] It is also important to note that many of the documents in my possession were stamped "secret." Postindependence African state archives present their own silences, absences, and erasures, issues with which historians of New World slavery have had to grapple within the context of colonial state archives.[32] The pan-African collaboration between Rastafarians and the Tanzanian state happened amid the larger fight for African liberation when Tanzania was still at the very center of armed struggle. The state accommodated freedom fighters from the liberation movements of southern Africa and created silences in service of survival, strategy, and safety. The war against the Portuguese and South Africa represented an anticolonial war in the postindependence period, and it was dangerous business. Additionally, it is possible that the Tanzanian government never intended for this particular history to see the light of day, as Rastafarians received access to Tanzanian citizenship and land through executive action.

Men are at the center of the oral and written sources I use to tell this history. As those who spearheaded the effort to set up Jah Kingdom in Tanzania, Karudi and Mkhululi offered revealing written and oral accounts detailing their thoughts. Along with the perspectives of other men, they established the political work of repatriation as a male undertaking. As with all nationalisms, Rastafari's pan-African nationalism was about liberation while condoning certain forms of repression. The men placed much of the work of nation building and the racial uplift that was its corollary upon the backs (and wombs) of women. Sharing much with the Garvey movement in this regard, the black nationalism of the patriarchal Rastafarians in this study included defined gender roles, as well as understandings of sexuality that were closely intertwined with issues of morality. I have engaged in extensive analyses of the particular brand of masculinity espoused by the male Rastafarian actors. But these men were not alone, and the revolutionary work of the repatriation was as much woman's work as it was theirs. Karudi, for instance, imagined the political mission of repatriation to Africa as a patriarchal project. When his relationship with his wife deteriorated, he found solace in an understanding that, as a "suffering servant of Jah," he had made the ultimate sacrifice. The testimony of his wife, Kisembo Karudi, disrupts her husband's narrative, changing our perspective of the repatriation and of Rastafari more broadly. Rather than merely a passive recipient of Ras Bupe's revolutionary impulses, Kisembo was a Rastafarian and pan-Africanist in her own right, and even in the midst of great hardship she "was never disappointed" because she knew that Africa was where she belonged. In large measure she emerged as the necessary pragmatist who sustained Karudi and their two children financially.

The other women left no written accounts of the repatriation, and many attempts to solicit oral interviews failed. The women's code of silence actually reflected their efforts to control the archive. Having gleaned much about the reasons they have chosen silence from a male Rastafarian who encouraged them to speak, it is clear that they remain deeply concerned/skeptical about a historian's depiction of Rastafari. They also remain invested in protecting the way in which history records Rastafarian repatriation. While acknowledging their presence, I have avoided speaking for the women in definitive ways that privilege the perspectives of the men or my own analysis. I have also refrained from treating Kisembo's perspective as one that represents all Rastafarian women. I have provided historical context for the debates concerning women's roles in Rastafari, including the presence of one polygamous family arrangement within the Rastafarian community in Tanzania. Above all, I have resisted the impulse to succumb to neat categories that see Rastafarian women as either victims or radicals. As Kisembo's own rendering of her experience shows, rigid categories fail to capture the complexities of a fully human experience. In the end she reminds us that the history of Rastafarian repatriation to Tanzania is inextricably tied to complex histories of marriage, family, and love. This yields important lessons about the tensions surrounding how gender identities are constructed within groups—including different forms of nationalism.

An Interior History of Rastafari

Certain widespread, fundamental assumptions, tenets, and goals unite all Rastafarians. Yet, as a decentralized movement, Rastafari has historically defied easy categorization. This renders every uncomplicated effort to apply the term "Rastafari" to a large group of people problematic. Further complicating the matter is the presence of three major groups within the larger movement referred to as mansions or houses: the Bobo Shanti, the Nyabingi, and the Twelve Tribes of Israel.[33] These three mansions emerged in Jamaica at different times and have been crucial to defining Rastafari's internal plurality. In large measure, different group affiliations faded in significance among Rastafarians as they focused on adjusting to life in Tanzania. Still, it is worth noting that several of them were in fact juggling multiple Rastafarian identities, which became detectable in various ways. The group of Rastafarians who went to Tanzania included members of both the Nyabingi and the Twelve Tribes of Israel. Beyond that, several of the most influential men had trod to Tanzania through England. While there, they had joined one of the many organizations formed by Rastafari in England, the Universal Rastafari Improvement Association (URIA). The group acted as a critical institution that raised funds for the repatriation, and its newsletter captured the thinking of those who made the trod to Tanzania. *Jah Kingdom* privileges the particular viewpoint of the members of URIA.

Based in Bristol, URIA was made up of individuals (and the descendants of individuals) who had migrated from Jamaica and (to a lesser extent, other Caribbean islands) to England in the wave of immigration that came after the Second World War. Their ever-evolving politics reflected the specific issues of the global black struggle in this period, the role of England as a radicalizing space for pan-African mobilization, and the studiousness with which Rastafarians witnessed and theorized about the liberation struggle.

That URIA was based in England reveals the extent to which it became a central node in the repatriation. England became crucial to the history and evolution of the Rastafarian movement, and emerged as a launch pad diaspora that linked this history of Africa and the Caribbean to black Europe.[34] By the 1970s, Rastafari had become a "major force" among black people in England.[35] As was the case in Jamaica, Rastafarians "entered into official explanations of black deviancy and pathology," and by the 1970s the symbols of Rasta "achieved a mass character in Britain's black communities" and was very much associated with criminality.[36] A vitally important site for histories of Rastafari's evolution outside Jamaica, the scholarly treatment of its history there includes the exact approach to which this study is opposed. Ignoring the important developments occurring within the movement, the scholarship on Rastafari in Britain has, in large measure, highlighted the relationship between the state and the movement. In addition, it has focused on Rastafari as popular culture. Instead of seeing Rastafari as a serious philosophy with doctrinal tenets that establish criteria for membership, Paul Gilroy argues that "by looking at the broad and diverse use to which the language and symbols of Rastafari have been put, it is possible to conceive it as a movement in which the lines dividing different levels of commitment are necessarily flexible." Through this framework, Rastafari expands "beyond Afro-Caribbean young people who wear locks, colours and wraps, or smoke God's herb, to old people, soul boys and girls, some whites and Asians." Based on this approach, which privileges Rastafarian symbols and representation, Gilroy argues that Rastafari's influence "increased steadily in Britain between 1970 and 1981." By 1981, he contends, "Rastafari did not disappear but its ethical dominance was broken."[37]

Gilroy's analysis depends solely on a framework that sees the history of the movement in terms of its interaction with the British state and public. As an assessment of Rastafari in Britain that is limited to popular culture and not based on the ideas of Rastafarians themselves, it ignores developments within the movement that were taking place during its purported heyday and beyond. Furthermore, Gilroy demonstrates a clear bias against Rastafari as a religion and dismisses repatriation when he concludes that Rastafari was unable to meet the challenge of British society after 1981 because "the officially recognized and sponsored leadership, drawn preponderantly from theologians and dogmatists rather than artists and musicians, was ill-equipped to meet the historic challenge posed by negotiation with rather than (mental or physical) escape from Britain's Babylon."[38]

There is no doubt that Rastafari spread throughout the world as popular culture. Many have been exposed to Rastafari through the reggae music of Bob Marley and others beginning in the 1970s. It is crucially important to note, however, that the international travel of Rastafarians themselves has constituted the most significant catalyst for the entrenchment of Rastafari around the globe.[39] Germane to Gilroy's approach is the effort to destabilize and/or dismiss aspects of Rastafari that are foundational and enduring: black radical politics, pan-Africanism, religion, and repatriation. The marginalization of black radical politics and pan-Africanism suggests that such a politics was no longer meaningful based on the linear idea that the 1960s gave way to less radical decades in the 1970s and beyond, and thus that pan-Africanism lost its relevance. This assumption has implications for the treatment of repatriation, in particular, by scholars. As historian Robin Kelley has noted, "back-to-Africa proposals in principle are almost universally dismissed as 'escapist' or associated with essentialist, romantic ideas about black cultural unity."[40] Additionally, the veneration of Haile Selassie has not been taken seriously by a range of scholars: from those with Marxist antireligion frameworks to those who accuse Rasta theology of pandering to absurd standards of hermeneutics and exegesis and others who chastise Rastafarians for refusing to see Haile Selassie as a mere mortal within the context of contemporary Ethiopia. Yet, even as some of these critiques necessarily challenge and critique Rastafari, the wholesale dismissal of these Rastafarian fundamentals ignores the ways in which they have been transformative for Rastafarians and imposes a myopic assumption that the movement has been a static one. Furthermore, it marginalizes an entire history of pan-Africanism, in which exodus politics and movements remained relevant, and the role of Rastafari in their survival.

The developments within the movement in Britain from the 1970s onward have everything to do with these critically significant aspects of Rastafari. The history of Rasta is not limited to how, as a culture, it has resisted Babylon, and how Babylon, has, with varying degrees of success, worked to quash its revolutionary power. In direct contrast to Gilroy's view, in 1982 prominent Rastafarian elder Jah Bones informed a British court that Rastafari was established in Jamaica in the 1930s, "developed subsequently in England in about the 1960s and got very powerful in the 1970s and even more so in 1981."[41] Though the histories of how Rastafari has been "routinized," or the processes that defined its shifting interactions with the "mainstream" remain important, the interior histories of Rastafarians' efforts to transform their lives must be taken seriously.

The Era of Decolonization: Its Triumphs and Struggles

This history of Rastafarian repatriation happened within the context of a complex global landscape between 1961 and 1992. It starts with the colossal shift that occurred when political independence from colonial rule became a reality for many continental Africans and diasporic Africans in the Caribbean. Beginning in the late 1950s, Africa and the Caribbean were essentially remade, a heady historical moment that saw black nation-states make their debut on the world stage. It was a moment of redefinition when formerly colonized elites declared European colonial rule out of vogue and claimed the right to self-government. The nation-state triumphed as the mechanism to symbolize that freedom, and newly installed black leaders worked to define citizenship while attempting to navigate a complex geopolitical landscape defined by the Cold War and the relentless tentacles of international capital.

Pan-Africanism had been a part of anticolonial activism long before independence and did not disappear after the transition to nation-states was hailed as a victory. Some leaders harnessed its power when it became clear that political independence was by no means a shotgun moment of liberation. Even as the early 1960s saw many victories, the Portuguese colonies of Angola, Guinea Bissau, and Mozambique remained under colonial rule, as did Namibia, South Africa, and Zimbabwe (then Southern Rhodesia). But beyond the ways that black leaders used pan-Africanism to deal with the international situation, statehood had serious implications for the development of pan-African politics, which had entered a new phase. The newly formed states were central to this development, as those with a pan-African agenda such as Ghana and Tanzania became the impetus for diasporic mobilization. On the one hand, the rise of black leaders opened up pathways for greater pan-African movement, exemplified by the extent to which Tanzania became a hub of pan-African activity after 1963.

On the other hand, the workings of the state apparatus saw black elites suppress grassroots expressions of pan-Africanism within their borders, a reality with which Rastafarians were all too familiar in Jamaica.[42] This division between state officials and nonstate actors was captured most poignantly in the planning and execution of the Sixth Pan-African Congress (PAC), which was held in Tanzania in 1974. When Nyerere chose state diplomacy and supported the decision not to invite nonstate actors from the Caribbean, Eusi Kwayana, coordinator of the Caribbean steering committee for the Sixth PAC, denounced the congress.[43] For Caribbean militants, "it was not a pan-African congress, just a meeting of governments and guests acceptable to the Tanzanian authorities."[44] The Tanzanian government's decision only put the spotlight on an issue that had long worried some militants within nation-states in Africa and the Caribbean. As the official call of the congress revealed, freedom from economic imperialism after political independence was meant to be a major focus of the agenda. But the conference planners were also aware that the transition to political independence had given rise to its own brand of intrablack conflict. C. L. R. James, a major player in drafting the call, explained that the Sixth PAC was meant to "draw a line of steel against those, Africans included, who hide behind the slogan and paraphernalia of national independence while allowing finance capital to dominate and direct their economic and social life."[45]

The congress also highlighted the fact that pan-Africanism housed many different ideological positions. One of the chief conflicts was the fissure between cultural nationalists and the radical Left—an issue that had resonance across Africa and its diaspora. It emerged when the Senegalese contingent, in support of cultural nationalism, officially stated its rejection of Sekou Toure's denunciation of Negritude,[46] and it had long been a point of debate in radical Caribbean spaces like Jamaica where antireligion Marxists debated god-fearing Rastafarians.[47]

Jah Kingdom challenges the rigid distinction between state and nonstate actors during the 1970s and beyond. When Joshua Mkhululi first approached the Tanzanian state in the late 1970s, he initiated a pan-African relationship with the very state that was at the center of the momentous divide between black states and black Caribbean militants. To be sure, the repatriation was shrouded in the inherent contradiction of the Rastafarian diasporic ideal that rejected the nation-state as the arbiter of identity construction while seeking legitimacy and support from the Tanzanian state. This practice of diaspora certainly exposed a persistent tension between Rastafari's pan-African ideals and the realities of the nation-state. Still, and notably, it also unveils a collaboration that constricts the space between state-actors and the grassroots.

The interaction between Rastafari and the nation-state was not limited to Tanzania. When the Rastafarians began to petition the Tanzanian government for the "right of entry" in 1976, they benefited from a history of linkages between Jamaica and Tanzania, facilitated largely by the personal and political friendship between Julius Nyerere and prime minister of Jamaica Michael Manley. Julius Nyerere's writings had made a tremendous impact on Manley's thinking. This provides evidence of the influence of African leaders on the formation of the Third World as a political block. More than this, Manley's personal struggle over his own perceived distance from blackness, as a member of Jamaica's "brown" elite, belied his acceptance in pan-African circles across Africa. Given that Manley's pan-African politics were constructed after he appropriated Rastafarian symbols and consciousness into his political campaigns, Rastafari was absolutely central to generating the brand of politics surrounding race, color, and class in both national and transnational spaces.

The repatriation also defies the idea of a rigid divide between cultural nationalists and the radical Left. In search of moral and financial support for the mission, Ras Bupe Karudi forged relationships with black activists such as John Henrik Clarke and Jacob Carruthers, both likely comrades who made their mark on the African American freedom struggle as cultural nationalists. But Karudi received even more substantial support from James, a stalwart of the black radical Left with very little patience for religion.[48] In the final analysis, many different ideological positions crisscrossed under the umbrella of pan-Africanism. Still more than just a quest for racial liberation, Rasta has always been invested in dismantling capitalist structures and through that commitment found common ground with the radical Left.

Jah Kingdom also considers other contradictions attached to state building in Africa and the Caribbean. The very colonial condition out of which these states emerged created a project that was, in some ways, rigged from the start. Those who emerged as political elites campaigned for independence within the framework of a Eurocentric paradigm of constitutionalism, liberal humanism, democracy, and other Enlightenment ideas. The political elites in Jamaica and Tanzania were educated in the Western intellectual tradition and were fluent in the language of the colonizers. The impact of European ideas on Africa and the Caribbean led to the paradoxes present in African and Caribbean epistemologies and philosophies.[49] Rastafari was not immune to this. Though it represented a grassroots pro-Africa discourse, colonial domination had made an impact on the thinking of all levels of colonial society. Furthermore, the incorporation of Christianity into Rastafari has sometimes served to undermine its aim to completely decolonize the (black) mind.

Yet despite its shortcomings, Rastafari was a dynamic and influential movement, and through repatriation it engaged with and affected the critical pan-African preoccupations of the period of decolonization. Though used widely to refer to agitation for independence, I emphasize a definition of "decolonization" that also includes struggle following formal independence from colonial rule. As such, the term suggests that efforts to decolonize continued on various levels, including the attempts to address economic realities, the quest for mental emancipation from colonial thinking, and the fact that independence was delayed in some places. For Rastafarians in particular, independence did not symbolize true freedom. As Africans, their ultimate and complete liberation could not be found in a diasporic nation-state.

The period between 1961 and 1992 fits the broad category of a postindependence history. But this is not to suggest that the different decades within these temporal markers did not yield significant historical shifts—often captured, for example, as the roaring, radical 1960s, the crisis-driven 1970s, and the conservatism of the 1980s as exhibited in the administrations of U.S. president Ronald Reagan and British prime minister Margaret Thatcher. *Jah Kingdom* relies upon shifts within Tanzania's economic and political system to mark historical time. Reflecting wider global shifts while also providing the Tanzanian contexts for different stages of the repatriation, the unbridled optimism of Tanzania's 1960s rhetoric had been undermined by economic decline and crushing poverty during the 1970s. In 1986, no longer able to avoid the International Monetary Fund, the country underwent a shift to liberalization.[50] Though the Rastafarians continued to benefit from his tremendous impact and power, Nyerere stepped down as president at the end of 1985, initiating shifts within the governmental structure that would later take effect.

Ras Bupe Karudi and Joshua Mkhululi did not bring about a large-scale repatriation from Jamaica; various hardships, including economic problems, prevented their community from growing beyond twenty-six members. But Rastafari's significance and impact have never been commensurate with its numerical representation. When Jamaican state officials appropriated its symbols during the 1970s, Rastafarians had never accounted for more than 3 percent of the population. But that did not stop them from becoming, in the words of Walter Rodney, "the largest single force opposed to white cultural imperialism in Jamaica after independence."[51] Furthermore, that Rastafari became the face and language of black consciousness in Jamaica belied its numeric reality.[52] This disparity between small numbers and colossal impact extended to the global context. While numerically small in scale, Rastafarian repatriation to Tanzania carries much larger, game-changing implications for how we document and remember pan-African politics during an era characterized by both "possibility and constraint."[53]

· · · · · ·

We begin our own "trod" through this history of Rastafarian repatriation to Tanzania. I necessarily start in Jamaica, where Rastafarians formulated the philosophy that sent them trodding in search of Africa. Rastafari's internal complexity encompasses all facets of the worldview: from religious imaginaries and rituals to political commitments and strategies. I situate the Rastafarians who went to Tanzania amid this plurality with a view to explaining who these particular Rastafarians were.

The next stop is Tanzania, which usurped Ethiopia as the promised land. Though some Rastas place less emphasis on repatriation than others, Ethiopia's position as the promised land in the Rastafarian imagination had never been seriously challenged. This history changes that. Tanzania's longstanding pan-African engagements made it ready for the Rastafarians' request. Rastafarians found their home in a hub of pan-African activity that had become a site of diaspora aspiration. As a nation-state, Tanzania had forged pan-African connections with other states, including Jamaica.

The repatriation unfolded within the context of this collaboration among states. The tangible bond that developed between Nyerere and Manley aided Rastafarians in their efforts to repatriate to Tanzania. Rather than the fixed divide between state and nonstate actors that had seemingly been entrenched after the Sixth PAC, the repatriation blurred the lines in illuminating ways. This history of repatriation transgresses analytical boundaries between state and nonstate actors.

Nevertheless, there was a clash between Rastafarian diasporic dreams and African nation-state realities. Even as the Rastafarian notion of diaspora transcended the state, Rastas were at the mercy of the Tanzanian state apparatus. The state granted them official "right of entry" in 1985, but it was not codified into law, and this made for a less than smooth process. The fissures that came to the fore turned on the legal, economic, cultural, and religious realities of repatriation. Notwithstanding these difficulties, Rastafarians and Tanzanian state officials continued to trod diaspora and to make claims about the relationship between race and citizenship. Tanzania specifically extended the invitation to *wajamaika weusi* (black Jamaicans). This implied that nonblack Jamaicans may not have qualified for citizenship in Tanzania. In the end, Nyerere's elevation of race as an important issue in this negotiation spoke volumes about the continued relevance of race in this period and made a statement about how citizenship expanded in pan-African terms.[54]

Land, above all else, signified belonging. Tanzania finally made good on its promise when it issued a land grant to Rastafarians in 1989. Now secure at home, they were prepared to reap what they had sown. The process was, like life itself, filled with both trials and triumphs. They wrestled with epidemiological threats, economic woes, and family dynamics. In the midst of hardship, they further injected Rastafari into various pan-African activities and circles. They contributed to Tanzania's development in the areas of education, journalism, and accounting, imparted Rastafari as a serious philosophy to local Tanzanians, supported African liberation movements, and forged alliances with pan-Africanists worldwide.

Karudi's relationship with James unequivocally displays the various pathways that Rastafari has trod to make its mark in pan-African circles. In 1964, James highlighted the "absurdities" of Rastafari. Additionally, in contrast to all that Rastafari represented, he remained ambivalent about African heritage and identity. By 1986, however, he was corresponding with Karudi frequently and sending money to him in support of the mission. This collaboration is critical to my exploration of how Rastafari inserted itself into the intellectual history of pan-Africanism.

The Rastafarian movement has made its mark around the world as a cultural phenomenon. Yet the focus on its cultural representations has neglected the history of Rastafari's evolution as an expression of black radicalism, and has relegated its militancy to a bygone era when its association with popular cultural could not have been foreseen. Through Rastafarian repatriation to Africa, *Jah Kingdom* insists on a history driven less by outsiders and more by the men and women for whom Rastafari remained an enduring and ever-evolving political project.

1 Without Vision the People Perish
The Divine, Regal, and Noble Afrikan Nation

Ras Bupe Karudi set his passport ablaze. As a Rastafarian, the passport of a nation-state in Babylon was merely a document that allowed him to travel. It had never symbolized freedom or belonging. Now that he was home, in Africa, this incendiary act celebrated his literal departure from Babylon—for good. His use of fire to mark the end of his trod through the wilderness was not a random choice. It connected him to the age-old propensity of Rastafarians to use the image of a raging fire as a symbol of their denunciation of the Western world.[1]

When Rastafari emerged in the early 1930s, Jamaica was a British colony. In 1956, one colonial governor saw the movement as "some kind of distorted negro nationalism."[2] Another governor saw the Rastafarian "cult" as consisting of "some of the riffraff of the country" who were "mentally imbalanced."[3] Their "madness," which was also deemed criminal, was their understanding of European slavery as the genesis of an institutionalized and systemic system of oppression that had targeted Africans. Rastafarians deduced that this system was governed by "a doctrine of Afrikan inferiority and European supremacy." Throughout the years, the defining characteristic of "Babylon" was its tendency to constantly promote "a completely negative conception" of black people, as well as "misguided and slanderous myths in order to discredit" African heritage. Rastafarians saw Babylon's construction of African inferiority as dialectically related to the construction of European superiority. The "long-standing myth" of European "invincibility" was based on Europe's "conceited vanity."[4] Far from mad, Rastafarians unveiled the insanity of the colonial project's invention of Africa and Africans to serve its own purposes.

Based on the anti-Africa ethos of slavery and colonialism, Rastafari's defiant pro-Africa stance was inherently anticolonial. Considered outcasts who threatened the stability of colonial society, the colonial state criminalized, persecuted, and ridiculed Rastafarians. Nonetheless, a wholesale celebration of African heritage remained Rastafari's raison d'être as it evolved from the 1930s into the period after independence from colonial rule. As a worldview, orientation, and set of daily practices, the movement encompassed a sweeping critique of colonial dominance and enlisted an extensive array of weaponry in its arsenal, including religion, aesthetics, and language.

As one of its defining characteristics, Rastafari has accomplished unity without uniformity; those who claim it share a particular worldview and consciousness. Generally, Rastafari connected with and diverged from previous expressions of the link between Afro-Jamaicans and Africa. Ethiopianism, Garveyism, and Revivalism set the stage for Rastafari, which selected elements of each as it shaped something distinctive. But Rastafari as a collective is complicated by smaller group affiliations as well as each member's individual autonomy to interpret it as a singular experience. The Rastafarians who went to Tanzania represented a shining example of this complexity. The Universal Rastafari Improvement Association (URIA), based in England, emerged as the Rasta group that came to represent—and act as a critical launch pad—for those who repatriated to Tanzania. URIA's concerns must be filtered through the specificities of the history of Rastafari in England. The group was one of several groups formed by Rastas in England during the 1970s and 1980s, such as Rastafari Universal Zion, Rasta Unity, and Rasta International. The different groups formed in England underscored Rasta's internal plurality and also reflected an effort of many Rastafarians to create umbrella organizations that would help them to mobilize around pressing issues such as repatriation.[5]

As was the case with many of the members of these umbrella organizations, the members of URIA had been or remained connected to one of the core Rastafarian mansions that were intertwined with the movement's evolution in Jamaica. In true Rastafarian form, these overlapping identities made for an internal intricacy not easily parsed. The different identities melded together for the greater goal of repatriation while also making for distinctive experiences and interpretations that had bearing on how the repatriation unfolded.

Under the aegis of URIA, the repatriates were clear about their desire to build a "divine, regal and noble Afrikan nation."[6] It was also a male-centered one preoccupied with black manhood. The men in URIA generally advanced prescribed gender roles that sought to protect and assure the survival of the race. Among other things, this meant affirming motherhood as the primary role of women, policing sexual conduct, and establishing a link between gender norms and morality.

They also grappled with the particular realities faced by the black struggle for freedom during this period. Though Rastafarians had offered critiques of capitalism in the early years, the rise of independent black nations with exploitative elites served to heighten their awareness of black people who worked against a collective black freedom. In the end, the Rastafarians who traveled to Tanzania were devoted to repatriation, the veneration of Haile Selassie I, the cause of African liberation, and advancing a nuanced and global race-first analysis that understood racism as endemic to capitalism.

Rastafari and the Link to Africa in Jamaica's History

Rastafarians understood their philosophy as a vision of freedom. Having properly identified the colonial "foe" and its power, they worked to rid themselves of its control.[7] Through this prism, Rastafari was an anticolonial discourse and set of practices. Yet based on the idea that the descendants of Africans in the New World all had a Rasta consciousness within them, Rastafarians saw the recognition of Babylon's evil as the beginning of a process by which diasporic Africans could embrace who they really were. Rather than conversion, it was an awakening. Rastafarians in Jamaica linked their experience to the descendants of Africans in the diaspora and to continental Africans, seeing themselves as a part of a global struggle for liberation. The idea that all black people came from Africa, coupled with a shared, latent Rasta ethos, empowered Rastafarians to develop strategies to work toward a collective destiny.

Rastafarians understood that colonial conquest had been as much a spiritual calamity as it was a physical and political one. They saw colonial oppression and racism as the "dread result of a devilish conspiracy" in which religion played an important role. Their assertion that missionaries were actually "mercenaries" spoke to the role of Christianity in Britain's history of imperialism, in terms of the imposition of a biblical hermeneutic that supported white supremacy, as well as the Anglican Church's participation in the economics of slavery.[8] Rastafarians rejected this particular use of Christianity. The movement was named for its divine figure, Ras Tafari Makonnen (Haile Selassie I), the 225th descendant of king Menelik of Ethiopia. In 1930 he was crowned "king of kings," "lord of lords," and "conquering lion of the tribe of Judah," and to those auspicious titles Rastafarians added "Jah" (God). Instead of the British monarch, who was also the head of the Church of England, Haile Selassie was a divine figure and also the king of Ethiopia. Whereas many Afro-Jamaicans nurtured loyalty to the queen of England and saw themselves as British subjects, the Rastafarian movement clearly articulated a different position: they were Africans, not British subjects. Rastafarians had swapped the British Empire as "God's earthly kingdom" for the kingdom of Jah in Africa.[9] Rastafari presented a clear statement that enslaved Africans' identities did not begin in the New World and that Africa, not the plantation, was the source of identity construction.

Indeed, enslaved Africans made the journey from west and west central Africa to the Caribbean with the religious cosmologies, gods, and spiritual practices of the cultures from which they were taken in tow. In Jamaica the enslaved, their descendants, and the Africans who arrived under indenture after emancipation in the nineteenth century underscored the African cultural presence through their dynamic religious expression, creation, and re-creation.[10] Religion was certainly a vessel through which Afro-Jamaicans simply asserted the right to be human, first in a slave society and then under colonial rule. In this sense the very connection to religious ways of knowing and existing in the world acted as a form of resistance to slavery's unrelenting efforts at dehumanization. Afro-Jamaican beliefs and practices included a cosmology that merged the sacred and the secular, invoked ancestral spirits in the land of the living, encouraged spirit possession, and utilized venerable power for both good and evil. Herbs, brews, baths, dreams, visions, and prophecy contributed to a depot of reliable sacred wares to bring about healing and agency.

The presence of African religions became a preoccupation of slaveholders and others both during and after slavery.[11] British colonizers deemed all the religious practices and worldviews that symbolized African heritage as backward and uncivilized. Indeed, such practices became the scaffolding upon which Europeans hung their construction of Europe as a counterpoint to the Caribbean. Without a nuanced understanding of the rituals and practices of the enslaved, slaveholders flattened all existing belief systems with the term "obeah," and even created laws to prosecute its practitioners and clients.[12] After Tacky's Rebellion in 1760, which used thaumaturgical beliefs as a mobilizing force, slaveholders and colonial officials became more preoccupied with policing the religious beliefs and practices of the enslaved.[13] As a legal term, "obeah" took on a life of its own, which had very little to do with the range of African-derived religious practices of Afro-Jamaicans, who rarely even claimed the term as their own.[14]

The broad category of obeah obscured a far more complex reality. African and African-derived religions in Jamaica underwent a process of evolution by which the religious practices of different African ethnic groups melded together to create something different. Additionally, African religious cosmologies also blended with Christianity to create various versions of

Africanized Christianity. The effort to precisely mark the moment when one religious form gives way to another has never been a perfect science, but it appears that different ethnic groups came together to produce revolts based on pan-African cooperation toward the end of the eighteenth century. The religion created by this blending of different African cosmologies was "Myalism." The Anglican Church had not worked hard to convert the enslaved population in Jamaica before the 1820s, but the arrival of black American Baptist missionaries Moses Baker, George Gibb, and George Lisle after the start of the American War of Independence in 1776 signaled the start of serious Christian evangelizing. The actual process by which African religious practices joined with Christianity in different ways and to varying degrees is debatable. The language of conversion, which assumes a linear shift from one belief system to another, has never accurately captured what has been a far more complex process.[15] The adoption of Christianity did not preclude African religious practices even as certain developments became publicly apparent. The proselytizing of the black American Baptist missionaries, which began in the late 1700s, led to the formation of Jamaica's Native Baptist denomination, which took root by 1830.[16] With the arrival of other missionaries, the Baptist, Methodist, Moravian, and Wesleyan missionaries jostled for influence, and Afro-Jamaicans incorporated, rejected, shaped, and reshaped rituals and biblical interpretations.

The Great Revival of 1860 also constituted a turning point as Myalism was transformed into Revivalism, which was divided into two branches: Zion and Pukumina. Zion was closer to Christianity in its adoption of Christian symbols and greater reliance upon the Bible. While practitioners acknowledged the existence of spirits, they shunned dangerous spirits through their religious practices and the display of sacred relics. On the other hand, practitioners of Pukumina displayed much greater distance from Christian symbols; they respected all spirits and invited spirit possession.[17]

Altogether, these African-derived religions in Jamaica connected with Africa through "spiritual" practices, including spirit possession. Rastafari did not qualify as African-derived religion in the same way because it spurned an African spirit world. As Taitu Heron and Yanique Hume rightfully conclude, "the practice of divination, food offerings and animal sacrifices to divinities, and ideas of spirit possession/participation are often perceived as 'devil business' by Rastafarians."[18] This was not always the case. Barry Chevannes has demonstrated a convincing link between early Rastafarians and Revivalism. During the early years, Rastafari's decentralized structure very much resembled that of Revivalism. Furthermore, the founders of Rastafari exhibited characteristics that can be traced to the earliest manifestations of Myalism. Early leaders such as Leonard Howell and Joseph Hibbert were known to be "scientists," which, in Jamaican parlance, meant they possessed special gifts associated with Myalism, ranging from prophecy to the power to use esoteric knowledge and spiritual literacy to control worldly circumstances. The followers of another leader, Robert Hinds, hailed him as a prophet and recognized him as one who was prone to visions.[19] The link to Revivalism continued into later periods as the leader of the Twelve Tribes of Israel, Prophet Gad, was a Revivalist before he made the shift to Rastafari in 1968. The members of the Twelve Tribes held Prophet Gad, their autonomous leader, in high esteem, and his appeal was boosted by the widespread belief that he was indeed a gifted prophet.

By the late 1940s, however, many aspects of Revivalism had been purged from Rastafari. Scholars generally agree that this was tied to the rise of a younger generation that built upon and also diverged from the Rastafarian practices of the movement's founders. One interpretation of this shift maintains that a Rastafarian organization, the Youth Black Faith, which emerged in 1949, consciously rejected practices such as the burning of candles, a ritual that had long been associated with the Revival tradition.[20] The members of Youth Black Faith did away with the structure of Revivalism and used the book of Revelation to denounce "supernatural" practices. Without attempting to rank the multiple ways in which Afro-Jamaicans have engaged with Africa, it is worth noting that African-derived religious cosmologies and ritual practices offered a different form of resistance from Rastafari, which emphasized consciousness.[21] Still, the disdain that many Rastafarians (there are exceptions) share for African-derived spiritual practices, including spirit possession, reflects the impact of Western intellectual discourses on Rastafari and on Caribbean thought more broadly.[22] This constitutes a major contradiction within Rastafari.[23]

The link to Africa during slavery also took the form of Ethiopianism, which became an ideological pillar of Rastafari and was crucial to the transnational history of black nationalist thought. The earliest manifestation of Ethiopianism hailed from biblical references to Ethiopia. Grounded in scripture, which proclaimed that "princes shall come out of Egypt, Ethiopia shall soon stretch forth her hands unto God" (Ps 68:31), Ethiopianism became the basis of a black theology. The references to Ethiopia in the Bible spawned the association of Ethiopia with black redemption and spoke to the notion of a downtrodden race that would receive divine deliverance. This was supported by the idea that "blacks were a chosen people with a special and distinctive destiny" and that "God would deliver New World Africans from slavery."²⁴ Ethiopia became synonymous with all of Africa, and Ethiopianism engendered a connection between Africans on the continent and throughout the diaspora.

Though fundamentally embedded in the Christian tradition, Ethiopianism did not remain static in black thought. By the late nineteenth century Ethiopianism, which had been "confined to the circle of Negro church people," became an "intellectually respectable" philosophy, spearheaded by Edward Wilmot Blyden, who set about vindicating the black race by pointing to sources other than the Bible to prove that Ethiopia was a highly civilized ancient nation. Blyden's work ushered in an intellectual (less mythical) Ethiopianism, and according to St. Claire Drake, "after 1900 Pan-Africanism gradually became the dominant political myth of the Black world—replacing the Ethiopianist pre-political myth."²⁵ The rise of a more secular Ethiopianism was significant, but this was not a linear evolution from one form to the next. The religious basis of Ethiopianism was summoned by Marcus Garvey's theology during the interwar years, and later by Rastafarians.

The Rastafarian movement relies heavily upon the religious/mythic component of Ethiopianism. When Ras Tafari Makonnen was crowned in 1930, Rastafarians were convinced that he had come to fulfill biblical prophesy. To support this claim, they relied upon Revelation 5:5, which reads, "And one of the elders saith unto me, Weep not: behold, the Lion of the Tribe of Juda, the Root of David, hath prevailed." They were, in fact, building upon a tradition of Ethiopianism that had been in existence in Jamaica long before the 1930s.²⁶ Though the historical record is scant on the history of Ethiopianism in Jamaica during the nineteenth century, it is likely that the biblical form was a part of the hermeneutics of what became the Native Baptist denomination.²⁷ In the final analysis, Ethiopianism represented an ideological progenitor of Rastafari that underscored both the local and the (black) international context for the movement's formation. Garveyism, also influenced by Ethiopianism, extended that link into the twentieth century.

Garveyism also became a foundational ideological pillar of Rastafari. Garvey's emphasis on messages of "race first," self-determination, race pride, repatriation to Africa, and his call to see God through the "spectacles of Ethiopia" all found resonance in Rastafari.²⁸ His emphasis on race as a tool of analysis and his insistence that "Africans at home and abroad" should take pride in African heritage has shaped Rastafarian psychology. Many early Rastafarians were either Garveyites or supporters of Garvey's movement, and for many Rastafarians even today, he ranks second only to

Haile Selassie.[29] Evidence of Garvey's elevated position within the movement can be found in statements made by prominent Rastafarians, in celebrations of his life, in references to his greatness captured by reggae songs, and in articles that have appeared in Rastafarian periodicals over the years.[30]

Garvey and Rastafarians also shared a disdain for Revivalist religions.[31] Garvey praised Africa while lashing out against "religions that howl, religions that create saints, religions that dance to frantic emotion."[32] Within Jamaica, belief in the spirit world and rituals that acted upon this belief came to signify class differentiation. In the wisdom of the times, such activity represented lower-class status as the masses performed spirituality in a way that was not considered respectable by colonial standards. This elitist critique was also common among black intellectuals on an international level as they engaged in racial uplift.[33] Additionally, for those who had socialist and communist affiliations, religion was a hindrance to true liberation.[34] In this way, though both Garveyism and Rastafari were generally associated with grassroots expressions, they were aligned with elitist dismissals of African-derived styles of worship. Yet while Garvey praised the pope and respected Catholicism, Rastafarians saw the Church of Rome as evil and the pope as the Antichrist. This was cemented after the pope endorsed Italy's invasion of Ethiopia in 1935. Rastafarians further departed from Garvey with the veneration of Haile Selassie.[35] Even so, Garvey occupied a very important place among Rastafarians generally, was celebrated as a prophet, and was instrumental in imagining a black god. He occupied a part of the holy trinity for a Rasta group named the Bobo Shanti, and the members of URIA referred to him as a "prophet" and a "saint." From Garvey's motto, "one God, one Aim, one Destiny," they fashioned their own: "One Jah, One Aim, One Destiny."[36]

Rastafari Livity

Rastafarians generally experience Rastafari as a comprehensive worldview that governs daily life. Crucial to the Rastafarian rejection of British cultural dominance is the Rastafarian language, known as dread talk.[37] Incorporated within Jamaican nation language (as opposed to "standard" British English) is a Rastafarian lexicon that powerfully articulates the Rasta worldview. The movement speaks truth to power and understands that Rastafarians' oral expression serves as a correction to the erroneous colonial written histories of Jamaica. Though written sources for the history of Rasta have in recent years gained in importance, the movement's genesis was very much connected to the larger history of how the Afro-Jamaican population defined itself through oral culture.[38] Rastafari highlights the politics of language, noting its relationship to culture, tradition, and identity, and its lexicon captures fundamental concepts. The word "Babylon" refers to the Western world and its oppressive, exploitative nature. Slavery and colonialism lie at the core of this understanding of the West, which, from the standpoint of Rastafari, is a clearly racialized one. Historically, Babylon has produced polarizing notions of black and white based on the racial hierarchy established during the period of slavery. As the movement evolved from the colonial into the postcolonial period, the Rastafarian notion of Babylon maintained its racial analysis in reflecting the continued salience of the conditions of (racial) inequality imposed on the African descended by slavery and colonialism. Ever adaptable and committed to the present and the past simultaneously, Babylon expanded to include the United States in order to accommodate its rise as an imperial power after the official colonial rule of western Europe began to wane.

In the lexicon, the opposite of Babylon is Zion, which refers to Africa—to home. As a word, "Zion" represents the true home of Rastafarians and forever establishes them as people who reside in Jamaica only temporarily. Zion allows them to be in a diasporic space of exile, without being *of* that space, while also naming the place to which they hope to return. The Rastafarian subversion of colonial sensibilities through language is also evident in a word like "downpression," which stresses that there is nothing *uplifting* about "oppression." A cornerstone of the Rastafarian lexicon, "I-n-I" functions on various levels and captures key Rastafarian concepts. On one level, the "I-n-I" affirms the subjective "I" as a way to emphasize the agency of the individual. Within the context of Jamaica's history of enslavement and colonialism, this represents a "rejection of subservience in Babylon culture and an affirmation of self as an active agent in the creation of one's own reality and identity."[39] The "I-n-I" also speaks to the connectedness between the individual and people. Along with the assertion of self is a profound awareness of the ways in which the individual is connected to others. On yet another level, the "I-n-I" speaks to the idea that every individual embodies the divine; it signifies the unity between God and man, the Rastafarian idea that "man is God and God is man." When Rastafarians proclaim "Rastafari," they are applying the name "both to God and to themselves" because "in affirming that his name is Rastafari, the Rastaman is claiming an identity with his God that is more than merely nominal. He is expressing a conviction that his is a part of the Godhead itself."[40] This emphasizes humans being godlike and empowered, with emphasis on the idea of humans becoming divine rather than God becoming human. This concept underscores the status of Rastafari as a religion focused on the realities of the present, an idea that was very much in sync with the this-worldly interpretations that characterize the movement. For Rastafari, "God is a living human, heaven is on earth in Africa, the apocalypse is now and the Anti-Christ is Rome; its deliverer the reigning monarch of Ethiopia."[41] Again, this asserts the power of the individual to affirm self, while also underscoring the relevance of the history of biblical figures anointed in order to carry out God's work.

Rastafari's expression of its philosophy extends to aesthetics. Though not all Rastafarians wore locks, many did, and the association of the movement with the mane of the "natty dread" was widespread. Dreadlocks have been connected to the Rastafarian use of the lion as a symbol of strength and (black) power. As a hairstyle that broke with conventional standards of grooming in colonial Jamaica, locks did not become a core Rasta identifier until the 1940s with the emergence of the Youth Black Faith. They understood that British cultural dominance included the glorification of a European standard of beauty. From the exaltation of a blue-eyed and blond-haired Jesus to the link between straight hair and "acceptable" ways of grooming, the skin colors and hair textures of Afro-Jamaicans were denigrated. Locks signaled pride in African heritage and triumph over the audacious whiteness of British cultural imperialism.

The oral histories of Rastafari contain multiple explanations concerning exactly how and why locks became a feature of the movement. One history argues that Rastafarians were inspired by the Mau Mau warriors of Kenya, the dreadlocked images of whom appeared in newspapers across the African diaspora as symbols of anticolonial struggle on the African continent. Underscoring East Indian influences on the Rastafarian movement, another explanation sees Rastafarians as having been inspired by images of Sadhus, Hindu holy men.[42] The Bible also offers an explanation, as many Rastafarians invoke the Nazirite vow as written in chapter 6 of the book of Numbers. This biblical justification includes proscriptions such as "no razor may be used on their head," and "they must let their hair grow long."

The widespread use of ganja (marijuana) in ritual practice among Rastafarians is well known. Referred to by many Rastafarians as "herb," ganja is believed to facilitate not only communion but spiritual enlightenment. As such, the act of smoking it is an essential part of the ritual of "reasoning," a "form of collective and visionary discourse in which individuals explore the implications of a particular insight, which could be based on subjects as diverse as a Bible passage or an event in the day's news."[43] Rastafarians also extol the healing and medicinal properties of ganja, accessible not just through smoking but as an ingredient in food and as a tea. Aside from ganja, Rastafarians see the healing properties of plants and herbs generally. This is in keeping with their pursuit of a natural lifestyle that depends on nature's bounty and translates into an "ital" diet, which consists of organic, unprocessed foods and, usually, the omission of salt as an ingredient. Yet Rastafarians differ in terms of dietary practices and observances. For example, while most Rastafarians do not eat pork, dietary restrictions vary significantly. The ital lifestyle encompasses a variety of positions, ranging from being strictly vegetarian to eating meat and/or fish.

Beyond these general characteristics of the Rastafarian movement are the mansions/houses that affect ritual practices. The Rasta community in Tanzania included members of the Nyabingi and the Twelve Tribes of Israel. Joshua Mkhululi and Ras Bupe Karudi, the two men who led the repatriation, were members of the Twelve Tribes of Israel, the Rasta organization with the largest international following. Although the Twelve Tribes shares much with the wider movement, it is, in significant ways, a unique expression of Rastafari. Founded by Vernon Carrington, also known as Prophet Gad, Brother Gad, or Gad Man, it initially operated as a charter (Local 15) of the Ethiopian World Federation (EWF). He was inspired and felt called to "do this work" after reading the bible from Genesis to Revelation twice.

Along with some early members including Brother Dan, Sister May, and Noel Douglas, Prophet Gad began to hold meetings under the governing body of the EWF in 1968. The EWF was founded in New York in 1937 by an Ethiopian called Melaku E. Beyen. With the full support of Emperor Haile Selassie, the EWF emerged in response to the outpouring of support when Italy invaded the country and Africans on the continent and in the diaspora rallied in support of Ethopia and its emperor. Furthermore, in connection with the EWF, Haile Selassie issued a land grant in Shashamane to Africans in the diaspora in 1955.[44] By 1972, Prophet Gad had officially broken with the EWF, having concluded that the Chicago-based branch with which he was affiliated was probably fraudulent and illegitimate.[45] As he moved forward under the name of the Twelve Tribes of Israel, he gathered members by holding weekly meetings. As more people joined, they formed what came to be known as the executive body of the Twelve Tribes of Israel. This body consisted of twelve men who represented the twelve sons of the biblical figure Jacob, one woman to represent Jacob's only daughter, Dinah, as well as twelve women. In addition, each member of the executive body had a "shadow," which established forty-nine executive members including the representative of Dinah. In the language of the organization, the executive members had to be "seated on the bench" and after the forty-nine were "sealed," the executive members began to hold monthly as opposed to weekly meetings.[46] In 1979, the organization used the membership dues and donations to purchase its headquarters on Hope Road in Kingston. This became the consistent venue for Twelve Tribes' events after having held meetings in many different locations since the very first meeting at Davis Lane in Trench Town.[47]

For the Twelve Tribes of Israel, "repatriation is a must."[48] The former link with the EWF showed up in the group's focus on repatriation to Ethiopia, a defining preoccupation of the Twelve Tribes of Israel.[49] Within Rastafari, the Twelve Tribes stood out for its organized efforts to collect funds from its members to aid with the cost of repatriation to Shashamane. Each member was given a card called a "dues book," which proved membership and recorded the member's financial contributions to the fund for repatriation and other expenses. Because members were chosen for repatriation based on when they joined the organization (earlier members going first), the dues book also provided a record of when each person became a member. For the members of this particular Rasta group, repatriation was a realistic goal to be carried out through a systematic process. By 1971, Prophet Gad had gone to Ethiopia twice, accompanied by a member of the executive body. In September 1972, the organization supported the departure of its first repatriate, Eric Smith (Asher Burks).[50] Between 1972 and 1980, the Twelve Tribes of Israel sent a total of twenty-seven men and women to Shashamane, Ethiopia. By 1982, the members of the Twelve Tribes who went to Ethiopia included a few like David James and Milky Zebulon who departed from one of the Twelve Tribes' branches in the United Kingdom.[51]

The Twelve Tribes of Israel is a centralized group within the wider movement, with an autonomous leader and an executive body. Within the organization (often referred to as the "organ"), there is reverence for Prophet Gad, whom the members embraced as one of the prophets of Israel and to whom they looked for spiritual instruction and doctrinal clarification. His position as a spiritual leader and trusted definer of the group's doctrine was clear. He encouraged the members of the Twelve Tribes to read the teachings of both Haile Selassie and Marcus Garvey. Most importantly, though, the members of the Twelve Tribes considered themselves students of the Bible, which they saw as a religious text, as well as "a history and a prophecy for the Twelve Tribes and the world."[52] Whereas some Rastafarians remain conflicted about the extent to which they should claim the name "Christian," the Twelve Tribes proudly asserts its connection to Christianity, and in keeping with this, the Holy Bible was central to the group's theology. One prominent member of the group declared on the occasion of Prophet Gad's passing that he would be remembered as the "chief individual who brought Rastafarian doctrine in line with the full teachings of the Holy Bible."[53]

Prophet Gad's dominance notwithstanding, the Twelve Tribes of Israel does in some ways represent the doctrinal diversity within the wider Rastafari movement.[54] This became clear after the prophet uncharacteristically agreed to a radio interview in 1997 and clarified the group's precise theological position.[55] His definitive statement that Haile Selassie was not the second dispensation of Christ led to a crisis among the members of the founding branch of the Twelve Tribes in Jamaica.[56] Though he had enjoyed autonomy as a leader, he had also encouraged the members of the Twelve Tribes to read the Bible a chapter a day in order to find the truth revealed therein.[57] This resulted in at least two different truths within the Twelve Tribes: one saw Haile Selassie as the second dispensation of Christ (Almighty God), while the other saw him as a representation of Christ on earth. Despite this complexity, it is important to note that the organ's heavy use of the Christian Bible affected the way in which both Ras Bupe Karudi and Joshua Mkhululi experienced and thought about the repatriation to Tanzania. In going to Tanzania as individuals, they had broken with the Twelve Tribes of Israel's well-established approach to repatriation. They had, however, not broken with its particular form of religiosity.

Karudi and Mkhululi led the attempts to bring about a large-scale exodus of Rastafarians from Jamaica to Tanzania, and for both, repatriation was a mission ordained by Jah. For Mkhululi, physical repatriation to Africa represented the fulfillment of prophecy. He saw his personal repatriation as inextricably linked to the repatriation of all Rastafarians and worked to bring about a mass exodus from the West to Tanzania. His personal writings about his journey established that even after thirty-three years in Tanzania, he remained wedded to the religious expression of Rastafari. According to Mkhululi, "It is a special time for I and I because at the end of every dispensation something significant happens that changes the earth—Adam, Noah, Christ. Rastafari came in 1930 to shorten the days for the sake of the elect. He is the Shiloah—the scepter shall not depart from Judah until Shiloah come, and unto H.I.M shall the gathering of the people be. The scepter is now handed to I and I, together with the people, to set-up Jah Kingdom, as shown in Revelation 7."[58] On one level, his use of "I-n-I" affirms the subjective "I" as a way to emphasize his agency as an individual. As a Rastafarian, Mkhululi's complete embrace of this concept is evident in his attempts to realize not only an ideological and spiritual return to Africa but also a physical one. "I-n-I" also meant that along with his assertion of self came a profound awareness of the ways in which he was connected to others. Mkhululi understood his responsibility as an individual but also knew that he would go about the work of setting up Jah's kingdom "together with the people."

Mkhululi's assertion that the scepter had now been "handed to I and I, together with the people, to set-up Jah Kingdom" meant that as was the case for anointed kings and prophets before him, he had been anointed and appointed to not only spread God's message but to establish his kingdom. For Rastafarians, the word "messiah" was commonly perceived to refer to the prophets or kings of Israel who were anointed by God. This meant that these prophets and kings were inhabited by the spirit of God and as a result were able to "proclaim HIS message and lead his people in the establishment of HIS kingdom on earth."[59] In this capacity, prophets and kings were "custodians of the temporal kingdom" and were different from Haile Selassie, who was "the Shiloah." The term "Shiloah," sometimes spelled "Shiloh," appears in the Bible as both a messianic title and as the name of a town.[60] Used by Mkhululi as a messianic title, "Shiloah" referred both to anointed human beings like himself and to *the* Shiloah, Haile Selassie, a "supreme man who is divine in a primordial way."[61] Haile Selassie's lineage, for which Rastafarians find ample support in the Bible, proved that he was the Shiloah, and Mkhululi used a verse from the book of Genesis to support the claim that Haile Selassie, who received the title of "Conquering Lion of the Tribe of Judah" at his coronation in 1930, represented the coming of the Shiloah. This represented another dispensation as the "scepter," which referred to the power or authority of the Almighty God, "shall not depart from Judah" until the coming of the messiah.

Ras Bupe Karudi also consistently framed his repatriation narratives in religious terms. All of his personal memoirs about the repatriation, and the letters he sent to others from whom he sought financial and moral support for the mission, underscored the centrality of Rastafari as a religion in his life. As he stated in the opening of one document, "let everlasting praise in uprightness be given unto the Holy One of Creation; let upfull praise be given unto JAH (God) who alone doeth great wonders; ceaseless praise be given unto JAH who made great lights, the sun to rule by day, and the moon and the stars to rule by night; never-ending praise unto JAH who remembereth I-n-I [us] in I-n-I [our] low estate, and hath redeemed I-n-I from I-n-I cruel enemies, for JAH loving mercy endureth even forever! Jah Rastafari!"[62]

Karudi reiterated the religious significance of repatriation when he thanked Jah "for divine inspiration, guidance, and protection." In response to the difficulties of repatriation, Karudi relied upon his faith: "as it was said already, let it be done right now, ever bringing to remembrance the prophecy of JAH—'What I-n-I sow in tears, I-n-I shall reap in joy,' for of a certainty, 'Righteousness will prevail, even in the fullness of this time! Prophecy must be fulfilled!'"[63]

The specific religiosity of the Twelve Tribes of Israel was not the only characteristic of this group that had bearing on the repatriation; the group also changed class dynamics within Rastafari. The emergence of the Twelve Tribes marked the point at which middle-class Jamaicans began to join the Rastafarian movement, which had previously been associated with the grassroots background of its early members.[64] Middle class members of the Twelve Tribes of Israel underscored the reality that black consciousness and issues of cultural identity appealed to a wide cross-section of the African-descended in Jamaica. This did not mean that the vast majority of its members were from the middle class. In fact, the humble beginnings of Prophet Gad reflected that of the founders of the wider movement and of the vast majority of its followers. Furthermore, the Twelve Tribes aimed to eschew class divisions via the intermingling of members from different backgrounds, a mix that was reflected in the leadership among the executive body and in relationships, both platonic and romantic. But it is the first point at which many with the background of Mkhululi, who had been university educated, began to join the movement. Many of them had been radicalized as students at the University of the West Indies at a time when Jamaican youth were influenced by the black power movement in North America and by Jamaican forms of black consciousness/radicalism that were connected to but independent of external forces.[65] Mkhululi, who worked as a college professor in Tanzania, represented middle-class presence within Rastafari, and this presence led to conflicts within the movement when some Rastafarians dismissed the Twelve Tribes as a less radical form of Rastafari. Mkhululi and other Rastafarians were not a part of the peasantry and did not live in the Jamaican "ghettos." This was a real difference. Some Rastafarians of the wider movement were also critical of the Twelve Tribes' openness to white members, which was perceived to be an indication of the group's conservatism and general "uptown," middle-class nature. Yet middle-class members of the Twelve Tribes essentially aimed to commit a form of "class suicide" as the Rastafarian consciousness they embraced aimed to transcend such differentiation. In the end, they represented a grassroots movement with grassroots sensibilities. Class differences did not create a problem among the Rastafarians who repatriated to Tanzania. Neither did the different group affiliations, as some identified with the Nyabingi order.

The Nyabingi mansion of Rastafari represents an aggregate rather than a centralized group. The term has been traced to an East African movement. Histories of Nyabingi have been difficult to reconstruct. Still, certain themes have been associated with this movement, which has been linked to narratives of public healing and religion across the Great Lakes region of eastern Africa.[66] One understanding of the Nyabingi movement with which early Rastafarians may have been aware holds that it originated in Kigezi, Uganda,[67] and was associated with the worship of the goddess Nyabingi, who appeared among the Bakiga people of Uganda during the eighteenth century.[68] She came to be associated with resistance to foreign domination, and historians have argued that this link was strengthened in the nineteenth century when the Bakiga were faced with significant social challenges across the interlacustrine region.[69] By the time of European encroachment, "Nyabingi became the embodiment of the ideal of Kiga autonomy and served as a vehicle for anticolonial agitation and the expression of anti-European sentiments."[70] Accordingly, when Rastafarian men began to refer to themselves as "Nya-men," it is possible that they were positing a connection with the view of Nyabingi as an anticolonial movement.[71]

Additionally, Ken Post argues that the concept of Nyabingi became a part of the Rastafarian worldview in 1935 after an article in the Jamaican publication *Plain Talk* stated that Haile Selassie took over the Nyabingi movement and would lead its followers in a black revolt against whites.[72] This was a flawed but particularly poignant idea, as it coincided with Italy's invasion of Ethiopia.[73] Though a precise explanation of how and why the concept of Nyabingi became absorbed into Rastafari is elusive, it is important to note that it represented an East African influence upon early Rastafari, which ventured beyond Ethiopia. As chapter 5 will show, this link became meaningful to Tanzanians who embraced Rastafari through their relationships with the Jamaican Rastafarians.

What became known as the Nyabingi order within the movement began to take shape with the emergence of the Youth Black Faith, which was formed in Trench Town in the late 1940s. This marked the point at which dreadlocks and beards became common among Rastafarians, and the Youth Black Faith came to represent "a more intense rebellious spirit."[74] Several

Rastafarian groups from this period trace their genealogy to Leonard Howell, recognized by many as the first Rasta.[75] These include the Rastafarian Repatriation Center of Samuel Livermore Brown, the groups in the Jamaican neighborhoods of Dungle and Salt Lane, and the Church Triumphant of Ras Shadrack on Foreshore Road, to which two of the repatriates to Tanzania belonged. Within the Nyabingi, rather than a concretized set of guidelines, elders have been instrumental in passing information about Rastafari from one generation to the next. The religious practices of the Nyabingi developed in the Dungle, Trench Town, and Back O'Wall communities.[76] These rituals relied on Nyabingi drums (*akete*), which included the *base*, the *funde*, and the repeater. These Rastafarians also developed a particular form of worship referred to as the *bingi* when they chanted praises (including psalms from the Bible) to Jah within a circular tabernacle. The Rasta colors of red, gold, and green, along with photographs of Haile Selassie and an altar, were prominently displayed at these gatherings, which went on throughout the night. By contrast, members of the Twelve Tribes of Israel such as Karudi and Mkhululi did not perform the *bingi*; their monthly gatherings occurred outdoors on the lawn of the headquarters and included the Ethiopian anthem, Christian hymns, readings from Bible passages, and announcements. The specific group to which they belonged did not interfere with recruitment processes as they encouraged other Rastafarians to join them in Tanzania. When Ras Iman Mani, Ras Kwetenge, and Ras Daniel Heartman and his son Ato Kidani Roberts joined Karudi and Mkhululi, they represented a Nyabingi presence. This would make a lasting impression on Tanzanians who learned about Rastafari from the repatriates.

The Universal Rastafari Association and the Gendered Afrikan Nation

The members of URIA were clear about their desire to build an "Afrikan nation." The vision was also a masculine, heteronormative one that included a great deal of moralizing. For the Rastafarian men of URIA, the progress of the race was closely intertwined with issues of gender and sexuality. Crucial to their ideas about racial progress were clear views about the role of women in the building of a nation. These ideas were generated by perceptions of gender norms in precolonial African societies, various currents of colonial thought, the experiences of black women during slavery, and continuities with Garveyite thinking. These men argued that patriarchy had never been a feature of African life across the continent, and that European civilization was founded on patriarchy; they understood a patrilineal system to be a European one and insisted that it established the father in a family as the "supreme ruler." Under this system, European women were oppressed and subjected to "sexual exploitation, domination and restriction." Africa, by contrast, promoted a matriarchal and matrilineal system, which ensured that women were equals. This thinking provided the basis for their conclusion that the Western trends of the 1960s and 1970s, which they associated with free love, hot pants, miniskirts, and the pill, did not apply to the African woman—who, they maintained, had "always been liberated in all things through the system of equality and through her own virtue, sense and love of high morality."[77]

In keeping with this dichotomous understanding of gender relations in Europe and Africa, these Rasta men argued that, beginning with slavery, African women were subjected to the immorality of European men. Enslaved women had been "subjected for centuries to many outrageous acts of perversion during the days of slavery by European slave masters." In response to the exploitation of women and the stereotypes about black hypersexuality that were rooted in slavery, they determined that Rastafarian women were better protected and respected by Rastafarian men.

The men of URIA worried about the impact of sexual deviance on the construction of the morally sound African nation they sought to build, and the lion's share of this burden to uphold the moral rectitude of the African nation fell on Rastafarian women themselves. As the men saw it, sexual deviance pertained to the "choice" to use contraceptives, to abort babies, or to engage in sexual activity solely for pleasure. The history of white British men perceiving of black women as available for rape led these Rastafarian men to abhor prostitution in particular. For them, the "presence of the Afrikan mother parading on the streets of Babylon as a common whore" was a "terrible and dreadful indication" of the psychological impact of Western values. In light of the history of white men assaulting black women, they found it incomprehensible that a black woman would choose prostitution and thereby "degrade her nation, culture and self." They chastised these women, designating them the "dregs left in the bottom of a barrel."[78]

This was also tied to their denouncement of miscegenation, another link to Garveyism. As Michele Mitchell demonstrates about Garveyism in the African American context, after Reconstruction Garveyites "could not recognize their goals without the actual biological perpetuation of the race." In other words, if Garveyites were going to succeed in creating a nation that was black, "sexuality had to be monitored and controlled so that it benefited the race."[79] As it did for Garveyites, the Rastafarian commitment to the African race depended on the sex lives of Rastafarians. These Rastafarian men posited that, in order to strengthen the African nation, Rastafarian women had to seek their model of womanhood in reproduction and the "traditional" African devotion to children. The role of the woman, therefore, was crucial to their understanding of how to bring about the "upliftment" of the race.

While the men of URIA do not represent all Rastafarian men, male dominance has a well-established history within the movement, accompanied by a plethora of biblical passages used to boost its power. Though women have historically dominated religious spaces in Jamaica, this has not been the case within the Rastafarian movement.[80] The area of gender equality has been a striking and easily identifiable analytical space in which Rastafari does not employ a revolutionary hermeneutic when reading the Christian Bible. Diane Austin-Broos argues that Rasta "draws significantly from a biblical poetics in which the transcendence of the man is thought to come through feminine subordination."[81] Similarly, Imani Tafari-Ama finds that "traditionally, the male leadership in Rastafari has portrayed the role of women as supportive and subordinate to the male."[82] Women have been excluded from participation in key rituals such as reasoning.[83] Rastafarian men—and in some cases, women—uphold the general idea that "man is the head of woman,"[84] and the teachings of St. Paul have given Rastafarians ammunition to assert that women were in need of male instruction. As they understand it, St. Paul maintains that women should not be in positions of leadership because Eve proved her inability to lead when she ushered sin into the world.[85] Scripture has been used quite literally to endorse the notion that men were the arbiters of spiritual instruction, captured in the phrasing of a "Rastaman's woman" as opposed to a "Rastafarian woman" in her own right. The widespread use of the word "daughta" to refer to Rastafarian women also demonstrates the belief that women are not spiritual or moral equals to men. The book of Leviticus has been used to justify seclusion during menstruation when women are thought to be unclean, and certain Bible verses have also been used to govern a modest dress code for women (Deut. 22:5; I Tim. 3:8–10).

The Christian Bible is not the only source for constructing gender roles within the Rastafarian movement. Jamaican peasant culture and efforts at (African) cultural innovation also influence thinking on such matters, and this further complicates the quest for a definitive assessment of women's roles in the movement. Additionally, the literature on Rastafari has reinforced patriarchal assumptions about the movement by focusing on male actors and masculine accounts of Rastafari's history and culture. The early historiography of Jamaica, writ large, was afflicted with similar male-centered narratives.[86] Yet scholars have demonstrated that women were not only present but were active in all areas of struggle during slavery and after emancipation.[87] As Mimi Sheller argues, "in the case of Jamaica, one is confronted head-on with the unexpected but critical participation of women in not only behind-the-scenes cultural resistance, but also in public activities such as collective labor protest, petitioning, demonstration and riot."[88]

There is no denying that gender inequity exists within Rastafari. Yet, the movement has evolved and has made great strides based on efforts by both Rastafarian women and men. Reflecting shifts within Jamaica and beyond, such as the women's rights movement of the 1970s, many Rastafarian women began to pose more visible challenges to male dominance. Scholars also argue that the entrance of middle-class women into the movement in the 1970s contributed to such changes.[89] The rise of the Twelve Tribes of Israel, which had women as a part of its leadership, has also been marked as a turning point for Rastafarian women. Beyond the significance of women being represented in Rastafari leadership, this assessment assumes that the presence of a greater percentage of educated women in the Twelve Tribes has meant less tolerance among those women for patriarchal norms. This assumption appears to hold weight when compared, in a general way, with female members of the Bobo Shanti who were secluded during menstruation. But such crude class analysis does not hold completely. Interviews with Twelve Tribes women revealed a wide spectrum of viewpoints concerning women's perceptions of their own place within the movement. For example, some women accepted the idea that the man was the "head of woman" and used biblical scripture to support this understanding of gender dynamics. In this case, religion trumped class and level of education, as women from all walks of life accepted this idea. Yet, for many, this came with a condition: men had to uphold their end of the arrangement by providing for their families and consistently practicing Rastafarian ideals in everyday "livity."[90]

Rastafarian women have been framed in two main ways. One interpretation sees male dominance as "built into the basic nature of Rastafari in such a way as to constitute its central contradiction."[91] This interpretation finds that the movement undermines its own critique of Jamaican society by reproducing its patriarchy. On the other hand, there is the view that the paradigm of a built-in male dominance in Rastafari denies female agency and is invalid in instances when a Rastafarian woman fully understands and accepts prescribed gender roles.[92] In such a diverse movement, it is likely that both interpretations carry weight, yet this polarity constrains analytical framings for the experiences of Rastafarian women. Some do not see themselves as necessarily reconciling their existence within patriarchy because they rely upon their own tools of hermeneutics and exegesis. Beyond the questions of how Rasta women deal with patriarchy and why they choose to remain in such a movement is an entirely different analytical space that takes seriously their ideological commitments. This space allows for their independent thoughts about Rastafari, which are emancipatory and outside of the organizational and theological structures erected by Rastafarian men. For example, some women proclaim that Haile Selassie's wife, Queen Omega, occupies an equally significant position and serves as a role model in her own right, citing references to her in Leonard Howell's *The Promised Key* as proof of this. Some also evoke Queen Nyabingi, highlighting the history of female religious leadership behind the chosen affiliation (the Nyabingi order) of a large percentage of Rastafarians. Whether or not these women are aware of the details of the history of the Nyabingi movement, its evolution involved gender wars arguably similar to those that have been waged within Rastafari. Within the context of the evolution of the Nyabingi movement in southwestern Uganda, Iris Berger argues that "many women sought empowerment through her [Nyabingi's] spirit" during the nineteenth century.[93] Rastafarian women have also interpreted the Bible differently as they created/solidified alternative woman-centered myths that reflected their perceptions of themselves. Furthermore, paradigms that center Rastafarian women may destabilize the metanarrative of men as the progenitors of the movement. Sister May, a respected elder and member of the executive body of the Twelve Tribes of Israel, maintains that along with the widely accepted founder of the group, Vernon Carrington (Prophet Gad), she was also a founder.[94]

Rastafari Chants Down Capitalism

Rastafari's understanding of Babylon was not only about race. Notably, the members of URIA saw racism and capitalism as inextricably linked. They insisted that racism was "entwined" and "interwoven" into the "basic fabrication of Europe's foundation of capitalism," and they saw capitalism as carrying within it the seeds of its own destruction. This was exemplified by the Great Depression of the 1930s, which "demonstrated the evident weaknesses of capitalism and how this finely balanced system can so easily be self-destructive." In essence, they blamed Western democracy, with its free market and "anything goes" mentality, for creating the conditions for immorality and myriad forms of exploitation. In light of historical shifts and the changing geopolitical landscape, these Rastafarians identified America as having "secured a capitalist death grip" on developing countries like Jamaica. In a biting critique of tourism in the postindependence era, they argued that Jamaica had become one of the new "garbage bins for the depraved dollar rich European tourists who flock to" the island.[95] This analysis of tourism resembled the one offered by Frantz Fanon in which he forewarned that tourism would essentially establish "brothels" for Europe.[96]

URIA's anticapitalist viewpoint was not new to Rastafari. Rastafarians were critical of capitalist approaches to development in Jamaica, and this aspect of their philosophy did much to secure their position on the margins of Jamaican citizenship. Rastafari posited that capitalism was inextricably bound to slavery and in the colonial and postcolonial periods remained an exploitative, individualistic system that thrived on the destruction of those of African descent globally. The capitalist way of life, captured in the term "Babylon," had been decried by Rastafarians in favor of an often vague, utopian alternative that was its very antithesis: "Zion." Yet, though Zion was ultimately Africa, Rastafarians offered a critique of capitalist development in Jamaica, which "was embodied and lived, not merely stated."[97]

Several scholars have made references to a link between Rastafari and socialism.[98] One even argued that the repatriation to Tanzania warranted closer examination particularly because of what it could illuminate about the "degree of compatibility between Rastafari knowing and socialist thinking."[99] When Leonard Howell, hailed as the first Rasta, established a commune named Pinnacle in St. Catherine, Jamaica, in 1940, he was clear about his aim to lead a "socialistic life."[100] Howell was born in Clarendon, Jamaica, on June 16, 1898. He had traveled to Colon, Panama, and to Harlem before he returned to Jamaica and set-up what has been described as a "great Ras Tafarite kingdom."[101] Under the banner of the Ethiopian Salvation Society, Howell held meetings that were monitored by the colonial government, and in February 1938 he was "certified insane" and placed in a mental health facility until December of that year. By 1940 Governor Arthur Richards had concluded that Howell's activities were dangerous because they caused "racial feelings" that were a potential threat to public safety.[102] Howell's commune at Pinnacle was cause for great concern. Though he was an autonomous and arguably autocratic leader who owned the land and directed his followers, Pinnacle was "based on communal principles where work was done in common and goods equally shared." This chosen exile from Jamaican society offended the colonial order, and this resulted in the police raiding Pinnacle, harassing its inhabitants, and arresting Howell on multiple occasions. In recognizing Pinnacle as a symbol of self-determination, one scholar placed the commune within the tradition of the Free Villages that were formed in Jamaica after emancipation from slavery in 1838.[103] With the aid of Baptist missionaries, the first Free Village was formed in Sligoville, St. Catherine—the same parish in which Pinnacle was founded.[104] In a tense climate that saw plantation owners and other elites actively working to maintain the social and economic order by keeping the formerly enslaved tied to plantation labor, the Free Villages represented an unwelcome repudiation of the status quo.[105] Free Villages facilitated the rise of a peasantry, which made important political, social, economic, and cultural contributions to the development of Jamaica. Beyond the psychological and social benefits of leaving the plantation after emancipation, the creation of a peasantry allowed some to acquire land and to cultivate crops for trade and export.[106]

Slightly more than a hundred years after emancipation, Pinnacle resonated with the Jamaican authorities in a similar manner: it signified a desire to pursue a different, independent way of life. To the writers of the 1960 *Report on the Ras Tafari Movement in Kingston, Jamaica* (commonly known as the University Report), Pinnacle appeared to "have been rather more like an old Maroon settlement than part of Jamaica [as] its internal administration was Howell's business, not Government's."[107] Indeed, despite the contradictions that undermined the pursuit of communalism at Pinnacle, Howell aimed to create a "community of believers," and his very approach—which saw him encourage peasants not to pay taxes—was a form of "defiant anticolonialism."[108] Needless to say, the colonial government did not take kindly to such effrontery. Within the context of colonial Jamaica, the crime committed by Howell was sedition. Along with his lieutenant, Robert Hinds, Howell was arrested by the colonial regime on January 1, 1934, as a result of speeches delivered by both men in 1933. The government found the idea that Ras Tafari was the "Messiah returned to earth" laughable. The "seditious speech," which "excite[d] hatred and contempt for His Majesty the king," created "disaffection among the subjects of His Majesty," and "disturb[ed] the public peace and tranquility of the island," was, however, no laughing matter.[109] Of grave concern in 1940 was also the idea that Pinnacle was an "isolated abode" that functioned as a "socialist colony" and its members constituted "a group apart, practical communists in the midst of a land where democracy rules happily."[110] Having arrested Howell multiple times, the Jamaican government finally destroyed the commune once and for all in 1954.

The precise ideological underpinnings of Howell's conception of a "socialistic life" are not clear. There is evidence that he formed a relationship with towering radical Left thinker George Padmore in 1938. The mail Howell sent from within the walls of the Bellevue psychiatric hospital in which he was detained shows that he had written at least one letter to Padmore. It also shows that he had subscribed to *Negro Worker,* the organ of the International Trade Union Committee of Negro Workers.[111] In 1981, Jah Bones, a leader among Rastafarians in England, referred to the Rasta community at Pinnacle as a "separatist village" where the "distinctive Rasta lifestyle developed." It was, he continued, "a bit like Marxism."[112] Evidence suggests that some Rastafarians identified with Marxism, but it is not conclusive.

Scholars have used both "socialism" and "Marxism" in reference to Rastafari. By the 1950s, colonial officials sought to understand the ideas that animated Rastafari with a view to devising suitable strategies to ensure the movement's demise. Reflecting the international climate of the 1950s, they were specifically concerned about a link to communism. In 1956 Governor Hugh Foot worried that the "local communist clique" would "make use" of Rastafarians, and by 1959 Governor Kenneth Blackburne seemed sure that "certain individual members of the cult" held what he referred to as "communist beliefs."[113] In addition, the Special Branch of the Jamaica Constabulary Force issued an intelligence report in 1957 in which it posited a link between Rastafarians and Communists. In particular, the Special Branch reported that the Communist People's Freedom Movement had reached out to Rastafarians in St. James and Kingston, and that another Communist group had ordered books for its bookshop and had circulated them among Rastafarians.[114] The absence of a detailed and/or unified Rastafarian statement on the movement's critique of capitalism prevents analytical precision. It is likely that in their thinking on Babylon's exploitative nature, Rastafarians shared beliefs with members of the radical Left, a group that in and of itself encompassed a wide range of orientations including Marxist, scientific socialist, and socialist. Rastafari's enduring denunciation of capitalism guaranteed this association with the radical Left. Additionally, though most Rastafarians did not live in communes, the association with communal living remained a widespread part of Rastafarian consciousness, and of the scholarly perception that there was indeed a link.

Following in the footsteps of Howell's commune, the next Rastafarian attempt at cooperative living took shape in 1958 with the emergence of the Ethiopia Black International Congress, the Bobo Shanti, founded by Prince Emmanuel Edwards. Though committed to repatriation to Africa, the Bobo Shanti made a real effort to establish a more acceptable way of life within Jamaica. This manifested in the very ritualistic lifestyle promoted at its commune in the Hills of Bull Bay, Jamaica, which was "organized in the tradition of Howell." Described by Barry Chevannes as a "utopian community," a spirit of self-reliance and industry was promoted within this group, which engaged in its own industry of broom making.[115]

By 1960 the Henry Affair once again brought the association between Rastafari and socialism to the fore. Born in the parish of Manchester in 1903, Claudius Henry claimed to have had visions as a child. He was arrested by the colonial government and placed in an asylum when he was twenty-six years old. He was later found to be well enough for release, and he then emigrated to the United States in 1944, where he became a preacher. He returned to Jamaica in 1957, and it was then that he embraced Rastafarian teachings and began to preach that Haile Selassie was the second dispensation of Christ. He also advocated for repatriation to Africa. Along with Edna Fisher, who led a Rastafarian group with which Henry associated, he founded the African Reform Church, which represented his own version of Rastafarian practice. His church did not incorporate all of the distinguishing characteristics of Rastafari,[116] but he continued to encourage repatriation to Africa, and this related to the incident that would most define him in Jamaican history. Henry preached that October 25, 1959, would be "Decision Day," when repatriation would happen miraculously.[117] Thousands of his followers abandoned their possessions and gathered to await repatriation, which never occurred.

Then, on April 7, 1960, the police raided the headquarters of the African Reform Church and reportedly found weapons, as well as two letters addressed to Fidel Castro. Henry was charged with "felony, treason, intent to intimidate and overawe Her majesty's government and to invite in a foreign power."[118] The letters, which informed Castro that Rastafarians were leaving for Africa and asked him to take control of the island, reinforced the Rastafarian lack of allegiance to the Jamaican nation and raised questions about the relationship between Rastafari and socialism (or communism). When the University Report was released that same year, it did not use the word "socialism" but warned that some Rastafarians nurtured a "marxist interpretation and terminology" and that, in some cases, this orientation "predominated over the racial and religious" interpretations."[119] In such a diverse movement, the idea that both positions were oppositional is plausible and could very well have been a source of conflict within the movement. But, beginning in the late 1960s, Rastafarians collaborated with members of the radical Left in ways that provided tangible evidence of their capacity to build alliances across ideological differences.

A few periodicals published in Jamaica during the late 1960s demonstrate coexistence of a multiplicity of viewpoints within a wider pan-African agenda. A young Rastafarian, Robin "Jerry" Small, began to publish a monthly periodical, *Black Man Speaks*, in 1968. The son of a Garveyite, Small was a part of a group of young radicals who were students at Jamaica College, a high school in Kingston. Small's home in August Town, which was close to the University of the West Indies, became a meeting place for Rastafarians and other radicalized youth, and *Black Man Speaks* became an outlet for historical articles, news, and poetry. Influenced by the Nation of Islam's *Muhammad Speaks* and Marcus Garvey's *Black Man*, Small's *Black Man Speaks* was one of two Rastafari-inspired periodicals that emerged in 1968; the other one was Frank Hasfal's *Our Own*. The group around Small decided to publish under the name African Youth Move, which represented a blanket term for all the youth engaged in the movement of the time. Though *Black Man Speaks* was fundamentally a Rastafarian paper, African Youth Move encompassed varying ideological viewpoints that found common ground in a general black consciousness and concern for the social and economic plight of African peoples on the continent, in the Caribbean, and in the United States.[120]

Black Man Speaks and *Our Own*, which were heavily influenced by Rastafarian philosophy, were risky in a hostile climate that sought to suppress all "subversive" ideas. Though certain events in the early and mid-1960s had helped to improve the wider society's image of the movement, police brutality and state discrimination against Rastafarians continued during this period. The periodicals emerged during a time when the works of black power authors such as Stokely Carmichael and Malcolm X were banned in Jamaica. *Black Man Speaks* and *Our Own* were published while "one eye was open watching out for the police and the other arranging for publication with all the difficulties involved in that process."[121]

During the 1960s, black consciousness and the pursuit of black power and self-determination in Jamaica were expressed by a diverse group of people, and this period saw the intermingling of ideas from varying perspectives. Although expressions of black consciousness were by no means limited to

Rastafarians, the movement had a tremendous impact on Jamaican radicalism, particularly among the urban poor. After spending January to October of 1968 as a professor of African history at the University of the West Indies in Jamaica, scholar-activist Walter Rodney concluded that the Rastafarian movement was at the forefront of radicalism during this period.[122]

Rodney was among the radicals who frequently convened at Small's August Town home and contributed articles to *Black Man Speaks* and *Our Own*. As Rodney and Rastafarians collaborated in the production of the two periodicals some disagreements emerged. In the case of *Black Man Speaks*, which was heavily Rastafarian in content, Rodney's Marxist-Leninist orientation disagreed with what he considered to be the conservatism of Rasta. Rodney advocated for *Black Man Speaks* to publish articles that were, in his point of view, more radical and less wedded to Rastafarian philosophy.[123] One night at the Wembley Sports Club, where the youth often gathered to talk and to listen to Rodney's lectures, Rodney stressed that decisions concerning the content of *Black Man Speaks* should not be dominated by any one person or group and suggested that control of each issue be rotated in order to reflect the different ideological emphases within the group. Though these conflicts led to ebullient debates, the group agreed to rotate the editorship of the paper. Small remembers that the issues edited by Rodney and his allies reflected Rodney's Marxist-Leninist outlook and had "purely Socialist articles." One such issue featured an image of Julius Nyerere with a caption that read "President Nyerere, President of Socialist Tanzania." Though Small understood the importance of the word "Socialist" in that context, he did not approve of what he perceived to be a de-emphasis on race. Similarly, when Small and his Rastafarian counterparts edited the July 1968 issue, which was dedicated to Haile Selassie (in celebration of his seventy-sixth birthday), it did not represent the approach that Rodney would have taken. These debates represented moments when Rodney and Rastafarians pandered in some way to the binaries (e.g., Marxism versus cultural nationalism) that had become important in pan-African discourse even as they remained respectful of each other and continued to rotate the editorship of *Black Man Speaks*.

At the heart of the conflict was the way in which Rastafari's broader pan-African agenda was rendered unique by the worship of Haile Selassie. While Rastafari's inherent internationalism underscored notions of pan-African unity, active engagement with non-Rastafarian radicals also highlighted the movement's particularity by reconstituting its religious ideas and beliefs. Yet, to pit Rastafarian religion against the radical Left in stark terms misses the reality that Rastafari's critique of colonial society was "very much akin to the socialist analysis of the capitalist system, in which those who own the means of production exploit the laborers to maximize their profits."[124] The Rastafarians who went to Tanzania offered insights about the evolution of the ideological link between Rastafarian thought and socialism. In the midst of newly independent African and Caribbean states that chose a form of socialism, Rastafarians made their allegiance clear. They explained their support of Tanzania's political project, *ujamaa* (African socialism), and argued that Nyerere's chosen political platform made Tanzania's brand of nationalism compatible with the Rastafarian way of life.

・・・・・・

The history of the Rastafarian movement reveals its internal dynamism and adaptability across different historical periods. It also highlights the varied and intricate ideological strands that make up the whole. The Rastafarians who went to Tanzania represented this multiplicity: they were individuals, members of the Twelve Tribes of Israel, members of the Nyabingi order of Rastafari, and members of URIA. This underscores Rastafari's complexity in ways not always captured by approaches that reduce analyses to Rastafari as a form of popular culture subjected to redefinition by non-Rastafarians.

Repatriation offers a rich and generative window through which many different aspects of the movement's evolution become clear. The particular African geographical space that constitutes Zion is one such area. Tanzania destabilizes the long-entrenched vision of Zion as Ethiopia. The repatriation began in 1976 when Mkhululi departed from the Ethiopia-focused return plans of the Twelve Tribes of Israel and headed to Tanzania. In the wake of the Marxist coup that removed Haile Selassie from his Ethiopian throne in 1974 and his subsequent death in 1975, Mkhululi sought to repatriate to a more "peaceful place."[125] Tanzania, a beacon of black pride with a reputation for welcoming diasporic Africans, would become Zion.

2 Tanzania
Site of Diaspora Aspiration

In 1971, African American poet, playwright, and activist Amiri Baraka declared that "Tanzania must be one of the strongest examples of African peoples' will to self-determination existing in the world today." Having been invited to the tenth anniversary celebration of Tanzania's independence by Julius Nyerere, Baraka found it "truly inspiring for African Americans to be present to observe intimately and in great detail the dynamic and courageous social evolution . . . which the Republic of Tanzania is undergoing."[1] These remarks, published in 1972, spoke to a historical moment when the black world was captivated by Tanzania. Though Baraka referred specifically to the impressions of African American black power advocates, his observations reflected a wider fascination with Tanzania that had gripped the black world since the late 1960s.[2] This fascination was related to the fact that as a newly independent African state, Tanzania embarked upon a path that boldly recalled black nationalist ideals of self-determination and self-reliance. Such a path beckoned the enthusiastic support of diasporic Africans, which contributed to the rise of Tanzania as a veritable hub of pan-Africanism.

The focus on Tanzania was intensified by the fact that it rose in the wake of Ghana's fall. The coup that ousted Kwame Nkrumah from power in Ghana in 1966 dealt a severe blow to the optimism of pan-Africanists around the world and represented a pivotal moment in the process by which the joys ushered in by independence had been dampened by the tribulations that seemed to haunt the African continent. When Ghana gained independence in 1957, it quickly became a symbol of African pride and pan-African unity, as Nkrumah invited "a large number of African, West Indian, and African American dignitaries" to attend the festivities. It was clear that "for people of African descent the world over, Ghana's independence lent momentum to rising demands for freedom and self-determination." As Kevin Gaines has documented, during the height of the civil rights movement, "from the late 1950s to 1966, scores of African Americans" moved from the United States to Ghana.[3] Nkrumah's Ghana had a lasting impact on the many African American and Caribbean expatriates who helped it become a mecca of pan-African solidarity. Ghana was transformative for the black world generally, as it provided a model of pan-African unity.

Following Ghana's decline, Trinidadian scholar C. L. R. James, burdened by his assessment that in "African state after African state you have this degeneration, this decay [and] this complete decomposition of the government," found in Tanzania a heartening reason to reignite his hopes for the African continent. For James, Tanzania was the "highest peak reached so far by revolting blacks." He argued that the government in Tanzania was one that "has understood what is happening and has made and is making a definite attempt to change it."[4]

In the late 1960s the hopes and dreams of pan-Africanists around the world found renewed inspiration in Tanzania. By 1968 Tanzania's declaration of *ujamaa* (African socialism), as defined by Nyerere, meant that the nation aimed to nurture an inherently African identity, and such a vision for society "offered black people a viable alternative" to the life they lived in the racist and capitalist West.[5] Furthermore, the state's declaration of nonalignment in the midst of Cold War tensions, and its unflinching support of African liberation movements as the headquarters of the Liberation Committee of the Organization of African Unity, appealed to progressive black people globally.

This chapter begins by explaining the shift from Ethiopia as the promised land for Rastafarians to Tanzania. It moves on to explore Tanzania's role as *the* mecca of pan-Africanism after 1966, with a view to placing the repatriation within the context of the ongoing dialogue between Tanzania and the African diaspora during the age of decolonization. In addition to an explanation of how and why Tanzania's political platform appealed to diasporic Africans, it shows the role of pan-Africanism in the making of Tanzania's national identity even before independence from British colonial rule. The chapter also provides context to Rastafarian repatriation to Tanzania by highlighting the ways in which Rastafarian thought found resonance in Tanzania's *ujamaa*. It engages Tanzania's participation in actual pan-African struggle while also demonstrating the seams and tensions within pan-African practice.

Repatriation Is a Must

Ethiopia has been well established as *the* promised land since the Rastafarian movement presented repatriation as a main goal. The impact of Ethiopianism as an ideology that saw diasporic Africans focus on the greatness of Ethiopia was boosted by Ethiopia's victory over Italy at the Battle of Adwa in 1896. This further enhanced the idea of Ethiopia as a source of black solidarity, as Adwa became a symbol for racial pride and black defiance.

The twentieth century saw Ethiopia shine brighter as a beacon of pan-Africanism. Not only was Ethiopia the home of Haile Selassie, but he had also offered a land grant to diasporic Africans through the Ethiopian World Federation in 1955.[6] The oral tradition of Rastafarians has historically referred to a grant of five hundred acres, which encouraged Rastafarians in their efforts to translate repatriation dreams into the realm of the pragmatic. Yet in 1959 an official from the British embassy in Addis Ababa informed the British Foreign Office that Haile Selassie actually gave "5 gashas" (two hundred acres) of land.[7] In the end, the precise acreage mattered less to Rastafarians than did the gesture from the object of their veneration.

As a result of this history, even colonial officials saw Haile Selassie as a pan-Africanist figure by the 1950s. In 1956, flummoxed by the Rastafarian "allegiance to the Emperor of Ethiopia," the custos of St. James Parish in Jamaica suggested that Governor Hugh Foot acquire a "refutation of their claim that Haile Selassie is God."[8] Three years later, after Foot had been replaced by Kenneth Blackburne, the idea of soliciting such a statement from the emperor finally made it to the British embassy in Addis Ababa. But an embassy official declared that it was "most unlikely" that Haile Selassie would make such a statement. He seemed certain that the emperor "would hardly be attracted to the idea of a statement that he had no interest whatever in a group of coloured people in the West Indies who regard him as Messiah." Such a statement, the official noted, "would appear to them [Selassie and his government] as contrary to the ideals of pan-Africanism."[9]

As the movement evolved, Rastafarians started to pay attention to Haile Selassie's teachings as an important aspect of their veneration of him. This became particularly significant during the 1960s and 1970s, when Haile Selassie's pan-Africanism and anticolonialism led others such as Julius Nyerere to label him a "great protagonist of African unity."[10] Additionally, Haile Selassie's work on behalf of other African countries allowed Rastafarians to see the emperor within the context of the wider continent and therefore made repatriation to areas other than Ethiopia plausible. Offering the experience of an African country that had a history of independence, Haile Selassie became actively involved in the continent's activities.[11] He enjoyed a reputation as an astute diplomat and effective statesman, and was respected by other African leaders, including Kwame Nkrumah of Ghana and Jomo Kenyatta of Kenya.[12] A number of Mau Mau freedom fighters, also from Kenya, were granted refuge in Ethiopia, and Haile Selassie awarded scholarships to Africans from other countries to study there. In terms of actual independence disputes, Ethiopian troops were sent to assist struggles in the Congo, and Haile Selassie served to mediate tensions in the Sudan and between Algeria and Morocco. His diplomacy had also helped to broker peace among competing notions of pan-Africanism on the continent at the Addis Ababa conference that established the Organization of African Unity (OAU) in 1963.[13] Such activities, and the fact that Ethiopia was the headquarters of the OAU, only served to enhance the emperor's image among Rastafarians while also opening up the idea of Africa to include places beyond Ethiopia. If Haile Selassie championed African unity, then other areas of Africa were worthy of investigation. The earlier idea of Ethiopia as all of Africa gave way to another interpretation in the modern era whereby Ethiopia was involved in efforts to unify the continent.

By 1974 the civil war, which culminated with the ousting of Haile Selassie by the Marxist Derg, made for a volatile climate in Ethiopia. Furthermore, the international media's coverage of famine and drought, juxtaposed to the affluence of the monarchy, served to tarnish Ethiopia's image abroad. Though the emperor's image suffered,[14] Rastafarians generally remained convinced that this was yet another ruse perpetrated by Babylon to discredit Haile Selassie and to perpetuate negative stereotypes about Africa. This skepticism continued into 1975, with the news of Haile Selassie's death, but as time went on his physical absence led some Rastafarians to examine their eschatological beliefs. Still, though the movement was shaken, Haile Selassie's lineage secured his divinity and continued to perform the ever-important task of connecting Africa to biblical history. In the end, while the upheaval in Ethiopia did not lead the vast majority of Rastafarians to abandon their faith, it did call into question Haile Selassie's identity as it related to biblical scripture for some Rastafarians, and it led individuals like Joshua Mkhululi to consider other areas of Africa as he sought to relocate to a more peaceful location.

Tanzania, known for its political stability on a largely unstable continent, provided Mkhululi with the peace he sought. Inspired by the example of the land grant in Ethiopia, he set about securing land in Tanzania for Rastafarian repatriation. Embedded in the shift from Ethiopia to Tanzania is much more than a geographical move that signals the Rastafarian embrace of the wider African continent beyond Ethiopia. As early as the 1940s, some Rastafarians in Jamaica had petitioned the colonial government for financial help to repatriate to Ethiopia.[15] Those who framed their sense of belonging in terms of Ethiopian "nationality" revealed that they were not opposed to nationalism as a construct, but to Jamaican nationalism in particular. Decades later, after black nation-states had become a reality, Rastafarian expressions of nationalism included a perspective that transcended (and was in opposition to) the nation-state and its territorial borders. In contrast to this, the nation-state was obviously an important part of Tanzania's conception and practice of pan-Africanism.

Tanzania and Pan-Africanism

Most analyses of *ujamaa* have been conceptualized within the framework of the nation-state. Yet, Tanzania's brand of African socialism was created and developed within a global context, which helped to shape it and on which it had an impact. Nyerere's concepts were not cultivated in a (national) ideological vacuum. *Ujamaa*, as Priya Lal argues, "contained numerous elements common to a continental repertoire of African socialism and a global repertoire of Third World—or postcolonial—socialism."[16]

Nyerere's expression of African socialism was one among the offerings of a number of African leaders who couched their postcolonial path forward in socialist terms. Along with major theorists such as Ahmed Sekou Toure of Guinea and Kwame Nkrumah of Ghana, Nyerere belonged to the first generation of African leaders who championed and created African socialism in the 1950s and 1960s.[17] To broaden the analytical frame is to see the global intellectual projects with which Nyerere was in conversation and to expose the transnational contours of Tanzania's history.

Pan-Africanism was a crucial aspect of the transnational dimensions of *ujamaa*, and Tanzania's involvement with the powerful global imaginary of pan-Africanist ideas calls for a more capacious approach to the nation's history. Its engagement with pan-Africanism before independence reminds historians that the nation-state was only one option on the road to independence. Frederick Cooper has shaken up linear narratives of decolonization by refocusing attention on the possibilities that were considered in the years preceding independence.[18] As the repatriation makes clear, it would also be unwise to focus on the nation-state as the only point of analytical departure after it happened to triumph over the other options that were available in the 1950s and 1960s. This also demands archival innovation and recognition of the fact that postcolonial national archives are incomplete and fail to contain the histories of the interactions that transcend the state.[19]

Ujamaa was indeed a national project, but it also operated within a pan-

African framework. Nyerere developed *ujamaa* with the rest of Africa and its diaspora in mind.

Pan-African ideas entered Tanzania long before independence. The presence of various strands of pan-African thought introduced into colonial Tanganyika during the interwar years situates Tanzania amid the "remarkable upsurge of political, social and intellectual renaissance, both on the African continent and in the transatlantic diaspora" during this period.[20] For Tanganyika, this influence has been associated with James Aggrey and Erica Fiah. From the Gold Coast, but educated in the United States, Aggrey was influenced by Booker T. Washington and his Tuskegee-based ideas.[21] Much like black nationalist thinkers of the nineteenth century, Aggrey pondered global African advancement within the confines of colonial rule. Yet, mirroring his own geographically varied experience as an itinerant West African, he offered global conceptions of race and the transnational struggle. Along with other destinations across the African continent, he toured Tanganyika as a member of the Phelps-Stokes Commission in 1924. For Aggrey, the African race referred to people with black skin whose origins were on the African continent. Aggrey imparted a message of racial pride and solidarity, and though he spent only two weeks in Tanganyika, his ideas about racial identification had a serious impact on East African intellectuals.[22] Aggrey proposed conservative attitudes to colonial rule and pushed for interracial cooperation, but East African intellectuals extracted the "more radical lesson of racial solidarity" from his platform. As Aggrey's "sentiments reached deeply into educated African households," they even became a part of the intellectual genealogy of individuals who went on to be ministers in independent Tanzania.[23]

Another dose of pan-Africanism, linked to Garveyism, hit Tanganyika in the 1930s with the activities and ideas of Erica Fiah, a Buganda shopkeeper and journalist who settled in Tanganyika during the First World War. In 1934 Fiah founded the African Commercial Association. This group rivaled what it perceived to be the elitism of the African Association, which was founded in 1929 and, as the ancestor of the Tanganyika African National Union (TANU), "was the institution through which many diverse ideas and ambitions were woven into political nationalism."[24] John Iliffe argues that in 1936, influenced by Garvey's Universal Negro Improvement Association, Fiah renamed his organization the Tanganyika African Welfare and Commercial Association (TAWCA). As was the trend with the spread of Garveyism around the world, Fiah adapted Garveyism's basic tenets to the local circumstances in Dar es Salaam, including the privileged economic status of East Indians.[25] TAWCA provided burial services for those without family ties in Dar es Salaam, fought for Africans to gain representation on the township authority, and claimed to speak for all Africans.[26] Fiah also went on to do journalistic work when in November 1937 he founded *Kwetu* (Our home), the official newspaper of TAWCA, which served to disseminate information among the "sons of the soil," to encourage unity, and to attend to social and humanitarian issues. Fiah upheld certain European values that saw him striving for a "future civilization" that used a "Western model" of Christianity and education.[27] Still, as Iliffe concludes, he represented the "radical side of African thinking" during the late 1930s.[28] Based on a police report, N. J. Westcott shows that the authorities saw Fiah as a "devoted reader of Garvey's Black Man" and saw a clear link between Garveyism and Fiah's activism.[29] Like Garvey, he argued that African progress was tied to an understanding of the link between economic development and politics.

Garveyism did not take root in Tanganyika as it did in other parts of Africa, from Kenya to Zambia and the Eastern Cape, where it symbolized the reach of global trends coupled with the particularity of local interpretations.[30] James Brennan has warned against exaggerating the impact of organizations like TAWCA and the African Association, as they inspired only "weak local support." The point here is that Fiah and the pages of *Kwetu* provide evidence that Garveyite ideas, at the very least, circulated among elites in Tanganyika, and this constitutes a meaningful link to pan-Africanist thought, especially since Fiah "played a central role in Dar es Salaam's political and intellectual life in the late 1930s and 1940s by editing and publishing" *Kwetu*. Notably, the pan-Africanist ideas that circulated in Tanganyika among the elites formed a part of the intellectual inheritance of some individuals who were active in subsequent postindependence political circles.[31]

Nyerere crafted *ujamaa* within the context of a decolonizing Africa where models of African unity had been considered. He had been a part of a cohort of continental Africans who had seriously imagined a unified Africa while studying abroad in Europe and the United States.[32] Like Nkrumah and others, Nyerere went into national independence with pan-African solutions in mind.[33] In particular, he was engaged with the idea of an East African federation, an attempt to unite Tanganyika, Kenya, and Uganda.[34] By 1960 Nyerere was prepared to delay Tanganyika's national independence in service of East African federation, and hoped that unity would not be derailed by the "temptations of nationhood and the intrigues of those who find their strength in the weakness of small nations."[35] Numerous experiments with federation were very much a part of the history of decolonization across the African continent and in the West Indies.[36] Like the attempt at West Indian federation, the plans for an East African federation collapsed. Though faced with the particular issues of East Africa, federation crumbled under several of the issues that plagued its West Indian counterpart: clashing personalities, location of the federal capital, citizenship, and the worry over economically stronger territories carrying the burdens of weaker ones.[37] The dream of federation in both East Africa and the Caribbean did not die, and several attempts at different unions were made. In 1974, Nyerere linked Africa and the Caribbean when he praised the establishment of the Caribbean Economic Community and compared it to the East African Community.[38]

Pan-African connections continued into the 1950s when a West Indian pan-Africanist, Dudley Thompson, assisted Nyerere with TANU's constitution. On September 15, 1974, Julius Nyerere spoke at the conference of the People's National Party (PNP) in Jamaica and acknowledged linkages that had been formed between Jamaica and Tanzania in an earlier period. He revealed that while he was a student in Britain, he was inspired by Norman Manley, the first leader of the PNP, which had been founded in 1938. Nyerere informed his Jamaican audience that TANU "owe[d] a great debt to the nationalist parties which blazed the trail," for "the P.N.P and other parties like it, made the idea of colonial independence respectable in principle at least, before our own party was even formed."[39] Nyerere emphasized even deeper linkages between Tanzania and Jamaica from the 1950s. He greeted PNP official Thompson, mentioning that the two had worked together before Tanzania gained independence from the British in 1961.

An Oxford-educated attorney, Thompson served as a member of the defense team for Jomo Kenyatta in the Mau Mau trials, and he also left his mark on Nyerere and TANU. Thompson left colonial Jamaica for a stint in Britain's Royal Air Force during World War II. This brought about his entrée into the world of anticolonial thought and pan-Africanism.[40] While on leave from the air force, Thompson was exposed to a circle of West Indian and African intellectuals from whom he gained the education that prepared him for his life's work. This circle, which nurtured many who went on to lead Britain's former colonies, included Ho Chi Minh, Jomo Kenyatta, Kwame Nkrumah, and George Padmore. It was at this point that Thompson met Kenyatta, who would later call upon him for legal assistance in his struggles with the British in the 1950s.

Thompson was most heavily influenced by George Padmore, who became his mentor. For Thompson, Padmore was "a virtual university for all colonial nationalists and for all resistance movements passing through London. To listen to him was to see the colonial empire unfold before your eyes."[41] Thompson also learned from his experiences as a soldier when he fought alongside poor Englishmen, and this shattered the notion of British superiority that had featured prominently in his colonial upbringing. After the war he returned to Jamaica, but was soon on his way back to Great Britain to study law at Merton College in Oxford on a Rhodes Scholarship. During this time he reconnected with his friends and became further entrenched in pan-Africanism and anticolonial politics. His circle expanded to include C. L. R. James and the Barbadian writer George Lamming. Upon completing his law degree Thompson refused an invitation to work with Norman Manley in Jamaica and decided instead to move to Tanzania.

In 1951, while living and working in Moshi, a town in northern Tanzania near the Kenyan border, Thompson was approached by Nyerere, then a struggling teacher, who had heard of Thompson's law practice and "had come for some advice." Thompson invited Nyerere to spend the weekend with him and his family and was "charmed by him at once." Nyerere informed him of his aspirations and dedication to the cause of independence, and Thompson advised Nyerere to "organize, organize, organize."[42] Though Thompson humbly accepts that he was "merely confirming a decision" that Nyerere "had already made," Thompson provided meaningful practical assistance to Nyerere at this stage of his political development. He helped Nyerere with TANU's constitution and, in an act of generosity, allowed Nyerere to gain the services of his secretary for two years, while Thompson continued to pay her.[43] Thompson also used the contacts he had established while a student in Britain to help Nyerere "internationalize" his movement. For Thompson, Nyerere was a "likeable politician" who possessed qualities he had seen in very few.[44]

In 1955 Thompson returned to Jamaica, but had certainly left his mark on East Africa and returned there many times to visit Nyerere, Kenyatta, and other friends. In his speech at the conference of the PNP in Jamaica in 1974, Nyerere remarked that while Thompson was in Tanganyika he "did not leave us ignorant about the P.N.P.!"[45] Notably, when Thompson returned to Jamaica and worked with the PNP, he did not leave them ignorant of Nyerere, Tanzania, or Africa in general.

This contribution of a Jamaican attorney to Tanzanian (then Tanganyikan) nation building in its early stages underscores the need for transnational approaches to African and Caribbean decolonization. Beyond the specificities of the struggle for independence in Tanzania and in Jamaica, these exchanges demand the recognition of a third analytical space: that transnational area where the histories of both intersect. The particular history to which Nyerere refers here provides an example of the cross-fertilization between formally schooled figures who went on to become prominent political elites in their independent nations after being radicalized in the seat of empire—in this case, Britain.

In addition, Tanzania and Nyerere came to play an instrumental role in the 1958 founding of the Pan-African Freedom Movement of East and Central Africa (PAFMECA), which was founded in order to coordinate and strategize for self-government in the region.[46] As PAFMECA became PAFMECSA (the Pan-African Freedom Movement of East, Central and Southern Africa) in 1962, the organization extended its membership to include southern African territories like South Africa and Southern Rhodesia. Based on its geographical location and the fact that it had secured its independence since 1961, Tanzania played a leading role in PAFMECSA. This involvement helped shape the image of Tanzania as a hub of radicalism, as well as the actual pivotal role it would play as a leading supporter of African liberation struggles after 1963. In the words of historian Azaria Mbughuni, PAFMECSA "helped advance the independence movements in the region and provided a platform for building regional unity with the ultimate goal of establishing continental unity."[47]

African First and Socialist Second

African socialism represented an adaptable discourse. For *ujamaa*, Nyerere chose from an array of ideological influences reflecting an eclectic mix, including Fabian socialism, classical liberalism, Marxism, pan-Africanism, and the ideas of Mao Zedong.[48] Scholars have also explored the culture of the Zanaki, the ethnic group to which Nyerere belonged, to gain an understanding of how he arrived at his conceptualization of the Tanzanian precolonial past.[49] Tanzania's variant of socialism certainly retained basic elements of the Soviet model of communism. This was made obvious by state-driven economic planning and nationalization projects. Yet Africa was *the* driving force that gave coherence and inspiration to the postcolonial path Nyerere sought to delineate. In a 1998 interview, he declared that if presented with the choice, he would have opted for a "free and united Africa before a fragmented Socialist Africa."[50] By unapologetically rooting socialism in indigenous African cultures, Nyerere offered an epistemological shift that became the defining feature of pan-Africanist discourse in this period. In harnessing precolonial ways of life as the basis of his philosophy, he asserted that Africa, and not Europe, would be the foundation of the postindependence path forward. In so doing he disrupted the well-entrenched backbone of the Western European intellectual tradition: the idea that civilization was the domain of Europe and that Africa existed outside of the purview of progress.[51] Scholars have been preoccupied with the extent to which African socialisms depended on romanticized notions of the precolonial African past and have utilized a national frame to assess the negative impact on the development of the postindependence African nation to which each was applied.[52] Yet the meaning and reverberations of Nyerere's elevation of Africa in the realm of the global black struggle for freedom also deserves sustained attention, especially since his (and other African socialist leaders') intellectual formations were the catalyst for widespread diasporic pan-African action.[53]

The black world was undoubtedly impressed by Tanzania's chosen path of *ujamaa na kujitegemea* (African socialism and self-reliance), which established Nyerere as an original African thinker who challenged Western dominance through his emphasis on the significance of the precolonial African past as the basis for development. Some felt that *ujamaa* served to place Tanzania's socialism "a notch above other countries' declarations of socialism" and that several of his policy statements gave Tanzania a "sophisticated legitimacy."[54] Beyond his role as leader of TANU and first president of Tanzania, Nyerere also filled the role of political theorist and strategist. He did not write every policy document—as was the case with "Mwongozo" (The Guidelines), which was largely the work of Kingunge Ngombale-Mwiru and released in 1971—but Nyerere was the main architect of numerous documents that outlined the government's policies and was as dedicated to delineating the ideas that provided a paradigm for policy as he was to leading the country.[55] Furthermore, in terms of diasporic perception, he embodied the Tanzanian state, and his role as a philosopher-king deepened the appeal of Tanzania. Though other African nations such as Zambia were also liberated spaces during the struggle to end white supremacy in southern Africa, Nyerere's Tanzania became a prominent player.[56]

Socialism appealed to Nyerere because it encouraged a society that was dedicated to maintaining equity among human beings. Yet apart from the fact that Nyerere refused to fall prey to a dogmatic reverence for any given political theory, he was adamant that socialism should serve Africa, and not vice versa. African socialism and self-reliance meant that Tanzania "could not adopt any political 'holy book' and try to implement its rulings."[57] For Nyerere there was no theology of socialism, and he rejected the dogma of those so-called scientific socialists who treated the writings of Karl Marx and Vladimir Lenin as the "holy writ."[58]

Tanzania declared its dedication to a unique conception of African socialism as early as 1962 with the release of the pamphlet *Ujamaa*. This document, which was written by Nyerere, advanced the idea of socialism as an attitude of mind. *Ujamaa* did not set out to define or to implement institutions that were pertinent to the creation and maintenance of a socialist state. The *Ujamaa* pamphlet was most salient in its assertion that Tanzania had chosen to develop as a characteristically African state and that it would ground its philosophy in the values of precolonial Tanzanian society. This made it clear that though the nation had adopted a socialist path, it was determined to see socialism through the specific eyes of Tanzania. According to Nyerere, in traditional African society "we were individuals within a community. We took care of our community, and the community took care of us." This meant that the urge to exploit other members of the community was "completely foreign" to Tanzanians.[59] Unlike socialist societies in European contexts that had reflected the Marxist notion of socialism emerging from capitalism, *ujamaa* was based on the idea that traditional Tanzanian society was inherently socialist. Nyerere insisted that though it had not gone through the stages of development as articulated by Marx and his followers, precolonial African society was based on ideas of communalism and human equality that would provide the basis for a socialist society in Tanzania. As it turns out, this view of socialism would mesh very easily with the Rastafarian notion of precolonial Africa.

For Nyerere, the basis of socialism was human equality, and this was its driving force. Though he read and gained inspiration from the work and experience of Marx and Lenin, he knew that their ideas had emerged from very different historical circumstances. Within the specific context of Tanzania, Nyerere argued that "to talk as if these thinkers provided all the answers to our problems, or as if Marx invented socialism, is to reject both the humanity of Africa and the universality of socialism." Furthermore, to reject the African foundation of socialism as he outlined it in *Ujamaa* was to accept the notion that Africa had "nothing to contribute to the march of mankind" and to accept the idea that "the only way progress can be achieved in Africa is if we reject our own past and impose on ourselves the doctrines of some other society."[60] This insistence that Tanzania depend on its own past for the journey forward was linked to Nyerere's overall emphasis on *kujitegemea* (self-reliance) as a major political objective. The fact that socialism, as a theory, had emerged in Europe, made its Africanization even more important for Tanzania's anticolonial struggle. Nyerere's decision to root *ujamaa* in Tanzania's precolonial past was related to his mission to restore the dignity of the African at the point of epistemology. In a 1998 interview, he declared that he had always been "African first and Socialist second."[61]

The most important document to be released after the *Ujamaa* pamphlet was the *Arusha Declaration* of 1967. This document, which enjoyed wider circulation than *Ujamaa*, was designed to solidify the ideas that had been introduced in the earlier pamphlet and outline the practical institutional steps required to build a society based on human equality. Nyerere stressed that the *Arusha Declaration* was primarily a "reaffirmation of the fact that we are Tanzanians and wish to remain Tanzanian as we develop." While acknowledging that development demanded changes and growth from the society, he was adamant that the "growth must come out of our own roots, not through the grafting on to those roots of something which is alien to them."[62] Nyerere was acutely aware of the cultural and psychological effects of colonialism and considered the celebration of African identity an important part of nation building. Even as they collapsed the cultural particularities of multiple ethnic groups in Tanzania, the concepts of African socialism and self-reliance were designed to empower Tanzanians by establishing a general precolonial African past as the place from which the Tanzanian way of life would be interpreted.

In addition, the *Arusha Declaration* outlined certain steps that the government would take in order to prevent exploitation and inequality in Tanzania. These included state control of the means of production, including the nationalization of banks, sisal estates, insurance companies, and multinational corporations. A strict leadership code that aimed to ensure that government officials led by example and remained connected to the people of Tanzania was an important feature of the declaration. To this end, leaders were prohibited from owning properties that were rented to others, from shareholding, and from serving as directors of private companies. The declaration emphasized the importance of self-reliance as a national objective for both domestic and foreign policy. This notion of self-reliance pertained to a wide range of issues, from the right of the country to determine its own road to development, to limiting its dependence on foreign aid. Nyerere explained that self-reliance did not mean isolationism; instead, "we shall depend on ourselves, not others."⁶³ The *Ujamaa* pamphlet and the *Arusha Declaration* were instrumental to the process by which Tanzania garnered the attention of many worldwide. By the time of the repatriation, however, Rastafarians had become aware of the ways in which Tanzania had failed to actually become self-reliant. In 1984, one year before the Tanzanian state officially welcomed Rastafarians, the members of the Universal Rastafari Improvement Association (URIA) observed that "not even within the borders of I-n-I ancestral home, Afrika, can I-n-I achieve equality and dignity" as, even within Africa, "I-n-I have become wholly and solely dependent upon alien nations for food, clothes and shelter."⁶⁴ Still, they respected what they deemed to be Nyerere's "consciousness" and found solace in his continued efforts, including his support of African liberation movements.

As president, Nyerere had been actively involved in African liberation work since the 1960s, especially after Tanzania became the headquarters of the Liberation Committee of the OAU, and the government's vow to "cooperate with other states in Africa in bringing about African unity" was a clause in the *Arusha Declaration*. Salim Ahmed Salim, former secretary general of the OAU and prominent Tanzanian government official, has argued that "it was in the liberation struggle where Mwalimu clearly exhibited the power of unity and its multifaceted impetus in the transformation of this continent."⁶⁵ Salim believed that Nyerere saw a "symbiosis between unity and freedom" and that he found it both a duty and an honor for Tanzania to be at the forefront of the struggle.⁶⁶

Before Tanzania's independence, TANU had existed as a liberation movement, and even a decade after independence Nyerere continued to think of it as such.⁶⁷ This was based on his belief that as long as Africans in other places remained in bondage, the continent was not free. In 1976, at a mass rally in Guinea-Bissau, which had won its independence from Portugal two years earlier, Nyerere saluted the African Party for the Independence of Guinea and Cape Verde and the people of the country for their "courage" and their "determination in the struggle." In keeping with his strong belief in the need for African unity, Nyerere reminded the people of the newly independent country that when they "liberated Guinea Bissau from colonialism" they were "extending the freedom of all of Africa—of our whole continent. And therefore of Tanzania also."⁶⁸ Through words as well as action, Nyerere consistently reinforced the idea that Tanzania's independence was inseparable from that of the entire continent.

In 1975, after the Liberation Committee of the OAU had helped Guinea-Bissau, Mozambique, and Angola to defeat the Portuguese, Nyerere hoped that in light of the struggles that continued in Namibia and Rhodesia, it would now be clear that "Africans will fight if that is the only way of gaining national independence, and . . . Africans can continue fighting until the objective is achieved."[69] On many occasions Nyerere explained that Africans did not favor wanton violence for its own sake. In one such instance he asserted that "no African people enjoy fighting for the sake of fighting. People everywhere want to live in freedom. It is only desperation that they feel forced to die for it." In 1963, when the Liberation Committee was founded, it was obvious that unlike the situation in Tanzania, where the transition to independence had occurred peacefully, "the peoples of Southern Africa, and of Guinea Bissau, had a different and much harder task" because "their attempts to win freedom and human dignity by peaceful means had already been suppressed ruthlessly. The only choice left to them was surrender, or armed struggle."[70] Nyerere stressed the violent nature of the colonial enterprise and the reluctance of the colonizers to adhere to the basic principles of human equality and social justice. He believed that freedom was a basic right for all human beings and that "men will not accept slavery as their lot. Always men will struggle against it." He saw violence as the only option in light of the fact that when African freedom fighters demanded that European colonizers respect the "universal principles of human equality and dignity," they were "answered with guns and bullets."[71] Armed force was thus the only match for the brutality of the colonizers.

The Rastafarians of URIA took a similar position. They were sure that "in the bitter struggle for the emancipation" of their "ancestral home," the "only solution" was "armed conflict." This declaration appeared in their monthly publication, which proved that they had followed the liberation struggles across the continent and understood the happenings in each territory in great detail. Nyerere and other state officials who had tried to negotiate with the Portuguese and the South African regimes had come to understand that such tactics were futile. Rastafarians had also concluded that the remaining colonizers would "never freely return what they had so mercilessly robbed, plundered and pillaged."[72]

Tanzania demonstrated its belief in the right of oppressed Africans to fight for their freedom. As headquarters of the Liberation Committee, Dar es Salaam welcomed the freedom fighters from the liberation movements of southern Africa. In addition, Tanzania hosted many conferences and meetings that focused on the liberation struggles. Nyerere's work on behalf of the committee and African liberation generally was so monumental that historian Gaudens Mpangala has argued that "the wider roles played by

Tanzania were to a large extent due to the individual efforts of Mwalimu Nyerere."[73] Nyerere campaigned tirelessly for the liberation movements of southern Africa. As chairman of the Frontline States, he made numerous speeches in all corners of the world in order to promote awareness of the liberation struggles and to solicit support.

Nyerere, Rastafari, and the Reclamation of Africa

The life and evolution of *ujamaa* as a form of African socialism was certainly a national story, and embedded in it was a definition of what made an ideal Tanzanian citizen. Through its rhetorical power, "African" was defined and redefined as a fundamental part of Tanzania's national cultural identity. As James Brennan notes, "Local thinkers in Dar es Salaam made sense of both colonial categories and Pan-Africanist arguments, but did so through the lens of local Swahili categories of thought."[74] Nyerere constructed noncitizens as "exploiters" and "parasites," and within the local context, these terms were applied to Dar es Salaam's East Indian residents, widely targeted for immoral and exploitative business habits.[75] In addition, within Nyerere's conception of African socialism, the nation was formulated as rural, with a rural citizenry, and as a result, "constructions of the city as decadent, unproductive, and emasculating constituted an important foil for TANU'S ideology." Furthermore, through a project launched shortly after independence, the postcolonial Tanzanian government aimed to define national culture (*utamaduni wa kitaifa*) in order to instill pride in African heritage. It was a poorly managed and financed state project but, like *ujamaa* more broadly, *utamaduni wa kitaifa* gained widespread rhetorical relevance. As Andrew Ivaska shows, within a framework that established rural citizens as the ideal Dar es Salaam became the site of culture wars, which saw the state target various perceived cultural intrusions including miniskirts, wigs, and Afro hairstyles.[76] In multiple ways, *ujamaa* set a framework through which debates over who belonged to the Tanzanian nation could be filtered.

Yet in Africanizing socialism to decolonize Tanzania, Nyerere also linked *ujamaa* to a wider pan-African tradition that centered the reclamation of Africa in opposition to global white supremacy. This showed that continental Africans were as engaged as diasporic Africans in using the African past to combat the transnational history of colonial anti-Africa discourses, racism, and capitalist exploitation. Just as Nyerere found the content of Tanzanian national identity and freedom in the African past, the Rastafarians of URIA were certain that "the truth of all forms of mental-spiritual awareness" must be found within "I-n-I noble regal and divine ancient continent and within the ancient history of Africa."[77] Rastafarians shared Nyerere's belief that in order to escape "colonization and neo-colonization" it was necessary to create a nation "based on the tradition, culture and ideology of the Afrikan."[78]

Nyerere argued that "of all the crimes of colonialism there is none worse than the attempt to make us believe we had no indigenous culture of our own; or that what we did have was worthless—something of which we should be ashamed, instead of a source of pride."[79] Similarly, Rastafarians understood this crime as the "falsification of recorded history" and were concerned about the "damaging long term effects on the inferiority [of] psychological conceptions of Africa by the vast majority of Afrikans at home and in bondage." This realization and the attempt to offer a deeper epistemological intervention aimed at affirming the dignity of Africans meant that Nyerere, like his diasporic counterparts, constructed an idealized Africa. His depiction of the communal nature of precolonial African society carried the very same connotations as the Rastafarian conception of Africa as "a civilization on an extremely high standard of virtue and morality."[80]

Much like the overarching focus of Rastafarian philosophy, Nyerere maintained that his utmost concern was with "the dignity and well-being" of all the people.[81] For Nyerere and for Rastafarians generally, the colonial African past provided the inspiration and root for the knowledge they valued and for the more just society they envisioned. As an expression of anticolonialism that sought to affirm the agency of Africans, the use of the African past demonstrated the validity of African origin. This rejected colonialism's pointed attempts to destroy African pride through the claim that precolonial Africa was without history and bereft of valuable institutions. After all, the construction of Africa as backward and unsophisticated constituted an important part of the process by which the colonizers attempted to ruin the self-image of Africans on the continent and throughout the diaspora. The idea that a fair and more egalitarian society—one that countered the inherently unfair and unequal colonial society—was characteristically African highlighted the irony embedded in the colonizer's claim that they had taken civilization to an "uncivilized" Africa.

In *ujamaa* Nyerere made it clear that a capitalist frame of mind was brought into Africa by colonialism.[82] The idea that Africans did not need to be "converted" to socialism because it was "rooted in our own past" meant that the African way was fundamentally socialist, and therefore, more just.[83] This notion, which was asserted in the *Ujamaa* pamphlet of 1962, echoed the Rastafarian idea that one did not "become" Rastafarian but that all Africans possessed an innate Rasta consciousness that they could come to realize. Rastafarians argued that "one already is Rastafari from the very beginning but one manifests the truth in the fullness of time when the self attains consciousness of itself."[84] In essence, both *ujamaa* and the Rastafarian movement initiated a call to memory. They posited that oppressed Africans had only to recall their true selves, which had been repressed by colonial forces, but not eradicated. The "true" or "conscious" self had everything to do with one's African identity.

Rastafarians and Nyerere beckoned to the people to remember who they were before they had been colonized. In the case of Jamaica, Rastafari's call to remember Africa represented an alternative agenda in a colonial society that thrived on forgetting Africa and suppressing any memory the people may have had about their homeland. In an attempt to destroy any modicum of African identity that would boost the strong sense of self sought by Rastafarians, the colonizers deliberately set about "forgetting" Africa. As Rastas saw it, this had caused some Africans to succumb to the chicanery of Babylon and they had therefore forgotten who they were. Indeed, the colonial distortion of the historical record had led many Africans in Jamaica to associate their African heritage with a sense of shame. Rastafarians were characterized by the fact that they dared to remember that which so many tried to forget. The colonial system had made tremendous efforts to tell Africans who they were—that is, to redefine them. But according to Rastafarian philosophy, those who internalized the mores of the oppressors had only to look within themselves to find the truth about who they really were. In the words of Walter Rodney, Rastafarians "served to remind the society of what the 'educated' blacks had been trying hard to forget: namely, that black people came from Africa, they were brought as slaves and they are still slaves."[85]

The Tanzanian case was different in that the Africans there had not been removed from the African space, and their experience with colonial rule was shorter than that of diasporic Africans, such as those in Jamaica. Still, the colonial system had encouraged the same type of "forgetting" that was rife in the diaspora. *Ujamaa* represented Nyerere's deliberate attempt to appeal to the memory of how Tanzanian societies functioned before the arrival of Europeans. As Toyin Falola has noted, "the idea of a successful African past was a powerful mobilizing agency."[86]

The striking similarities between Nyerere's conceptualization of Africa and that of Rastafarians underscore the extent to which continental Africans also participated in inventing a particular "Africa" as a part of mental and psychological liberation. They were also trodding diaspora. Indeed, Nyerere was saddled with the business of building a nation-state while Rastafarians focused solely on a form of nationalism that was inherently pan-African and without borders. This was a real difference. Still, their shared approach to the construction of "Africa" demonstrates the intellectual and political impact of the shared history of European oppression on Nyerere's thinking. This attempt to reclaim Africa was a vitally important part of Tanzania's appeal across the African diaspora. Its participation in African liberation struggles was also crucial.

Tanzania and the Challenges of Pan-African Practice

Tanzania's commitment to pan-Africanism yielded lessons concerning both its possibilities and its limitations. As the black power movement came into full swing in the United States, Tanzania had established itself as an ideologically progressive African state and as the base of the liberation movements of southern Africa. In 1972, Charlie Cobb, a former member of the Student Nonviolent Coordinating Committee (SNCC), astutely noted that the rhetoric of the Tanzanian state included "terms and ideological concepts that are attractive to blacks in the States engaged in any form of struggle and at almost any level of political consciousness. These ideas meet emotional as well as political needs."[87] The impact of Tanzania's unapologetically African-centered path made a tremendous impact on black power advocates in various ways. Cultural nationalists were inspired by *ujamaa*'s reliance upon precolonial Tanzanian culture as the basis of national identity. The use of Swahili as the national language intensified this appeal. With the European languages of the former colonizers serving as the national language in most newly independent African states, Tanzania's embrace of African identity through language was powerful. Several African American organizations used the language of *Ujamaa* and the *Arusha Declaration*, and the desire to learn Swahili became more widespread. As the most prominent organization for black cultural nationalists in the United States, the US Organization encouraged the use of Swahili, which its leader, Maulana Karenga, saw as a pan-African language.[88]

The appeal of Tanzania's experiment with African socialism and its assertion of cultural nationalism through Swahili were so captivating that the "cultural content of the pan African movement in the United States took on a decidedly Tanzanian (or Swahili) cast."[89] The impact of Tanzania's ideology set the stage for moments of collaboration between Tanzania and black America. In the area of print culture, the Drum and Spear Press, which was founded by former SNCC members in 1968, had an impact on African American cultural politics through its dependence upon *ujamaa* ideology while simultaneously contributing to Tanzanian nation building.[90]

Furthermore, as the black power phase of the African American freedom struggle signaled the open celebration of more militant strategies for liberation, Tanzania's willingness to take up arms in aid of liberation struggles enhanced its image among black power supporters. David Graham Du Bois argued in 1972 that the "momentous achievements of African liberation movements" had "provided black Americans with a unique inspiration" due in large part to the "idea of the black Freedom Fighter—spear, machete or gun in hand—ready to die for freedom and winning!"[91]

Based on the ways in which Tanzania's politics resonated with black power advocates, African American desire to travel to Tanzania represented a natural progression. It was no secret that President Julius Nyerere embraced African American enthusiasm. Black power activist Amiri Baraka reported that Nyerere and the TANU government had "made it clear and official that they welcome African Americans who can help them with the struggle for Self Determination, Self Reliance and a better life for Africans the world over."[92] As early as 1967, members of the International Affairs Commission of SNCC met with Nyerere and proposed the development of an African American skills bank with a view to sending skilled black Americans to "progressive" African nations to "assist in national development."[93] When this finally materialized in 1970 and African Americans began to travel to Tanzania through the auspices of the Pan African Skills Project (PASP), it represented a mutually beneficial arrangement for African Americans and for Tanzanians. African Americans contributed to pan-African solidarity, while Tanzanians benefited from the expertise of African Americans in areas ranging from health care to education.

Many prominent African Americans journeyed to Tanzania between 1965 and 1976, including Malcolm X, Angela Davis, Amiri Baraka, and Eldridge Cleaver. Tanzania had also offered a safe haven for Black Panthers, such as Pete O'Neal, who fled the United States in order to escape prosecution. He became part of a growing number of expatriates who referred to themselves as *warejeaji* (returnees).[94] This reflected the assertion of African identity that was widespread among the diasporic community in Tanzania, though it stemmed from many different strains of black nationalist thought.

The pan-African solidarity between the Tanzanian state and African Americans was not without its challenges. In some cases the expectations of African Americans were not met as smoothly and quickly as had been anticipated. Historian Brenda Gayle Plummer has reported that the "PASP recruited more people than it could place, since Tanzania made the placement decisions and proceeded cautiously." Some of the delay was based on the fact that African American radicals had deep respect and admiration for the Zanzibari revolutionary Abdul-Rahman Muhammad Babu, who was a member of the cabinet but had a tense relationship with the administration.[95] While Tanzania's mainland had made the transition to independence peacefully, decolonization in Zanzibar resulted from a violent revolution in which race played a key role. This garnered the attention of African Americans such as Amiri Baraka and Malcolm X. who both forged relationships with Babu.[96] The merging of mainland Tanzania (then Tanganyika) and Zanzibar in 1964 was fraught with tensions that continued to torment the union.[97]

Additionally, the Tanzanian state's practice of pan-African politics sometimes clashed with the new state's efforts to define a national culture. Nyerere had made it clear that culture was "the essence and spirit of any nation" and maintained that "a country which lacks its own culture is no more than a collection of people without the spirit which makes them a nation."[98] The state's welcome of diasporic Africans was challenged by some Tanzanians who worried about the impact of foreign cultures on the development of the new nation. As more and more African Americans spent time in Tanzania, black American politics and culture had an impact on Dar es Salaam. Their presence brought into sharp focus the tensions between internal debates in Tanzania aimed at defining Tanzanian culture and the state's commitment to pan-African politics. This meant that though the Tanzanian government welcomed African American expatriates, they faced "the ambivalence of a political establishment that was itself crisscrossed by local rivalries, struggles and agendas."[99] This conflict was evidenced by incidents ranging from a ban on soul music in 1969 to perhaps the defining moment in 1974, when hundreds of African Americans were arrested under suspicion that they were agents working for the CIA. This began with the incident known as the Big Bust, when the Tanzanian port police arrested two African American men who had previously worked at the Kirongwe Ujamaa Village. In addition to detaining the men, the police impounded a shipment that reportedly included "guns and bullets."[100] This marked a turning point for African Americans in Tanzania, and many left the country in response to the increased scrutiny.[101]

This reflected the reality that though African Americans did not receive the full benefits of citizenship at home, their status as Americans had serious implications in an international context. Black Americans were sometimes suspected of being aligned with the hegemonic/imperialistic power of the United States. This had been a reality with which African Americans were forced to contend in the 1960s, years before the Big Bust.[102] American foreign policy had been a concern across Africa, as the continent became a theater of the Cold War in various ways. Anti-America protests outside the American embassy in Dar es Salaam in 1966 were one expression of the fear among some Tanzanians that America was plotting against Tanzania. Their status as U.S. citizens caused African Americans to bear the burden of American imperialism, and they appeared to be disproportionately singled out for surveillance.

Though the pan-Africanist practice of this period made it difficult to distinguish between African American and Caribbean radicals, it is important to note that the Caribbean was represented in the network of radicals in Tanzania. The PASP actually became a point of connection for progressive diasporic black people in Tanzania. Jamaican-born scholar and activist Horace Campbell, though not affiliated with the organization, spent his first night in Tanzania in December 1972 in the PASP office.[103] Guyanese scholar and activist Walter Rodney was also in Tanzania and held a teaching position at the university. Though he had written a doctoral dissertation on West Africa, Rodney chose to go to Tanzania upon completing his degree. He explained that

> in 1966, when I went out to Tanzania, it was shortly after the coup in Ghana. This broke the period of several years in which Ghana held the focus as black people in America were concerned. It meant, for instance, that for those of us for a long time who had said we should go back to the continent—we should involve ourselves in one way or another—the fall of Nkrumah and the change in Ghana created a vacuum . . . we immediately sought another model—another point of attraction on the continent—and quite clearly Nyerere and Tanzania offered these points of attraction. . . . I went to Tanzania roughly during the same years that a number of black people were beginning to show a great interest in that part of Africa."[104]

Rodney "frequented the offices of the PASP and gave talks to incoming PASP recruits about African history and the political economy of Tanzania."[105] Rodney had served as a facilitator of pan-Africanism while a lecturer at the

University of the West Indies in Jamaica in 1968, and his "Walter Rodney and Friends" talks in Tanzania were "another way in which the PASP sought to attune its participants to the politics of Tanzania and inform them about their role and responsibilities as progressive solidarity workers in support of *ujamaa*."[106] The University of Dar es Salaam had begun to attract many expatriate intellectuals as a result of Nyerere's politics and leadership.[107] Rodney's time at the University of Dar es Salaam was one, he deemed, of "accelerated growth."[108] He became known as one of the left-wing expatriate scholars who, along with local radical scholars, made a significant impact on the university.[109]

Just as they had formed an important part of the expatriate community in Ghana, Caribbean intellectuals and activists flocked to Tanzania. There were sustained linkages between Tanzania and Africans in the Caribbean. For example, Nyerere's *ujamaa* had inspired Eusi Kwayana, one of the leading black power advocates in Guyana. In 1964, Kwayana, formerly Sydney King, founded the African Society for Cultural Relations with Independent Africa (ASCRIA), which "sought to promote the economic and cultural uplift" of Afro-Guyanese people. Influenced by Nyerere's ideas, his program for economic growth and development was based on cooperatives.[110] While a liberated space in Africa provided psychological benefits for progressive diasporic Africans generally, black people from the Caribbean related to newly independent African states in different ways. Unlike African Americans, they looked to African nations for a sense of how they themselves would fare as independent nation-states with large or majority black populations. Though the vast majority of Africans forcibly transplanted across the Atlantic were not from East Africa, the shared history of colonial rule created a sense of kinship between Tanzania and Caribbean nations. This did not mean their experiences were identical. Nyerere pointed out in a speech he delivered in Jamaica that Tanzania had endured British colonial rule for a much shorter period than had Jamaica, where colonial rule lasted three hundred years. He also noted the differences in terms of geography and population.[111] Still, he and the Caribbean leaders were convinced that theirs was a common struggle.

Tanzania had forged meaningful connections with Guyana, Jamaica, and Trinidad, which had experienced British colonialism, and with Cuba. The Tanzanian state had engaged in programs that not only allowed Caribbean citizens from Guyana and Jamaica to work in Tanzania but facilitated cultural exchanges.[112] The 1970s also saw Tanzanian newspapers frequently cover the news from Caribbean nations.[113] The Tanzanian connection to the Caribbean at the state level demonstrates forms of collaboration employed by those of African descent at a point in history when nonalignment and Third World politics became coterminous with pan-Africanism. Much of this collaboration at the governmental level centered on support for the liberation movements of southern Africa.

On the ground, some Tanzanian citizens and state officials were of the opinion that Tanzania risked too much to support African liberation movements.[114] Beyond the politics of the Cold War, they worried about the financial costs and the loss of human life as armed struggle intensified. Certainly, both Tanzanian officials and citizens were aware that the government's decision to be involved with the anticolonial war against Portugal and South Africa seriously affected Tanzanians at all levels of society. As Portugal's president Admiral Americo Thomaz continued to "defend his government's war effort in Africa" as one in defense of Western civilization, Tanzania's second vice president and minister of defense, Rashid Kawawa, reminded the nation that defense was the "responsibility of every Tanzanian."[115] Kawawa spoke in the wake of Portugal's invasion of Guinea Bissau and called for "vigilance," pointing out that defense was not limited to the use of firearms as "eyes and ears are most essential things and must be used in guarding our country."[116]

Additionally, the Lusaka Manifesto of 1969 had strained the generally good relationship between the Tanzanian government and the liberation movements. Penned by Nyerere and accepted by the Frontline States, the manifesto stated that it would pursue negotiations with South Africa and the Portuguese colonialists, and would discourage armed struggle if the regimes agreed to independence and majority rule. The liberation movements were displeased with this move, as they were convinced that the Portuguese and South African regimes would not respond to nonviolent approaches and they also resented the attempts of African heads of states to define the course of the struggle. The president of the People's Movement for the Liberation of Angola, Agostinho Neto, represented the position of many liberation movements in his fiery speech at the Third Non-Aligned Conference in Lusaka, Namibia, in late 1970. Neto appealed for "concrete aid in arms and funds to meet our pressing material needs." He underscored the actuality of armed struggle, which was very different from the slow pace of venturing from one conference to the next engaging in peace talks. According to Neto, "war is not compatible with the oratorical slowness of eloquent speeches or with time bureaucratically intervening between intention and decision, between decision and implementation."[117]

African leaders continued to deliberate over whether or not matters could be solved if the oppressive regimes of South Africa and Portugal were isolated,[118] and Nyerere led the commonwealth in pressuring Britain to stop selling arms to South Africa.[119] But by 1971 the freedom fighters had been proven correct. This was marked by the Mogadishu Declaration, which recognized the obdurateness of the apartheid and Portuguese regimes and replaced the Lusaka Manifesto with the declaration that armed struggle was the only choice. South Africa's prime minister, B. J. Vorster, had made it clear that he was not going to discuss apartheid, Portugal continued to justify its efforts to hold on to its colonies through violence, and Britain continued to supply arms to South Africa.

In large measure, diasporic Africans were enraptured by the utopian promise of Tanzania's ideology and deeply inspired by a one-dimensional concept of the nation's role in the liberation struggles of the day. Yet though a romanticized Africa lingered in the diasporic imagination, the setbacks to global African liberation, which were painfully clear by the end of the 1960s, had disabused many of relentless naïveté. By the 1970s, utopian ideas of Africa had been bludgeoned by a fierce dose of reality. So much had happened since the advent of independence euphoria in 1960 that alerted diasporic and continental Africans to the domestic and international threats to freedom.

In 1970 Nyerere addressed the pressures of the Cold War and affirmed the significance of the nonaligned movement, which was not without its own difficulties. In direct reference to the fact that decolonization had proven to be a protracted process rather than an uncomplicated move to complete liberation, Nyerere argued that "recent years" had provided "plenty of evidence of the urge to dominate," adding that "barely a month goes by without further evidence of externally organized or supported coups d'etat, and sectarian rebellions, or of economic blackmail." With reference to the nonaligned states, he argued that "our role arises from the fact that we have very definite international policies of our own, but ones which are separate from, and independent of, those of either of the power blocs." He explained that nonalignment served to remind the "big powers" that "we also belong to this planet. We are asserting the right for small and militarily weaker, nations to determine their own policies in their own interests, and to have an influence on world affairs." This was crucial because it accorded "with the right of all peoples to live on earth as human beings, equal with other human beings." Nyerere's concern was with the "right of all peoples to freedom and self-determination; and therefore expressing an outright opposition to colonialism and international domination of one people by another."[120]

Still, reflecting the ideological debates of the period, he acknowledged the diversity that encompassed the nonaligned states, recognizing that nonalignment said "nothing about socialism, or capitalism, or communism, or any other economic and social philosophy." It was "simply a statement by a particular country that it will determine its policies for itself according to its own judgment about its needs and the merits of a case." This meant that the members of the nonaligned movement "even differ in our foreign policies—and sometimes quarrel among ourselves!" In the end, he concluded that "only on opposition to colonialism and racialism do we all agree, yet even on that issue we differ on the tactics which should be pursued."[121]

It is also true that the considerable travel between Africa and its diaspora in this period helped to dispel romanticized notions of Africa and of Tanzania in particular. Diasporic Africans who traveled to Tanzania were often keen observers of the state's efforts to practice its ideology. From the office of the PASP in Dar es Salaam, Fred Brooks wrote to Walter Rodney, who had left the city, to inform him of "the biggest change in the structure of the government [in Tanzania] since independence." In reference to the policy of decentralization, which was meant to "give more power to the regional," Brooks opined that though "Mwalimu [Nyerere] had said some time ago that the structure in the government was going to be changed . . . know one [sic] knew the change would be of such proportion." After informing Rodney that the PASP was in the process of recruiting African Americans "with skills" for the "500 vacancies" the Tanzanian government sought to fill by July, he closed the letter with the hope that it would give Rodney "a brief idea of the situation . . . the African political scene change [sic] so fast that it [sic] difficult to tell what is old or new news."[122] Through this exchange it is clear that some diasporic Africans were not only aware of the realities of life in Tanzania but keenly observing the relationship between the state's rhetoric and its actions.

Continental Africans were also traveling to the diaspora and facilitating greater diasporic engagement with actual life on the African continent. Nyerere himself traveled to the Caribbean for the first time in 1974 and made stops in Cuba, Guyana, Jamaica, and Trinidad. In several speeches he admitted to the ways in which he had been naive and the measures taken to address missteps in policy.[123] In Trinidad he explained that he did "not wish to give the impression that Tanzania consists entirely of selfless and dedicated citizens, all leading austere and comfortless lives in the interests of the greater good and future!" He was transparent about the fact that it was a mistake to think that the government's "aims and plans" were "working out smoothly," adding that "those Trinidadians who have recently worked in our country know that this is not the case."[124]

In speaking at the University of the West Indies in Jamaica after receiving an honorary degree, Nyerere explained to his audience the "considerations which caused Tanzania to adopt its policy of Ujamaa na Kujitegemea." But he admitted that his government had been "very naïve" in its assumption that its goals "could be achieved without any fundamental change in the social, political, or economic organization we had inherited from our colonial masters." He admitted that "in 1961, and for some years afterwards, we thought that poverty in our country would be abolished by hard work on our part, combined with a large influx of capital from abroad." Yet, "by the end of 1966" the government "had been forced to the conclusion that these were false premises for policy making," admitting that what was taking place was a rather rapid growth of inequality" among the people. In truth, "a few individuals had become well-off, and could see the prospect of riches before them; but the masses of the people were hardly better off than at independence." TANU "had found that the ideas and plans of the government were being thwarted by the logic of our own policies."[125]

Still, notwithstanding these challenges, Tanzania's reputation as a mecca of pan-African activity was well deserved.[126] The government, as well as the people of Tanzania, had made many sacrifices in order to support the liberation of southern Africa. When Jamaican prime minister Michael Manley traveled to Tanzania in 1973, he visited the Kabuku Ujamaa Village in the Handeni District.[127] In welcoming Manley, the people of this village addressed him: "we the villagers of Kabuku Ujamaa Village feel greatly honoured by a visit of a revolutionary leader like yourself. Jamaica and Tanzania has [sic] a lot in common. This makes us appreciate your visit very greatly." They provided Manley with a history of their village and explained that sisal constituted their main industry. They were particularly proud of their sisal industry and explained to Manley that they were grateful to TANU and other government officials in Tanzania "for leading us in our sisal industry, especially in solving the sisal price problem." As "Africans were not allowed to grow sisal" during colonial rule, they were proud that they had managed to grow it successfully and thought their success represented a "big revolution towards economic independence." They also informed Manley that the government had provided the village with a reliable water supply and services such as a clinic, a school for children, and a dispensary. At the end of the visit they presented Manley with several gifts and sent greetings to the people of Jamaica. Beyond a demonstration of how agrarian reform functioned in Tanzania, the villagers also expressed pan-African sentiments.[128]

They even went as far as to entrust a monetary contribution to liberation movements in southern Africa to Manley, who had become a prominent supporter of African liberation struggles: "As a leader of the PNP, a liberation party like our TANU party, we the villagers of Kabuku, being devoted TANU members, do support fully the liberation of the African continent. Hence we request you to accept Shs. [Tanzanian shillings] 1,000/= being our contribution towards the freedom fighters in Africa."[129] The document that detailed Manley's visit to Kabuku Village reflects the complexities that surrounded the creation and maintenance of *ujamaa* villages in Tanzania, and particularly the relationship between the government and the people. While it was presented as a TANU party document, it was signed by the "Ujamaa Villagers, Kabuku, Handeni." This makes it difficult to figure out the extent to which the ideas of TANU represented the ideas of the people. Still, it is clear that, even outside of the urban space of Dar es Salaam, many Tanzanian citizens were aware of the nation's pan-African connections.

As headquarters of the Liberation Committee of the OAU, Dar es Salaam welcomed the freedom fighters from the liberation movements. This was the base from which they were able to train, and they often established schools and other facilities. When the Liberation Committee held a conference in Algiers in 1968, the various liberation movements were required to submit status reports. The Frente de Libertação de Moçambique (FRELIMO) presented a comprehensive report of "the situation of our struggle in Mozambique . . . including political, military, economic and social programmes."[130] The report was issued by the "provisional headquarters" in Dar es Salaam and spoke of the existence of adult literacy classes being run by FRELIMO in its "refugee settlements in Tanzania." Fourteen years later, after Mozambique had become independent, President Samora Machel, who had lived in Dar es Salaam as a FRELIMO fighter, returned to Tanzania on a state visit. Nyerere extended a warm and exuberant welcome to Machel, which was tempered only by Nyerere's sense that it was unnecessary to "welcome someone to their own home." Beyond the pan-African idea that there were no borders within the African continent, Nyerere felt as though Machel was returning home because he had lived in Tanzania for many years. In addressing Machel, Nyerere asserted "you lived with us for many years, using Tanzania as a rear base when participating in, and then leading, the armed struggle for the liberation of your country."[131]

The African National Congress (ANC) of South Africa also had a home in Tanzania. The Solomon Mahlangu Freedom College (SOMAFCO) was founded in 1978 in Dar es Salaam. The Tanzanian government provided one thousand hectares of land near Morogoro. Though the school benefited from funding from agencies, organizations, and countries that supported the ANC, "the environment provided by Tanzania was crucial to the foundation and survival of SOMAFCO."[132] The constant threat of an attack from South Africa meant that security was a serious issue for the Tanzanian people, and the government offered its national security forces to protect it. The area surrounding the school became a complex that included a hospital. Though this was an area designed to serve the ANC population in exile, the hospital served mostly local Tanzanians. The establishment of the ANC school in Tanzania provides an example of the extent to which the freedom fighters from other African territories set up residence in Tanzania and the exchange between Tanzanians and South Africans that transpired as a result of the sacrifices made by the Tanzanian government and people on behalf of African liberation.

・・・・・・

Tanzania became the "new center of the pan-African movement" after 1966,[133] and through its active engagement with pan-Africanism, the nation was "trodding diaspora." It was a nation-state that affirmed the continent as the home of those of African descent in the diaspora. It also became an African geographic space where pan-Africanism underwent many of its internal struggles and where bonds were tested, deepened, or severed. Nyerere's *ujamaa*, like Rastafarian thought, created a utopian vision that recalled the African past and was used in the service of postindependence transformation. Within the intellectual history of pan-African praxis, this interplay between elite discourses and the ideas of common people was important. As chapter 3 will show, interaction among states was also significant.

At the level of state politics, the bonds between Jamaica and Tanzania, were strengthened during the 1970s when both states collaborated to further the cause of African liberation, nonalignment, and pan-African solidarity.

Yet Rastafari provided the language and idioms of signification by which the Jamaican state understood and discussed pan-Africanism, and Rastafarian ideals helped to establish strong bonds between Tanzania and Jamaica. This provides essential context to the repatriation.

3 **The Wages of Blackness**
Rastafari and the Politics of Pan-Africanism
after Flag Independence

••

Following the death of Rastafarian reggae superstar Bob Marley, former prime minister of Jamaica Michael Manley reflected on the ways in which Rastafarian ideas and reggae music were inextricably bound, and he acknowledged the impact of this bond on his personal development: "I could never pretend that the lyrics of the protest music, which were the driving motivation of reggae, taught me things that I did not know. From an intellectual point of view they were confirmatory of all that I believed as a socialist and as a trade unionist. But I had not myself been born in the ghetto and was not personally part of that experience. Reggae music influenced me profoundly by deepening the element of emotional comprehension."[1]

Manley's acknowledgment of his own subjectivity as one who was "not born in the ghetto" represents a candid recognition of the social distance between him and the majority of people he served as prime minister. Rather than solely the recognition of distance based on social class, it was also a reference to race, because Manley struggled with his own status as a "brown" or "near white" Jamaican. He nurtured feelings of insecurity about the fact that he shared "very little social intimacy" with the people he represented locally and internationally. At the height of his involvement in pan-African politics in the 1970s, Beverley, the black, working-class woman to whom he was married, frequently reminded him that the "masses of people saw him as black and referred to him as black." Yet, his insecurities were not easily put to rest for, in the words of Beverley, he "wanted to be a black man more than anything in this world."[2]

Manley's time as prime minister of Jamaica during the 1970s was marked by a radical foreign policy that saw him emerge as a leading advocate of African anticolonial struggles, pan-Africanism, and Third World solidarities. His activism on behalf of the liberation movements of southern Africa, his support of armed struggle, and his unwavering antiapartheid stance facilitated the strengthening of pan-African bonds between Africa and Jamaica and raised his profile in pan-African circles during this period. Manley's foreign policy reflected his grasp of the connection between continental Africans and those in the diaspora. In his speech at the special plenary meeting of the UN General Assembly, which was devoted to the International Anti-Apartheid Year 1978, Manley explained that Jamaicans had struggled for their own liberation and had always known that their struggle was "particularly linked to Africa's struggle." He continued to explain that the people of the Caribbean were moved to such "internationalist concern" partially because "we seek the rediscovery of our own identities misplaced in history as the slave ships made their way through the Middle Passage between Africa and the Americas."[3]

When Manley traveled to Tanzania in 1973, the newspaper *Uhuru* reported that he arrived at the Dar es Salaam airport to the enthusiastic welcome of thousands of citizens singing and applauding. In a speech he delivered on that trip, Manley pledged Jamaica's continued support to the freedom fighters of the liberation movements of southern Africa, assuring his audience that along with financial help and medicines for freedom fighters, Jamaica was also willing to send personnel to speed up the liberation of the continent. As he had stated in prior speeches and written documents, Manley added that Jamaicans had their origins in Africa and had a desire to visit and learn from the continent. Furthermore, he underscored the bonds between Jamaica and Tanzania by adding that both countries had experienced British colonial rule.[4]

But as Manley celebrated blackness and constituted "diaspora" in terms of a singular framework of African origin, he was departing from both personal and political traditions. When he asserted that Jamaica was a part of the African diaspora, he rejected the platform of multiracialism that had dominated Jamaican politics, and his pro-Africa radicalism represented a remarkable shift in Jamaica's domestic and foreign policy. His celebration of blackness and of African roots belied his personal status as a "near-white" Jamaican whose family belonged to the privileged political elite that had dominated Jamaican politics in the modern period. As the head of an independent nation governed by an official antiblack discourse, Manley practiced black radical politics. To a considerable degree, Rastafarian thought shaped his own. To that end, this chapter traces the process by which the People's National Party (PNP), led by Michael Manley, appropriated Rastafarian language and symbols. Beyond the party's use of Rastafarian culture to connect with the people, Manley in particular enhanced his intellectual grasp of black nationalist discourses through Rastafari.

This reverberated internationally. Rastafarian ideas helped to establish strong bonds of pan-African politics between Tanzania and Jamaica. The black nationalist ideas of Julius Nyerere and Michael Manley, like those of the Rastafarian movement, were part and parcel of the black anticolonial tradition, which "ruptured the divide between the nation and the global community as a unit of analysis" and replaced it with a pan-African vision that united Africans on the continent with those in the diaspora.[5] This vision led to the creation of intellectual, political, and cultural linkages between Jamaica and Tanzania. As an older statesman, Nyerere inspired Manley, thereby substantiating Africa's role at the forefront of decolonization politics. This interchange between Manley and Nyerere demonstrates that *ujamaa* was situated not only in the repertoire of African socialisms but also in an array of Third World socialisms. As both faced the daunting task of leading a postindependence state, they underscored the linkages between Africa and the Caribbean while also revealing the differences. Their shared affiliation with Fabian socialism offers a view into their intellectual debt to Western Enlightenment universalism even as they challenged its Eurocentric biases. By the 1970s both leaders had become close personal friends and political allies. Manley was certainly attracted to Nyerere's ideas. But his sustained and significant relationship with Nyerere was linked to his own concerted effort to place Africa at the center of foreign policy, with dramatic local implications.

Manley's wife helped him to navigate the racial politics associated with his pan-African activism. In the final analysis, however, he borrowed most heavily from Rastafarian ideas in order to fashion his own (black) consciousness. Rastafarian thought shaped Manley's thinking on Africa, and Rastafarians gained inspiration from Nyerere's visits to Jamaica. When Joshua Mkhululi first posed the question of repatriation to Nyerere, Nyerere remarked that he had received the "warmest of welcomes" on his visits to Jamaica and had often wondered why the people were "not here in Africa."[6] Manley appropriated Rastafarian symbols and language, which in turn helped to strengthen bonds between Tanzania and Jamaica. In the end, those bonds provide important context for Rastafarian repatriation to Tanzania. They are also absolutely central for an understanding of this moment of decolonization.

The Word Is Love

In 1962 Jamaica gained independence from Britain through constitutional decolonization. Having cut their teeth in the world of trade unions and party politics since the 1930s rebellions, the "brown" elite took control of the struggle to gain political independence. As they constructed a national identity for independent Jamaica, they relegated blackness to the periphery of the nationalist narrative. Instead they chose to represent Jamaica as a "Creole" nation. As the bedrock of a nationalism that celebrated hybridity, Creole nationalism claimed to be a celebration of the "mixing" that characterized the Caribbean while failing to trouble the existing racial hierarchy. By eliding the reality of racial strife in Jamaica, Creole nationalism was used to buttress Jamaican exceptionalism, the vacuous notion that Jamaica was not plagued by the racial problems found in places like South Africa or the United States. It also left intact the denigration of blackness and African heritage. As Rex Nettleford observed in 1970, "the trouble with this solution to our race differentiation problems is that if the hybrid is norm, then the vast majority of pure blacks must be the aberration."[7] While claiming to locate its logic in the "mixing," Creole discourse reinforced racialized colonial ideals that glorified Europe while demonizing Africa.[8]

But the "brown" elites were not the only ones in the business of defining the Jamaican nation. As indigenous Jamaican forms of black nationalism meshed with the African American freedom struggle throughout the 1960s, the Jamaican government's response, in many ways, resembled that of the American government. Under the leadership of the Jamaica Labour Party (JLP), the government labeled all black nationalist activity subversive and took great pains to eradicate this perceived threat. Black power represented an engagement with the history and memory of enslavement, which had no place in the official imaginings of the Jamaican nation. The JLP engaged in repressive activities akin to the COINTELPRO-type attacks faced by African Americans engaged in civil rights and black power activities.[9] The government became known for its pointed attempts to undermine student movements, its harassment of progressive individuals, its banning of black power literature, and its brutality toward Rastafarians.[10]

Black consciousness and the pursuit of black power and self-determination in Jamaica were expressed by a diverse group of people. In fact, this period saw the intermingling of ideas from varying perspectives such as those of Marxists, cultural nationalists, and Rastafarians. In addition, Jamaican radicals, broadly defined, fostered an internationalist approach to black struggles, engaging African anticolonial movements, the North American variant of black power activism, and Jamaican expressions of black consciousness, including Rastafari.[11] Yet the movement had a tremendous impact on Jamaican radicalism, particularly among the urban poor. The revolutionary fervency of the 1960s, and Rastafari's central role in it, culminated in the

Rodney Affair of 1968. Guyanese scholar Walter Rodney was banned from Jamaica and refused entry into the country when he tried to return from the Black Writers Congress in Montreal on October 15, 1968.[12] After spending ten months in Jamaica, from January to October 1968, Rodney deduced that "in our epoch the Rastafari have represented the leading force of this expression of black consciousness," noting that Rastafarians had "rejected this philistine white West society" and "sought their cultural and spiritual roots in Ethiopia and Africa."[13]

Walter Rodney was born in Georgetown, Guyana, on March 23, 1942. As a student he excelled academically and received a scholarship to Queen's College, a reputable secondary school in Guyana. From there he left Guyana to attend the University of the West Indies in Jamaica, where he studied history. While in Jamaica, Rodney made his mark as a skillful debater and was involved in student politics.[14] A paper trail provides ample evidence of Rodney's interaction with Rastafari when he returned to Jamaica as a professor in 1968, but a couple of his contemporaries have stated that he first "came face to face with Rastafari" as a student in Jamaica and that Rasta influenced his decision to study West Africa as a doctoral student.[15] In 1963 he earned a bachelor's degree in history with first-class honors and won an award to study at the School of Oriental and African Studies at the University of London. In 1966, Rodney completed a doctorate in African history and headed to Tanzania.[16] After about a year in Tanzania he returned to Jamaica in January 1968 to teach in the Department of History at the University of the West Indies. By Rodney's own admission, this was a mutually beneficial relationship, and he was transformed by his experience in Jamaica among Rastafarians. In fact, his time in Jamaica was crucial to his development as a scholar and a revolutionary.[17]

In a text published in 1969 about his interactions with Rastafarians in Jamaica, *The Groundings with My Brothers,* Rodney revealed that "above all, I would like to indicate my own gratification for the experience which I shared with them. Because I learnt. I got knowledge from them, real knowledge." Rodney understood the power of such a statement in a society where the Rastafarian critique of colonial mores and fearless embrace of an African identity were long considered the misguided preoccupation of the "uneducated" ignorant masses. Rodney's assertion that he had "learnt" from Rastafarians and his "own gratification for the experience which I shared with them" turned conventional thinking about who could produce knowledge on its head. He acknowledged that point when he noted that when one listens to Rastafarians "you get humility because look who you are learning from. The system says they have nothing, they are illiterates, they are the dark people of Jamaica."[18]

Beyond the Rastafarians with whom he interacted around the publication of the periodicals, Rodney had intellectual exchanges with leading and influential Rastafarians in Kingston. In Rupert Lewis's study of Rodney's intellectual and political thought, he writes, "Rodney shared the passion of Rastafarian brethren like Ras Negus from East Kingston and Ras Planno from West Kingston for political liberation in Africa. Ras Negus and Ras Planno were both in their own way as intriguing as Rodney and certainly as brilliant with words and ideas."[19]

Fearful of the growth in black consciousness and social protest, the Jamaican government saw Rodney as a harbinger of "subversive" activity and a serious security threat. In the wake of his banning, Rodney highlighted the irony of the fact that "the government of Jamaica, which is Garvey's homeland, has seen it fit to ban me, a Guyanese, a black man, and an African."[20] As early as 1960, when Rodney lived in Jamaica as a student, his "consciousness of West Indian society was not that we needed to fight the British but that we needed to fight the British, the Americans and their indigenous lackeys. That I see as an anti-neocolonial consciousness as distinct from a purely anti-colonial consciousness."[21] Rodney understood that this phase of the black liberation struggle demanded an understanding of the tradition of anticolonial activism that had depended on nationalism as a strategy, as well as the neocolonialism that had already begun to rear its ugly head in the Caribbean and in Africa. Neocolonialism related to both the ways in which the international system of capitalism continued to prevent advancement of African peoples globally and the ways in which political independence in Jamaica and other places had given rise to a petite bourgeoisie that sought to become a dominant class at the expense of peasants and workers.[22]

The JLP government, which had been installed since independence, bore the well-deserved brunt of the ire felt by progressive black people and provided proof of a newly independent black government that had succumbed to a neocolonial mentality. In truth, though the PNP under Norman Manley had declared socialism as its chosen path since the 1940s and was therefore politically left of the JLP, its vision for independence was not connected to black nationalist ideals. Yet when Michael Manley succeeded his father as leader of the PNP in 1969 and began to campaign for the 1972 elections, the younger Manley recognized that the Rodney Affair exposed a revolutionary tide that the state could no longer afford to ignore or attempt to thwart.

Manley and the PNP won a landslide victory in the 1972 elections thanks to a campaign that relied heavily upon Rastafarian symbols and language. Rasta cultural expressions (music, language, etc.) had articulated poor black people's disappointment over the failures of independence. Manley tapped into this protest and communicated with the people though the language and culture they had created.[23] This represented a brilliant strategy, which signaled that the PNP was the party of the "sufferer" and that Manley was Joshua, the deliverer of the people. Though Manley understood the importance of Africa before he became prime minister, his principled engagement with and support of black nationalist causes in the 1970s began with the co-optation of Rastafarian symbols into Jamaican politics. As the Rastafarian movement had endured a history of marginalization in Jamaica, the embrace of Rastafarian culture and politics by state politicians represented a notable intervention of grassroots black nationalist discourse into Jamaican statecraft.

Since 1969 Manley had also begun to court the wider Left, which included non-Rastafarian Marxists, scholars, and black power advocates. Many of these individuals were university students who would later form the New Left within the PNP. In fact, by 1974, much of the Left had been incorporated into the PNP, which came to represent the hopes and dreams of many radicals.[24] Yet the Rastafarian movement became the face of the transformation that was taking place within the PNP while also representing a cultural and philosophical link with grassroots radicalism and the black nationalist, African-centered strain within Jamaican leftist politics.

As has been richly documented by Anita Waters, Manley and the PNP relied heavily upon Rastafarian symbols and language in the 1972 election campaign. This represented a moment in Jamaican history when black nationalist politics—most stridently expressed by Rastafarians at this point, seriously influenced state politics. The Rastafarian symbols used by the PNP (and later the JLP) included "language and names, props, issues and connections with specific individuals."[25] As he engaged the public between 1969 and 1972, Manley used the unique and powerful Rastafarian lexicon to connect with the black poor of Jamaica. Along with the use of "I" words, Manley tapped into the signature Rastafarian notion of "peace and love" by beginning his speeches with the phrase, "The word is love."[26] This spoke to the Rastafarian emphasis as a people-centered politics that was grounded in love. To add to the appeal of Manley as a man of the people, he carried a walking stick that came to be known as "the rod of correction." Having become fodder for legend, the origin of the rod is difficult to trace, but was said to be a gift to Manley from Emperor Haile Selassie I of Ethiopia. This was never proven, but was a widely accepted notion that further connected Manley to Rastafarians.

Beyond the embrace of Rasta language and symbols, the PNP also associated with prominent Rastafarians. Manley and the PNP allowed Claudius Henry, the controversial religious figure, to participate in the 1971 annual conference of the party. In 1958 Henry had embraced two key aspects of Rastafarian thought: repatriation to Africa and the divinity of Haile Selassie.[27] As was mentioned in chapter 1, Henry had clashed with the Jamaican state in previous years. Yet Henry's Peacemakers Church played the drums in the arena as the names of the PNP candidates were called. This signaled a considerable shift in the state's relationship with Rastafari generally and with Claudius Henry in particular. Henry chose to endorse Manley after Manley began to support African liberation movements and encouraged the implementation of African-centered curricula within the educational system.[28]

Another Rastafarian who was close to the PNP and to Manley was none other than the most famous reggae ambassador, Robert Nesta Marley. Manley met Bob Marley in 1971, and Marley became part of a group of reggae artists who traveled across the island with the PNP as they campaigned during the 1972 elections.[29] According to Marley biographer Timothy White, Manley and Marley developed a relationship and Manley spent many evenings at Marley's residence on Hope Road in Kingston. By the early 1970s, Rastafari and reggae went hand in hand, and Manley understood the power of this combination. The prominent role of reggae and Rastafari in the election campaign convinced the Jamaican people that Manley and the party he led related to the culture of the people, understood their plight as it was expressed through Rastafari and reggae, and spoke their cultural language. The transformative power of reggae and its message were not lost on Manley, who believed that "the greater part of Bob Marley is the language of revolution." A year after Marley's death, Manley wrote that "everybody listened to Marley and his school of reggae protestors. Certainly, I listened and was reinforced in the conviction that we had to struggle for change." As he praised reggae music for having "established an audience for itself among the myriad of competing musical forms which jostle for space in the communication apparatus," Manley highlighted the role of Marley, the "uncompromising revolutionary."[30] In a powerful statement that acknowledged the legitimacy of Rastafari as a religion, a worldview, and a political philosophy, Manley declared that "the answer" to questions about how and why Marley was successful was indeed Rastafarianism.[31] For Manley, Rastafari was "as true a faith in the sense that its believers have taken that step beyond mere rationality into the acceptance of a view of the unknown, unknowable and unprovable which is faith." He saw that the Rastafarian had "traced his identity beyond mere history and geography to the ultimate source of all things, for the believer, the Creator himself."[32]

Manley analyzed Rastafari and reggae within the context of Jamaica's history of enslavement and colonialism, and found it successful because of its power to address the need for black Jamaicans to connect to their African past in order to move forward. Manley argued that Rastafarian thought allowed Bob Marley to "successfully journey into the past which released him to believe in his people's future." Here Manley demonstrated a keen understanding of the ways in which Rastafari affirmed African roots by engaging history as a means of transforming oneself in the here and now. He understood that Bob Marley, the "definitive exponent of reggae," was a Rastafarian and that Rastafari was the journey that allowed him to solve his "identity crisis" and to "become a complete human being."[33]

In addition, shortly after Manley won the election in 1972, Dudley Thompson, who was then the minister of foreign affairs, led a mission to Africa that included respected Rastafarian elder Mortimo Planno.[34] Having lived in East Africa where he forged meaningful relationships with Julius Nyerere and others, Thompson was ideal for this mission.[35] In addition, he would use his position to repeatedly emphasize the linkages between Tanzania and Jamaica, and Africa and the West Indies more broadly.[36] Thompson was a known pan-Africanist, but as the only Rastafarian member of the five-man delegation, Planno's presence underscored the seriousness with which the administration took the ideas of Rastafarians in its approach to Africa. Ras Planno and Thompson also had a personal friendship.[37]

By 1974, however, some Rastafarians had become keenly aware of the ways in which Manley as a state actor sometimes worked against the best interests of Rastafarians.[38] In 1973 Manley addressed the Jamaican nation and suggested serious measures to curtail crime. Much to the chagrin of Rastafarians who used ganja as a sacrament and petitioned for its legalization, Manley "tied the ganja trade and the increase in local crime to the international traffic in firearms and hard drugs."[39] With the assistance of Eli Matalon, then minister of national security, the government crackdown on crime included unreasonably harsh sentences through the new Gun Court and a partnership with the U.S. government named Operation Buccaneer,[40] through which the Jamaican government allowed the U.S. Drug Enforcement Agency access to Jamaica in order to provide "technical assistance for a program designed to interdict the narcotics traffic" between Jamaica and the United States.[41] This program, aimed at the eradication of ganja cultivation, gave the U.S. government access to Jamaica that, in the end, far exceeded the operation itself and did not differentiate between proper drug dealers and individual ganja smokers. For Rastafarians, the attack on ganja had begun around the time of the state's destruction of Leonard Howell's Pinnacle commune in 1954, and some were disenchanted with Manley's role in perpetuating state violence against them.[42] To make matters worse, many "young Jamaican dreadlocks" were incarcerated under the new Gun Court laws.[43]

Such contradictions were common as the state actors of Caribbean nations tried to balance their relations with First World powers and the demands of popular movements. Nevertheless, the profound impact of Rastafarian ideology on Manley's consciousness took shape in his politics as prime minister. As he began to document the ideas that guided his policy initiatives, it also became clear that he was connected to Africa in another way—through the impact that Julius Nyerere had on his political ideas.

Ideological Ties: Nyerere and Manley

By 1974 Manley was "known to be an admirer" of Nyerere.[44] In Manley's 1974 book *The Politics of Change*, he clearly revealed the extent to which Nyerere had influenced his political thinking. For him, Nyerere was the "greatest contemporary African political thinker." Manley drew inspiration from Nyerere's writings, which stressed that despite the universal significance of general socialist principles, such as human equality, the socialist path of a given country had to reflect that country's uniqueness and cultural grounding. In the same way that Nyerere adamantly refused to be limited by scientific Marxism or any other theory in his pursuit of Tanzania's brand of African socialism, Manley maintained that "political systems are better approached in terms of analysis than dogma." In recognition of this, Manley praised Nyerere's attempts to "construct a genuinely democratic model that is consistent with the logic of Africa's situation" and noted that the model he chose was a "one-party state, which is a logical extension of the "natural tendency of the Tanzanian people."[45] Manley so appreciated Nyerere's emphasis on the specificity of each situation that the official PNP document defining what the PNP recognized as democratic socialism in 1975 was titled *Democratic Socialism: The Jamaican Model*. This use of *The Jamaican Model* was a deliberate attempt to make it clear that though the two-party, Westminster-type government was suitable for Jamaica, Manley and the party certainly saw the validity of other forms of socialism being tested around the world, including Nyerere's one-party system in Tanzania.

Nyerere had declared that a one-party system was suitable for Tanzania based on its particular history and experience. He argued that "European and American parties came into being as a result of existing social and economic divisions—the second party being formed to challenge the monopoly of the political power by some aristocratic or capitalistic group." He explained, however, that political parties in Africa "had a very different origin," as "they were not formed to challenge any ruling group of our own people; they were formed to challenge the foreigners that ruled over us." For Nyerere, the critical point was that rather than a mere "party," TANU and other parties that fought for independence across Africa represented nationalist movements and "from the outset they represented the interests and aspirations of the whole nation." This was an important distinction that enforced his argument that TANU was not concerned with either supporting the "Labour Party of England or opposing the Conservative Party of England." The fissures within the British political system did not factor into Tanzania's politics, as English politicians "were all colonialists" and TANU's mission was to "rid ourselves of their colonialism." Nyerere was convinced that "where there is one party, provided it is identified with the nation as a whole, the foundations of democracy can be firmer."[46] Manley did not see the one-party system as a viable option for Jamaica, but he was inspired by Nyerere's unwavering dedication to creating a political system that catered specifically to Tanzania. Nyerere's defense of the one-party system represented another display of his determination to develop Tanzania based only on the history and proclivities of the Tanzanian people.

In *The Politics of Change*, Manley declared that the two-party system was suitable for the Jamaican people. Just as Nyerere had developed *ujamaa* based on the culture of precolonial Tanzanian society, Manley looked to what he considered to be the "natural" way of Jamaicans. He declared that the "natural tendency" of the Jamaican people is individualistic, disputatious almost to the point of destructiveness, but rooted in a great, historically acquired strength: the ability to accept that the vote is the natural end product of dispute and that a majority decision is conclusive of an issue." As was often the case, Manley's analysis of the Jamaican situation and its people was rooted in the historical context of enslavement and colonialism, which meant that Jamaicans were "emerging from a background of sustained and total tyranny." As a result, "it was inevitable that Jamaicans should enter the new condition of legal freedom with a profound distrust of authority which was, inevitably, associated with tyranny in the mind of every newly freed slave." As Manley saw it, the fact that colonialism ensured that the post-abolition period "continued to be oppressive" and Jamaicans continued to associate authority with the tyranny of enslavement.[47]

All of this meant that Jamaica's particular history led the people to favor processes that rested upon the "containment of authority." Manley attributed this to the experience of colonialism, the impact of the church in Jamaican society, and a history of social gatherings among the people where "men learned to sit down and debate and argue and take a vote to decide." Continuing his comparison to the Tanzanian model, Manley insisted that he thought democracy could be achieved through a one-party state, and that Nyerere had demonstrated that such a model could work. But the particular history of Jamaica dictated that "it is natural that the Westminster model should more readily accommodate the psychological needs of a people."[48]

Manley's writings confirmed that, like Nyerere, he set out to establish an ideology for the state. The pamphlet *Democratic Socialism: The Jamaican Model*, like Nyerere's *Ujamaa* pamphlet, asserted that socialism was an "attitude of mind."[49] Through his pamphlet Manley revealed the extent to which Nyerere had influenced him in terms of how the state's platform should function as an ideology. In addition, along with lengthy quotations of his own and from Norman Manley (his father and the founder of the PNP), Nyerere was the only other theorist quoted in the pamphlet. The actual quotation reflected the value that Manley assigned to Nyerere's ideas concerning the importance of specificities within different states in the development of socialisms: "the task of a Socialist is to think out for himself the best way of achieving desired ends under the conditions which now exist in his country."[50]

Ideologically, Michael Manley and Julius Nyerere were also connected by Fabian socialism. The Fabian Society had been formed in Britain in 1884 in response to concerns such as the plight of workers and the "concentration of wealth in the hands of a few."[51] Fabian socialism as a system of thought is difficult to pin down due to its ideological elasticity and the absence of a definitive set of rules—comparable to, say, Karl Marx's *Communist Manifesto*.[52] This reluctance to present a calcified orthodoxy became an actual feature of the Fabian Society in 1939 when it officially decided that members should not be allowed to issue formal, authoritative statements as to what constituted Fabian socialism.[53] Furthermore, since its emergence, the group endured its own process of evolution, having little concern for issues such as trade unions and foreign affairs in the early years but embracing them later.[54] Still, there are several basic assumptions that form the foundation of Fabian socialism. The society nurtured a rejection of classical Marxism with its emphasis on class conflict as the engine for movement in history. This was replaced by a belief in the value of research into social situations and the use of social science information for state action. Fabian socialists believed in the power of ideas, with the goal of merging ideas with action. They hoped that such ideas could be spread among the population through state-run educational initiatives such as publications and lectures. The state was central to the vision of Fabian socialists, whose politics was based on using the existing apparatus of the party and the parliament to bring about reforms and not revolution. Fabians were also driven by a strong sense of morality and social responsibility, which was related to their pursuit of egalitarianism and democracy.

Manley developed a strong appreciation for Fabian socialism while he was a student at the London School of Economics, where he came under the influence of Harold Laski. Manley biographer Darrel Levi has argued that Laski's impact on Manley was "second only to that of his parents."[55] Laski was born in 1893 and was exposed to the work of prominent Fabian socialists Beatrice and Sydney Webb as a young man.[56] He then joined the Fabian Society while a student at Oxford University. After graduating in 1914, Laski went on to teach at Harvard and Yale Universities, where his socialism brought him into conflict with the institutions. Laski was known for his efforts to combine socialism and democracy. He was also active in trade unionism and the left wing of the British Labour Party, serving on its national executive from 1937 to 1949.[57] Laski's influence on Manley was obvious when Manley returned to Jamaica and became an important trade unionist,[58] and when Manley became leader of the PNP, the party declared democratic socialism as its platform. Linking Manley's politics to Fabian ideals, Levi argues that the adoption of democratic socialism "was intended to restore moral purpose to the political process."[59]

Julius Nyerere's introduction to Fabian socialism came when he was a student in Great Britain and established a relationship with the Fabian wing of the Labour Party. After 1919 the Fabian Society decided to affiliate with the Labour Party exclusively, forgoing association with other political parties in Britain.[60] Having already become politicized as a student, Nyerere joined the Fabian Colonial Bureau, which was founded in 1940 and functioned as an interest group with the tasks of conducting research and gathering information on British colonial policy. In response to widespread discontent in Britain's colonies, the bureau sometimes challenged the government on matters like racial discrimination, land tenure, labor issues, and the exploitation of mineral rights. Still, many nationalists found it to be very lackluster in its efforts to bring about independence in the colonies. As a Fabianist group, the Colonial Bureau favored a gradual process to bring about reform. John Iliffe has argued that Nyerere joined the bureau because he "sympathized with the Fabian variety of gradualist Socialism."[61] Nyerere continued this relationship as he campaigned for Tanganyika's independence from Britain, which he achieved through peaceful means in 1961.[62]

Nyerere's connection to the Fabian Society continued after independence through the presence of his personal assistant and speechwriter, Joan Wicken. On the eve of Tanganyika's independence at the end of the 1950s, Nyerere asked Wicken, a British woman who was working for the Commonwealth Bureau (formerly the Fabian Colonial Bureau) of the British Labour Party to help him establish the Tanganyika Education Trust.[63] This resulted in the founding of Kivukoni College in Tanzania, to which Wicken contributed much. Wicken, who became Nyerere's personal assistant in 1960, was his chief assistant for more than thirty years and was the "organizer of his schedule" and "drafter of his speeches and policy statements."[64]

Without rigidly imposing its ideals on either Manley or Nyerere, Fabian socialism nonetheless constituted an important point of connection for both men. Fundamentally, both Nyerere and Manley were true idealists who believed in the power of ideas and had established an ideological basis for political praxis. In true Fabian socialist fashion, these ideas were rooted in a strong sense of morality and a devotion to political practice based on certain unshakable principles. Manley has written that "like all political leaders who belong to the idealistic stream, broadly defined, I have found myself constantly in the presence of a personal, moral imperative."[65] Nyerere has defended his principled politics against the charge of unrealistic idealism by maintaining, "The major challenge to the validity of the principles of love, sharing and work as a basis for society is made on the grounds that they are too idealistic, particularly for large groups where the members cannot know each other. This criticism is non-sensical. Social Principles are, by definition, ideals at which to strive and by which to exercise self-criticism. The question to ask is not whether they are capable of achievement, which is absurd, but whether a society can do without them."[66]

Both men embraced a form of socialism that was not wedded to Marxism. Though Manley acknowledged the existence of class tensions within Jamaican society, he thought it was "possible to negotiate the terms of class relationships in Jamaican society by creating a public discourse of equality and brotherhood."[67] This was related to his belief in the transformative power of ideas, something that was characteristic of Fabian socialism. Nyerere started out by arguing in the *Ujamaa* pamphlet of 1962 that class did not exist in precolonial Tanzanian society and made it clear that his vision for socialism in the nation did not depend on the Marxist model for epistemological guidance. By 1967 he had recognized that some tendencies toward class differentiation had developed in Tanzania and made efforts to prevent its growth with the *Arusha Declaration*. This was yet another display of the extent to which he believed that ideas based on certain principles could provide the impetus for change in society.

Both Manley and Nyerere used the state machinery to spread their ideas to the population. Nyerere declared that socialism was an "attitude of mind" and was clear that shortly after independence "our first step, therefore, must be to re-educate ourselves, to regain our former attitude of mind."[68] This pamphlet and many subsequent publications by Nyerere and TANU reflected the Fabian socialist tendency to attempt to utilize state initiatives to educate the people. Similarly, the 1974 manifesto of Manley and the PNP clearly stated that the party "felt that there was an urgent need to educate the nation to a more complete understanding of what the processes of change would demand of the people."[69]

Nyerere, Manley, and African Liberation

The ideological compatibility between Manley and Nyerere translated into political action. By 1973 Nyerere had found a trusted ally in Michael Manley. Manley expressed a deep understanding of Jamaica's connection to Africa and demonstrated that, like Nyerere, he cared about the freedom and dignity of Africans. Manley understood the problems of Jamaica within the context of pan-Africanism. He knew that "in Jamaica, foreign policy is a significant part of domestic politics" and that "black pride, black power and Rasta gave many Jamaicans an intense interest in Africa."[70] As a result, his foreign policy reflected his grasp of the connection between continental Africans and those in the diaspora.

Manley also posited a pan-African connection between black freedom fighters in Africa and in the diaspora. He made reference to the roles of

Caribbean-born George Padmore and C. L. R. James, who became "mentors of Kwame Nkrumah," and he underscored how Jamaican-born Garvey inspired Jomo Kenyatta and Nkrumah.[71] At a meeting of the UN Special Committee against Apartheid in 1979 that was held in Jamaica, Manley argued that "by holding this meeting in the Caribbean rather than in Africa we dramatize the international violation of ethics which racism in the southern extremity of Africa represents."[72]

Manley's antiapartheid activism was driven by moral indignation and fueled by his vision of a world founded on the principles of "justice and human dignity."[73] For him, apartheid was linked to the "origins and continuing nature of imperialism." Decrying South Africa's support of the oppressive Ian Smith regime in Rhodesia (now Zimbabwe) and its intervention in Angola and Namibia, Manley called for the UN Security Council to "declare without qualification that South Africa represents a threat to international peace and security. Manley argued that more direct action, including economic sanctions, was justified by the existing UN Charter. He called for the UN and the entire international community to become engaged in the struggle against apartheid because "total sanctions, diplomatic isolation and even blockade are not too high a price to pay now for the holocaust that will surely come."[74] Manley's work to end apartheid also included his efforts with the Gleneagles Agreement, which asked Commonwealth of Nations governments to fight against apartheid in the realm of sports.[75] For his contributions to antiapartheid struggles, Manley was awarded the UN Gold Medal on October 11, 1978.[76]

Manley demonstrated his belief in the connection between Africa and its diaspora, as well as his strong commitment to social justice through his tireless and bold antiapartheid activities and his work on behalf of the liberation movements of southern Africa. At the Fourth Summit Conference of Heads of State or Government of the Non-Aligned Movement in Algiers in 1973, Manley offered to send volunteers from Jamaica to fight alongside their African brothers and sisters. However, in the spirit of self-reliance, a concept to which Manley and Nyerere were committed, it was agreed that the fighting should be done by those directly involved in the struggle. Manley demonstrated his acceptance of this notion in Maputo when he affirmed that the role of those supporters of the liberation movements, who were not immediately involved, was one of "support" and not "instructions."[77] Unable to join the Organization of African Unity, Jamaica's contribution was limited to the liberation fund and Manley was happy to "give direct aid to the freedom fighters in ways that are acceptable to THEM and within our means."[78] On his trip to Jamaica in 1974, Nyerere lauded Manley and Jamaica for their "voluntary participation in the struggle."[79]

In 1977 the secretary general of the United Nations invited Manley to Maputo, Mozambique, to be a special guest speaker at the international conference in support of the peoples of Namibia and Zimbabwe. By this time Manley had begun to garner international recognition for his unwavering support of the decolonization movements across Africa, and the invitation was extended to him based on the stance Jamaica had taken in support of liberation movements and his overall "international position."[80] While in Maputo, Manley delivered a radical speech that heralded his unflinching support of African liberation struggles and his acceptance of armed struggle as the modus operandi wherever attempts at negotiations with the colonial powers had failed. He praised the freedom fighters of Angola, Guinea Bissau, and Mozambique for their victories against the Portuguese and commended them for their continued engagement in the efforts of those who continued to struggle in Namibia, South Africa, and Zimbabwe. Based on his conclusion that the "Rhodesian racists" would not "yield to moral suasion," he declared that "armed struggle provides the only realistic path to a solution."[81]

Manley's support of African liberation and his trips to Africa represented a foreign policy that aggravated many at home in Jamaica. At times he defiantly chastised critics who maligned him for helping "sufferers" at home and "African brothers" abroad, accusing them of "creating divisions" in the country.[82] He was also known to deliver fiery speeches outside of Jamaica. On one such occasion, the American agents who monitored his every local and international move described a speech he gave in Zambia as "rather demagogic oratory."[83] At the same time, the pressures he faced at home, intensified by the racial messages of his activism, also saw him downplay the role of race in African liberation. Even as he spoke about the Jamaican nation's ancestral ties to Africa, he sometimes tried to appease his critics by framing his determination to send troops to Africa in terms of a "colorblind" endeavor in pursuit of freedom. He even invited "white, black and brown" Jamaicans to volunteer to serve in Africa.[84]

Amid the sometimes contradictory interplay between local and foreign politics, in which racial issues were particularly fraught, Manley's profile abroad showed that he was respected in pan-African circles—including state officials, citizens, and freedom fighters of the liberation movements of southern Africa. An exchange between Manley and Joshua Nkomo of the Zimbabwe African People's Union in 1979 demonstrates that Manley had cultivated a relationship with at least one of the freedom fighters of Zimbabwe (then Rhodesia). Nkomo sent a letter to Manley updating him on the movement's attempts at negotiations with the British government and thanking him for his assistance, noting that the "attitude and approach of the British government has since proved disastrous to what we believed was the spirit of the Commonwealth countries." He was convinced that the British government was "not interested in any concrete agreement on major issues," and explained to Manley that the "security situation" back home in Rhodesia had become "untenable," as the "white civilians in Rhodesia" had been given "more than 155,000 weapons." It was clear to Nkomo that the British were "laying a series of mine-fields along the way to obstruct, if not destroy the Patriotic Front."[85] Having outlined the dire situation in which the Patriotic Front found itself, Nkomo acknowledged receipt of a letter from the PNP requesting some money owed to the Jamaican government by the Patriotic Front for the "handling and storage of goods" at the port in Jamaica. These goods had been donated to the Patriotic Front by Canadian support groups for the movement's refugees in Zambia. From Jamaica the goods were flown to Havana, from where they were then shipped to Angola and then finally to Zambia. Nkomo appealed to Manley to settle the account on behalf of the Patriotic Front, explaining that his appeal was "not mindless of the fact that you have assisted us so often in the past. It is just that we are in dire difficulties." Nkomo then signed the letter, "[Y]ours in the liberation struggle."[86]

In response to Nkomo's letter, Manley assured him that he had read his "account of the state of negotiations with interest and concern." In addition, Manley granted his request by informing him that "in so far as the charges for handling and storage of goods in Jamaica are concerned, I am pleased to advise you that you can forget that matter. We have taken care of it and are happy to treat this as a small contribution to a larger struggle."[87]

On an official visit to Mozambique in 1979, *Tempo*, a weekly publication that was founded in Mozambique in 1970 and was supportive of the Frente de Libertação de Moçambique (FRELIMO), featured Manley's visit, which "resulted in three days of celebration for thousands of people who . . . received, listened to and welcomed him all along the stops he made." Among his stops was a popular rally in Maputo, where he was received with "great joy, warmth and a sense of brotherhood as the leader of a country that, like ours, has a tradition of struggle against colonialism, neocolonialism, and imperialism." In a meeting with Samora Machel, the president of Mozambique, the Jamaican delegation and the Mozambican government engaged

The Wages of Blackness 95

in talks about ways to strengthen bonds of friendship and "existing mutual cooperation between the related people of Mozambique and Jamaica."[88]

Bond without Blood

Beyond their shared support of African liberation movements, the ideological bonds between Nyerere and Manley led to the manifestation of tangible connections between Tanzania and Jamaica. When Manley visited Tanzania in 1973, he was exposed to Nyerere's attempts at agrarian reform there. Tanzania's brand of socialism was marked by a strong emphasis on agricultural development in the rural areas. Nyerere sought to organize rural communities into *ujamaa* villages that were based on the principles of the "traditional African family" and explained that the development of a socialist Tanzania meant "co-operative living and working for the good of all."[89] As a result, the Tanzanian government was committed to a policy of villagization throughout Tanzania.

In a speech delivered at the University of Dar es Salaam during the same trip, Manley explained his own attempts to implement agrarian reform in Jamaica, having consulted Rastafarians about his plans. He explained that the process had started with the "massive taking in of idle lands and beginning the development of cooperative farming with those lands."[90] The Jamaican government had sponsored the Cornwall Youth and Community Development Project, which was being run by the Ministry of Agriculture's Project Land Lease Division and the Ministry of Youth and Community Development. The project area included three named community sites: Cacoon Castle; Ramble, or Haughton Grove Property; and Mafoota. The project was an innovative one that sought to settle young farmers in rural areas with a view to focusing on food crops and forestry. Like Nyerere, Manley stressed the importance of agricultural development and argued that agrarian reform was crucial to the process by which Jamaica would "achieve a measure of self-sufficiency in food."[91] In an effort to help Jamaicans feed themselves, Manley and the PNP launched Operation GROW in 1974. As one of the young women recruited for the Mafoota site, Grace Pennicott-Smith learned that "for us to survive, we have to rely on ourselves and agriculture was one of the main things to get self-reliance"; socialism meant "people come together and unite and work as one," and she was convinced that "Manley's plan was good."[92]

In conjunction with this food farm program, the PNP also launched Project Land Lease, which sought to persuade landowners who were not using their land to lease the surplus to the government, which would then redistribute the land to farmers. This was a direct attempt to address the social and economic disparities caused by the fact that all the best agricultural land was either foreign owned or in the hands of a small local minority. In keeping with his propensity to connect policy initiatives to the history of enslavement and colonialism, Manley hoped that the Land Lease Project would help the many farmers who were "still trying to survive on steep hillsides to which their ancestors had fled in 1838 after nearly 200 years of capitalist slavery."[93] The impact of this aspect of the Land Lease project was reflected in the experience of Joseph Christie, one of the farmers recruited to work on the Cacoon Castle site in 1974. As a farmer in this government-run program, Christie received agricultural training, a house, and a plot of land for farming. This was particularly meaningful for Christie, who had been born in Cacoon Castle at a time when the said property belonged to a wealthy white family with the surname Charlie. Since the days of enslavement, this had been the sugarcane plantation where Christie's ancestors had worked. Manley's rationale for the Land Lease Project resonated with Christie, whose family was forced to eke out a living in the hills on less arable land above the plantation: "My grandfathers, forefathers, grandmothers and aunties, di whole of dem slaved to build here and is up in dem mountain we used to live. We couldn't come on di level. If we come, some black man like wiself run we off di land for di white people dem." Christie gained access to the land that was once owned by the Charlies because "Michael [Manley] took it away from them," and this represented a clear case of social justice for Christie. He thought it grossly unfair that "they took us from Africa and bring us here and slave us and my forefathers slave to build here but we had to live in the hills." For Christie, whose experience had taught him that "a black man is an African [and] a white man is a robber," he was able to acquire land previously owned and occupied by the white planter class due to Manley's attempt at land redistribution.[94]

Once again, Manley demonstrated his admiration for Nyerere when he named the Cacoon Castle food farm in Hanover where Christie worked the "Nyerere Farm." As the first farm to be set up under the Cornwall Youth and Development Project, "Nyerere Farm" was supposed to serve as the "model of rural development and cooperate farming to be followed throughout Jamaica."[95] On his 1974 trip to Jamaica to participate in the national conference of the PNP, Nyerere visited the Cacoon Castle community, where he was asked to unveil a plaque, thereby marking the official opening of the community. As Nyerere toured the site of Nyerere Farm, he was heard commenting that it was "just like we have at home." The *Jamaica Daily News* article featured a photograph of Nyerere beaming with pride as he shook the hand of a Rastafarian resident of Nyerere Farm and noted that he encouraged these residents to "struggle against those who would always seek to oppress them."[96] This was a powerful and ironic message delivered on the grounds of Cacoon Castle, which had previously been the Great House of the Cacoon Castle Plantation.

"Salute Your African President": Nyerere's 1974 Visit

Nyerere's visit to Jamaica in 1974 was a momentous one. While there he enjoyed a warm reception that included a gun salute and keys to the city of Kingston. He was also awarded the Order of Jamaica and an honorary degree from the University of the West Indies. The pomp and circumstance that marked his arrival belied the controversy that preceded his visit. Michael Manley and the PNP had extended an invitation to Nyerere to speak at the party's annual conference and to have discussions with the executive of the PNP. Members of the opposition, the JLP, then led by Hugh Shearer, objected to what they interpreted as a blatant attempt by Manley and the PNP to involve Nyerere in Jamaica's party politics. The correspondence between Manley and Shearer concerning the conflict over Nyerere's visit was published in the *Jamaica Daily News*. Upon learning that Nyerere had accepted the invitation to speak at the PNP's conference and to meet with the party executive, Manley wrote to Shearer detailing the activities planned for Nyerere, and asked whether Shearer "might wish to have the executive of the J.L.P. benefit from the opportunity for a discussion with the president." Hugh Shearer responded by explaining that he and the JLP would "enthusiastically welcome President Nyerere to Jamaica and will give our fullest support to his state visit" if the program of his visit "is in accord with protocol and conforms with the well established precedents for such occasions and that it studiously avoids any overt or inferential involvement in the domestic affairs of our country and particularly involvement in the sensitive area of party politics." Shearer continued to explain that since Jamaica's independence in 1962, several heads of state had visited and were never expected to "identify themselves either overtly or covertly with a political party." In order to make the point that he and the JLP wanted Nyerere to visit Jamaica, Shearer also reminded Manley that in 1970, as Jamaica's prime minister, he had also extended an invitation to Nyerere, who had accepted but then had to later cancel his visit "due to a domestic situation in

Tanzania."[97] In response to Shearer's objections, Manley did "not concede that there is anything improper in such an arrangement provided the visiting dignitary meets all of the recognized elements of the political system of the country which is being visited." Manley refused to change the list of activities that had been planned for Nyerere and instead offered to reclassify the visit from a state visit to an official visit, adding that Nyerere had agreed to the change. This meant that Nyerere would not be visiting Jamaica in "his capacity as symbolic Head of State but as a working politician who is the head of a friendly government seeking strong ties in international affairs in Jamaica." Shearer was incensed by Manley's decision and accused the PNP of "employing subterfuge and engaging political sophistry in its endeavor to sustain an unorthodox and unprincipled decision." He added that Nyerere was in no way culpable, that the JLP did not blame him for the "distasteful position in which he will find himself," and assured Manley that the JLP had decided not to participate in any of the activities planned for the president's visit.[98]

With the official boycott of the JLP, the issue remained a hotly debated one up to the point of the visit. National hero and former leader of the JLP Alexander Bustamante also boycotted the event even though a meeting with him had been included on Nyerere's itinerary. Bustamante opined that Nyerere was "being dragged into party politics" in Jamaica.[99] The Jamaica Council of Churches (JCC) also weighed in on the debate, agreeing that it was inappropriate for Nyerere to address the PNP conference and asked Manley to withdraw the invitation. At the same time, the council encouraged the opposition to call off the boycott in order to "save Dr. Nyerere embarrassment while he is a guest in Jamaica."[100] In the final analysis, the JCC, though disappointed in the reluctance of both the PNP and the JLP to reconsider their respective positions, decided to "share in all public nonpartisan occasions of welcome." The organization based its decision on its "profound respect" for Julius Nyerere.[101]

In the midst of this ebullient exchange, the *Daily News* also featured articles that demonstrated the zeal with which the public prepared for Nyerere's arrival. The Agency for Public Information produced a booklet on Julius Nyerere that included a biography and detailed his political philosophy. The booklet, which was free of charge and available to the public, also looked at the similarities between Jamaica and Tanzania.[102] The agency also developed a television and radio program that looked at Nyerere's politics as well as "the part he plays in the Third World."[103] Nyerere's friend and minister of government Dudley Thompson agreed to share his impressions of Nyerere with the public.[104] As a part of the agency's attempt to prepare the public for Nyerere's visit, an exhibition that showcased books on the culture and history of Tanzania and other African countries was held at the Tom Redcam Library. A research paper on Nyerere, which was prepared by Karl Phillpotts with the help of Peter Phillips, delved into Nyerere's early life, his philosophy, and the history of Tanzania.[105] Both Phillpotts and Phillips were students at the University of the West Indies and Rastafarians. For Rastas and others who appreciated Nyerere's strong anticolonial stance, the debate between the political parties was of little relevance. The PNP youth organization offered a more radical cause for support of the visit, urging "progressive Jamaicans and the youth of the country" to ensure that Nyerere's visit would mark a "milestone in the struggle for democratic socialism against the forces of reaction in the Third World."[106] This plea from the PNP youth organization spoke to the socialist orientation shared by Michael Manley and Julius Nyerere, a point that had been avoided by the correspondence between Manley and Shearer. But Nyerere's anticolonial stance, his championing of a socialist path for Tanzania, his work on behalf of developing countries, and his tireless pan-Africanism served to solicit a heartfelt response from the Jamaican public.

Nyerere arrived at the Norman Manley International Airport in Kingston on September, 14, 1974 to "thousands of people waving Jamaican and Tanzanian miniature flags." Though the tribute planned for Nyerere reflected Jamaica's motto "out of many, one people" by offering what one newspaper reporter referred to as a "multiracial affair," the significance of President Nyerere's visit to Jamaica's African population was not lost. Rastafarians, representing the radical element in Jamaican society, were well represented. Rastafarian musicians such as Count Ossie, Mystic Revealers, and the Sons of Negus participated in the festivities, as did respected Rasta elder Mortimo Planno. Nyerere descended from the airplane to the sound of drums, which "drummed the welcome of various Rastafarian groups who came to pay tribute to a son of Africa."[107] He was flanked by signs and banners that displayed messages like We Salute You and Hail the son of Judah. The latter, bearing a palpable Rastafarian orientation and usually reserved for Haile Selassie, revealed Nyerere's importance as an African leader. In addition, as Nyerere was driven through Kingston, he was taken to Trench Town, known as the home of Kingston's downtrodden, where the Zap Pow band played Bob Marley's "Natty Dread." This was a display of great respect for Nyerere, who did not have dreadlocks, but whom many Rastafarians would have embraced as one with a "dread" (Rastafarian) consciousness.

Beyond the quarrel between the political parties, some worried that Nyerere's presence would spur on black nationalists, including Rastafarians. The justification for such fear could be found in the pages of the *Jamaica Daily News*: "Julius Nyerere is a prominent BLACK MAN who has liberated his people from colonialism and monopoly capitalism, and this must have a strong psychological effect on the advocates of Black Power, the Garveyites, the Pan-African movement, and the Rastafarians. One of the real fears is that the Rastafarians are having a problem with the Haile Selassie doctrine, and Julius Nyerere might provide a powerful psychological image for this group."[108] This was a particularly poignant notion in 1974, as Ethiopia was embroiled in a civil war and news of the coup that ousted the emperor was splattered across newspapers. Still, while Selassie's fate did lead some Rastafarians to question and revise the foundation of their theology, most remained faithful.

Not all Rastafarians supported Nyerere's visit. A very small contingent within the Nyabingi order questioned what they deemed to be Nyerere's criticism of the Organization of African Unity (OAU). While the specific critique to which they referred is not clear, Rastafarians had long associated the OAU with Haile Selassie and would have offered only scorn for anyone who dared to disrespect the emperor.[109] Still, the overwhelming majority of Rastafarians received Nyerere with joy, and several prominent Rasta groups welcomed him, making public pronouncements of their support. Planno and those in his circle in Trench Town took a strong position that was publicized in the media. In response to the JLP's proposed boycott, Planno issued a broadside that urged people to "beware of capitalistical [sic] inspired boycotting of your African president." "In a society where 90% of the population is of African origin," Planno continued, "Capitalist oriented politician have [sic] lost their vision of nationhood and what the visit of an African president mean [sic] to black people in a land where party politics have divided black people." In supporting Nyerere, Planno revealed his astute understanding of the local political scene in Jamaica while also making it clear that Nyerere's socialism constituted a part of his appeal to Rastafarians. As sophisticated and fluid as the members of the Universal Rastafari Improvement Association in his race/class analysis, Planno called on "all black people to boycott the propose[d] boycott" of Nyerere." At the end of his closing remarks informing the people that "your children must ask you about Nyerere's visit" and they should "come out and meet your black president," Planno used the Kiswahili word for "freedom" in his salutation: *uhuru*.[110]

In the annals of Jamaican history, perhaps only the 1966 advent of Haile Selassie compares with that of Nyerere's 1974 visit. One columnist asserted that Nyerere's reception "rivaled that accorded the former emperor Haile Selassie in April 1966."[111] A mere comparison to Haile Selassie's visit spoke volumes in light of not only the centrality of his divinity to Rastafarian thought but also to the significance of his visit. Rupert Lewis argues that "no other event in the 1960s, not even the Independence celebrations of 1962, had had such a catalyzing effect on grassroots Jamaica" as did Selassie's visit.[112] Another columnist argued that "with the eclipse of Emperor Haile Selassie the President must in fact be the most prestigious leader in black Africa today."[113] Individual Rastafarians and organizations such as The Rastafari Movement Organization and the Ethiopian African National Congress also expressed support for the visit.

After talks between Nyerere and Manley, both leaders issued a joint communiqué that demonstrated their ideological unity with regard to matters of international import. Placing great emphasis on the liberation movements in southern Africa and apartheid South Africa, they discussed the success of the freedom movement in Guinea Bissau and welcomed their membership to the United Nations. Among other matters they discussed were the Lusaka agreement between FRELIMO and the Portuguese government, which served to provide a timeline for the liberation of Mozambique from Portuguese rule. The communiqué marked the end of a visit that solidified important ties between Jamaica and Tanzania.

Race, Class, and the Interplay between the Personal and Political

Manley paid a heavy price for Nyerere's visit. High on the list of grievances expressed by his opposition was the concern that Manley's "stated admiration of Nyerere" symbolized his aim to move Jamaica to a one-party state.[114] Despite a plethora of announcements to the contrary, this idea persisted, and Manley was accused of pandering to the militant left wing of the party. In truth, this was a tantrum from the disenchanted middle class, longing for a return to the PNP of Manley's father Norman.

The career of Norman Manley, from whom Michael took over leadership of the People's National Party in 1969, had been marked by his support of multiracialism as the model for Jamaican society. As black power activism reached a high point in Jamaica in the late 1960s, he maintained that black power was a "foreign concept." He denied not only the real concerns of those of African descent in Jamaica but the pan-African connections that defied a provincial analysis of black power as a movement. Norman Manley's embrace of Jamaican exceptionalism was also clear in his personal life. Of mixed heritage and considered a member of the privileged "brown" elite in Jamaica, he had experienced blatant racism in England as a soldier during World War I and been refused entry into a restaurant in the United States. In the face of such experiences, he maintained that race was not an issue in Jamaica. When he was about to marry Edna, Michael's mother, a British woman who was born of a Jamaican mulatto mother and British father but who looked phenotypically white, Norman had quelled Edna's mother's fears about their union by assuring her that they would live in Jamaica, where such concerns were not relevant.[115]

Edna Manley, an influential part of the Manley dynasty, has been hailed as the mother of Jamaican art. Born and raised in Britain, she relocated to Jamaica upon marrying Norman. A celebrated artist, Edna paid tribute to the African cultural roots of Jamaica and asserted black subjectivity through her sculptures. As ostensibly "white" and the wife of Norman Manley, Edna was all too aware of her status (real and perceived) and of the colonial history that created Jamaica's social hierarchy. She reacted with discomfort to the privilege she was assigned and was keen to point out that African blood flowed through her veins. Yet, as her granddaughter (Michael's daughter) writes, the family maintained "quaintly British middle-class sensibilities."[116]

Seen in this context, Michael Manley's appropriation of Rastafarian symbols, language, and consciousness represented the main way in which he appropriated blackness in order to compensate for this, but he also gained much-desired social and political capital through association with his wife Beverley Manley. When they married in 1972 both were aware that according to the social standards of Jamaica the union represented the merger of two very different worlds. Beverley, a woman of African descent with working-class roots and little patience for bourgeois affectations, personified the political shift that was taking place in Jamaica House. In a place and space where the state's platform of multiracialism had historically served to marginalize black nationalism, Beverley's Afro and dashiki signaled a new day. From the Jamaican upper classes she received heinous disapproval in the form of letters demanding that she straighten her hair.[117] The masses, in contrast, offered her support and admiration.[118]

Though captivatingly charismatic, with an appeal that definitely endeared him to the people, Michael depended on Beverley to put him at ease whenever he interacted with the populace. On various occasions, as they walked through crowds, he begged her to hold his hand, ever aware of the political messages worn by her black, African-centered body. The symbolic nature of this was heightened by the fact that Beverley was the keeper of the rod of correction. In recognition of the power of the rod, Beverley believed that it

> invoked in the masses of Jamaicans this need to be able to say I'm black and I'm proud which had been subsumed for all types of reasons, we had to straighten hair, bleach . . . it became very powerful. They associated it as coming from Africa and Rasta and it had such an impact on them . . . like Michael, I believe that we will never be able to liberate ourselves until we own Africa. I don't mean Africa in terms of slavery but Africa before slavery. Putting Marcus Garvey into schools is just beginning to happen, we've been struggling for that since from the 1970s.[119]

Beverley's astute assessment of why the rod was a catalyst for a public response like she had never seen reveals her firm grasp on the politics of the day. Her relationship with Michael was a partnership that was mutually beneficial as they negotiated the politics of race, class and gender. In a real way, his family and the social circles in which he had been socialized rejected her while he felt that her social circles rejected him, and they helped each other to navigate the very different social locations in which they operated. In the final analysis, Beverley "blackened" Michael. In her words, "Mike was very aware of what I did for him and I was aware of what he did for me. It really worked."[120]

But Manley's consciousness came from Rastafari. On the one hand, his widespread acceptance in pan-African circles demonstrates a pan-Africanism in the 1970s that was less concerned with phenotype because it had become coterminous with nonalignment, Third World politics, and support of African liberation. Yet race remained a salient factor in local and international settings. Certainly Jamaican foreign policy concerning Africa had much to do with internal notions of race and identity construction within the new nation. His "near-white" status, observed as such among a majority black population in Jamaica, did not solicit the same type of privilege in a North American context where the "one-drop" rule reigned supreme. But from within his own context in a majority black country like Jamaica, a Tanzanian state official confirmed how very close Nyerere and Manley were while also remarking that Manley did not appear to be black.[121]

These variations underscore the complexity of identity within a transnational and trans-regional pan-African agenda in which local contexts carried very different racial politics. In the final analysis, Rastafari played a critical role in the politics surrounding race, color, and class in Jamaica, which set the stage for solid ties between Jamaica and Tanzania. In what many Rastafarians might interpret as a divine promise kept, when Jamaican Rastafarians began to repatriate to Tanzania, they were able to appeal to and benefit from Nyerere's experiences with Manley and Jamaica more broadly.

4 Diasporic Dreams, African Nation-State Realities

In his self-portrait *Not Far Away*, famed Jamaican Rastafarian artist Ras Daniel Heartman depicts himself looking into the distance toward Africa, with a palpable sense of longing. Repatriation was a dream that Heartman had nurtured as a Rastafarian, and beckoned as an artist. When Tanzania officially opened its doors to Rastafarians in 1985, Tanzania was deemed the promised land. But it did not occur to him that he would need a passport to make his dream a reality. After all, as a Rastaman, Heartman had rejected Jamaican nationality and identity. He was an African living in exile in Jamaica; why would he need a passport to go home? But Tanzania was a nation-state, and he had no choice but to get a passport. Repatriation was worth the compromise. So finally, in 1988, Heartman and his sixteen-year-old son Ato Kidani Roberts left Babylon behind, bound for the promised land.[1]

Another Rastafarian who repatriated to Tanzania in 1983, Ras Bupe Karudi, had willingly acquired a passport but did not consider the immigration laws of any African state. Before Tanzania validated his definition of diaspora by granting him the "right of entry" into Tanzania, he spent six years, from 1977–83, going from one African state to the next, including Kenya, Zimbabwe and Uganda, hoping to be welcomed into the continent of his ancestral origin. In a letter he wrote to C. L. R. James from Tanzania in 1986, Karudi expressed his frustration: "the only status under which I qualified for entry was that of a tourist/a foreigner" and "I failed to meet the financial requirements to qualify for a six-week tourist visa." Karudi believed that he "was penalized for being a poor Black Afrikan captive returning home" and he had come "to the harsh realization that Black Afrikans in captivity in foreign lands were neither provided for, or accommodated in Black Afrikan Citizenship or immigration Laws."[2]

• • • • • •

The experiences of both Heartman and Karudi dramatize the divide between their vision of freedom, based on a particular notion of diaspora, and the realities of African nation-states in the age of decolonization. The

Rastafarian embrace of an African identity, as an inherently transnational optic, destabilized the nation-state as the assumed path to postcolonial freedom.[3] Rastafari, arguably antistatist in both structure and philosophy, defied the nation-state and its emphasis on a territorially bound framework of solidarity.[4] In their local Jamaican context Rastafarians, as staunch pan-Africanists, had never sought to be citizens of the state. Indeed, Rastafari was at odds with the Jamaican nation-state project and represented a threat to its consolidation. This friction, well treated in the extant literature on the movement, defined the relationship between Rastafarians and the Jamaican state.[5]

The repatriation to Tanzania revealed a tension between the ideal of a stateless African identity and the political necessity of the state apparatus in effecting the return. Rastafarians quickly came to understand that to belong to the African continent in the postindependence period was to acquire permanent residency or citizenship in one of its states. The reality was that the age-old Rastafarian adage that one should "never trade a continent for an island" gave way to the necessity of acquiring Jamaican passports in order to begin the process of gaining such papers/documentation—not for a continent, but to secure rights in a nation-state in Africa.

Tanzania faced a similar conflict. Julius Nyerere and the other state officials who participated in the practice of pan-Africanism through repatriation did so within the confines of the nation-state they served. The power they possessed as state actors facilitated repatriation in ways that were not possible before the advent of political independence from colonial rule. Yet they exercised state power, particularly the rule of law, in inconsistent ways. Furthermore, that the Tanzanian state's offer of permanent residency or citizenship to Rastafarians was extended to "black" Jamaicans in particular shed light on how race—as both a sociopolitical construct and somatic reference—remained salient throughout the protracted process that was decolonization. The state officials' use of race as a criterion for citizenship had much to do with both the history of race making (and governmental regulation of race) in Tanzania and their flawed perception of the racial politics in Jamaica (and the West Indies more broadly). This highlighted the transnational meaning of race, its powerful global resonance, and how it traversed different locales.

The Rastafarian movement was at the center of not only how pan-African collaboration was imagined but how it translated into a lived reality. Rastafarians laid bare their definition of pan-Africanism and placed their expectations at the feet of continental African state officials. The history of how Tanzanian state actors responded to such expectations and how they, along with Rastafarians, trodded diaspora, reveal much about how pan-African theory, activism, and praxis took shape after flag independence in Africa and the Caribbean.

Movement of Jah People

Joshua Mkhululi arrived in Tanzania in 1976, ready to begin a position at the University of Dar es Salaam as a lecturer in the Department of Business and Administration. This was the beginning of a productive number of years at the university where Mkhululi used his expertise to contribute to Tanzanian nation building. But his presence and his work there also provided him with opportunities to help other Rastafarians repatriate to Tanzania. As a lecturer, he gained access to President Nyerere, who also served as the chancellor of the university at the time. Mkhululi first met Nyerere in 1979, when Mkhululi was elected the first dean of the faculty of commerce and management, and Nyerere as chancellor confirmed his appointment. This gave way to the second and far more critical meeting later that year, when one of Nyerere's sons took Mkhululi to have a personal meeting with Nyerere at his home in Msasani. It was at this meeting that Mkhululi first requested Nyerere's support for the wide-scale repatriation of more Jamaican Rastafarians to Tanzania. Mkhululi assured Nyerere that his brothers and sisters were waiting in Babylon to return to their motherland, and asked for Nyerere's thoughts on the matter. Nyerere responded favorably, mentioning that he had received the warmest of welcomes on his visits to Jamaica. Mkhululi left Nyerere's home after thanking him and informing him that Rastafarians in Jamaica would "prepare to receive this welcome."[6]

As Mkhululi strategized about the best steps to take after Nyerere responded favorably to his request, Karudi arrived in Tanzania in 1983. Born in England in 1952, but raised in Jamaica after his Jamaican-born parents returned to the island during his youth, Karudi returned to England later in life. When he decided to leave England for Tanzania, he was connected to an active and generative Rastafarian network that became a hub for the evolution of the movement and a critical launch pad for repatriation to Africa. As a launch pad, England was certainly central to the history of Rastafarian repatriation to Tanzania in particular.

The process by which Rastafari stepped into the very seat of Babylon happened within the context of Britain's changing relationship with Jamaica and its other colonies following the Second World War. The British government began to encourage immigration from its colonies in order to deal with the labor shortages it faced after the war. Additionally, the war had thrown into sharp relief the contradiction between the British Empire's rhetoric of egalitarianism and the reality of the racial discrimination faced by its subjects in the colonies. As a part of its efforts to reform the empire, the colonial office's Labour Party government tried to stymie agitation for self-rule in its colonies through economic development programs, social provisions in areas such as education, the expansion of local participation in governance, and an overall posture of paternalistic kindness. The British Nationality Act of 1948 extended citizenship to the subjects of the empire in the colonies and provided a legal framework for giving them the same rights as those living in the metropole. By the 1950s thousands of West Indians, including many Jamaicans, sought to escape crushing poverty by migrating to the "mother country." As a large percentage of the population lived in dire straits, the local government in Jamaica actually depended on migration as a main strategy for a serious problem of unemployment and underemployment. Jamaicans took full advantage of Britain's open-door policy and flocked to England in high numbers. Additionally, for many West Indians the desire to migrate to Britain from a British colony also represented "an imperial right, a condition of belonging within empire."[7] Marking its significant social, economic, and cultural impact, the wide-scale migration was immortalized in poetry by Jamaican poet Louise Bennett, who sarcastically referred to it as "colonization in reverse."

The mother country was not welcoming. As the Caribbean population in Britain grew, many Britons became unsettled and were disturbed by the invasion of "coloured" people. Black people had been in England for centuries before this particular migration.[8] Rastafarians were, however, a part of the growing black presence in Britain that started in 1948. Resistance to the changing racial and cultural landscape was significant across British society and even resulted in the emergence of right-wing groups like the Union Movement, which perpetuated stereotypes about black immigrants as criminals, savages, and drug dealers.[9] The discontent spread to disgruntled adolescents, including the infamous Teddy Boys, who blamed immigrants for their economic woes due to increased competition for jobs. The bubbling friction came to a head in the riots of 1958: Notting Hill and Nottingham exploded when immigrants fought back in response to the attacks from those who deeply resented their presence in Britain.

As British society nurtured its race-based xenophobia and the British government strengthened its resolve to police black people, Caribbean governments worried that Britain would begin to restrict immigration from the islands. In September 1958, Norman Manley, then premier of Jamaica, visited Britain in the wake of the unrest to "make an on-the-spot investigation of the riots in Britain." Convinced that Jamaicans constituted the vast majority of West Indians in England, Manley thought it important for him to make the journey but left with the impression that the "great majority of the English people are not against West Indians."[10] Upon his return to Jamaica about two weeks later, however, he had come to the realization that there was indeed a "very fair percentage of colour-prejudice in England," estimated by experts to be about a one-third of the population there.[11] At every step of the way he expressed his "absolute rejection of the restriction of immigration as a way of tackling the problem," even as some Jamaicans and other West Indians opted to return to the Caribbean.[12] Manley had gone to England "to give what help" he could to West Indians who turned out to be heavily influenced by Rastafari. In the meantime, he returned home to resume his part in the state-sanctioned repression of Rastafari, constantly reminding Rastafarians of "Jamaica's forces of law and order."[13]

Rastafarians faced similar state repression in Britain. In the midst of the "England-bound fever" that swept Jamaica in the 1950s, Rastafari's anticolonial stance was once again on display as they responded with the slogan, "Africa Yes, England, No!"[14] Still, some Rastas made the journey to Britain. Some of the young ones migrated with their families, while others saw England as geographically closer to Africa and so a step in the right direction.[15] Yet while they may have sought opportunities that were unavailable in Jamaica, they knew that England was the very center of Babylon and not the promised land imagined by many non-Rastafarian migrants. The pages of *URIA Voice* reveal the particular viewpoint of the members of the Universal Rastafari Improvement Association (URIA). Along with its international coverage, the comprehensive publication offered a window into the specifics of living in England and understood the British government's decision to open its doors to Africans "from Afrika and the Caribbean" as a means to deal with "the acute labour shortage due to their war losses." The members of URIA argued that those who thought they were going to the mother country were "deceived by promises, visions of plenty and mirages of streets paved with gold." Such commentary reinforced Rastas' propensity to juxtapose their vision of Africa to the vision that Africans who saw themselves as British subjects had of England. *URIA Voice* explained that black people were "classed as scroungers from a system that was created on I-n-I back." In this virulently racist society, they faced landlords discriminating against black people openly, verbal abuse, and the brute force of "marauding 'natives' seeking to use I-n-I structure as a punch bag and beating post."[16]

Jah Bones, a prominent Jamaican Rastafarian who migrated to England, offered his own view on why some Rastafarians undertook such a migration. He was convinced that "the overwhelming majority of Rastas" were fully aware that Britain was not a suitable place for black people. They understood that "Britain is Babylon" and that a move to Britain meant black people would "only be going deeper into slavery rather than getting out of slavery." According to Bones, despite this understanding of what Britain represented, "human 'I-man' nature being what it is, individuals' curiosities do get aroused from time to time and a few Rastas braved it." In the end, he argued, "these Rastas, the tiny band of courageous I-drins [brethren] who trusted, through faith, in the powers of the most high Jah" were indeed the "pioneers in expanding the frontiers of Rasta livity."[17] Bones failed to recognize the Rastafarian "sistrens" who were ever-present and crucial agents in the movement's growth, but he was correct about the "frontiers of Rasta livity" being expanded in England.

Serious developments within Rastafari have taken place in the international arena. Rastafarians who travel from Jamaica to other places participate in a process by which the movement adapts to different local circumstances. Yet, as was the case when Rastafari moved to Britain, its development took shape in conversation with Rasta communities in Jamaica and other parts of the world. For example, the Rastafarians in England who chose to function as Charter 37 of the Ethiopian World Federation (EWF) did so only after receiving permission from that same charter in Jamaica. Furthermore, the issue of whether or not Rastafarians should participate in politics was focused on "Rastafarian representation in the legislature of Jamaica" and not England. It also pertained to repatriation, which remained the goal, but those who supported participation in politics called for what they deemed a realistic approach to return and argued that it could only be done at the level of government.[18] Debates such as these were rife among Rasta communities in Britain, which were fully engaged in the movement's internationalization while remaining connected to the anticolonial, antiimperial politics that gave it life in the 1930s.

In keeping with the decentralized nature of the movement, there were many different Rastafarian groups in Britain, including mansions of Rastafari, as well as organizations formed for specific purposes. The Twelve Tribes of Israel had branches there that were closely tied to the group's headquarters in Jamaica. Prophet Gad, the leader of the group, frequently visited the branch in England, sometimes for extended periods. The Rasta organizations formed included Rasta International, the Rastafarian Advisory Service, Rastafari Universal Zion, and URIA, as well as chapters of the EWF.[19]

Rastafarian organizations in England were active in planning conferences, which have been essential to the evolution of the movement in England, Jamaica, and beyond. Many of the productive conversations and actions regarding the role of women in the movement occurred among these Rastafarians in England. In 1986 the Rastafarian Advisory Service held a conference that was coordinated by a Rasta woman, Sister Liveth Ivory.[20] The conference, titled "Rastafari Focus," brought eminent Rastafarians such as Ras Boanerges from Jamaica to England to "talk to people in England on the history of the Rastafarian movement."[21] The first such conference in Britain was held on January 11, 1975, at Loyola Hall in Tottenham and was spearheaded by Charter 33 of the EWF. The second conference, held on July 23, 1981, at the Brixton Town Hall, was organized by Rastafarian women and men from Kennington known as Rasta International. Several different individuals and groups, including Rasta Unity, Tree of Life, Rastafari Universal Zion, and Charters 11 and 33 of the EWF attended the conference.[22] Repatriation was a major issue, with a debate between Rastafari International, which advocated for immediate repatriation, and Rastafari Universal Zion, which supported organization and centralization before repatriation. Rastafarians in England created an intellectually vibrant and dynamic environment in which they vigorously debated black radical politics, pan-Africanism, religion, and repatriation.

Onward to Zion

As a dedicated Rastafarian, Ras Bupe Karudi decided that it was time to leave Jamaica for Africa in 1977, at the age of twenty-five. Propelled by the blind faith that defined his life, Karudi abruptly resigned from his job as a production manager at Grace Kennedy, a prominent company in Kingston. "Cold stone will be your pillow" were the words his father used to warn him about what he perceived to be a rash, ridiculous move. Undaunted, Karudi prepared for his departure. Though he would later write about the repatriation as though he embarked on the journey alone, his plans had always included his wife, Kisembo, with whom he had been involved since 1974. Though the idea to leave was his, they both decided that he would establish himself on the African continent before Kisembo and Kiyende, her daughter from a previous relationship, would join him. Also a committed Rastafarian, Kisembo shared her partner's deep desire to head to Africa, but, like Ras Bupe's parents, she also registered shock that he had so unceremoniously left a "good, good job."[23] Kisembo never romanticized Africa—she knew repatriation would be "no bed of roses"—but to her it was worth it; they were going home. Both were convinced that the plight of "black humanity" was "sad and sorry" and that repatriation to Africa was the only way to move away from the "ever-increasing trials and tribulation[s]."[24]

Unlike Mkhululi, Karudi's initial efforts to return to Africa were based on his conviction that immigration laws did not apply to him. There was precedence for this approach. Noel Dyer, the Rastafarian who probably most personifies the desire to repatriate, was born in Jamaica, migrated to England in 1960, and from there set out to reach Ethiopia in 1964. Though he eventually made it to Shashamane, Ethiopia, he experienced hardships along the way that were similar to those Karudi would endure when he began his journey in 1977.[25] From England Karudi was denied entry by several African countries, including Kenya, Zambia, and Zimbabwe.[26] On his first of many attempts to enter Kenya he "had much difficulty in gaining entry" because he "failed to meet the financial requirements to qualify for a six-week tourist visa." After pleading with immigration officials and relating the history of African captivity in the West, immigration personnel at Nairobi International Airport decided that he had enough funds to qualify for a two-week tourist visa. Karudi was outraged by the fact that "the only status under which [he] qualified for entry was that of a tourist/a foreigner." He resented having been treated as a Jamaican, not "an Afrikan born in captivity" and that he "was penalized for being a poor Black Afrikan captive returning home!"[27] Karudi's approach to repatriation, though grounded in the same notion of diaspora nurtured by Mkhululi and other Rastafarians, was strikingly representative of the tremendous fissure between his diasporic freedom dreams and the political realities of African nation-states. When he left Kenya and tried to enter Uganda, he was allowed to stay for a brief period. He applied for citizenship from the Ugandan government but was denied. He returned to Kenya, but this time the country refused him entry, and he tried once more to settle in Uganda. From there he was deported to England in 1978.

Kisembo was waiting to receive word from Ras Bupe, but she was surprised when the expected mail came from England and not somewhere on the African continent. He explained the circumstances under which he had been deported and asked her to join him in England. Along with Kiyende, Kisembo met Ras Bupe in England in 1978 and they wed in 1979. In 1980, Kisembo gave birth to their son, Nyamekye. Two years later they were ready to make another attempt at repatriation, and Ras Bupe finally returned to "Mother Afrika" in February 1982. This time he decided to take his two-year-old son with him when he went ahead of Kisembo. Zimbabwe was his first point of entry, and Kisembo and Kiyende joined him two months after his arrival.[28]

Ras Bupe Karudi returned hopeful that he would get help from newly independent Zimbabwe but was faced with the same problems he had encountered between 1977 and 1978: the difficulty of "gaining the right of entry," and permanent residency, rather than the status of a tourist. At this point Karudi claims to have been inspired by Jah (Haile Selassie I) and Marcus Garvey to "use the truth in defense," and he "set out to confront Black Afrikan Governments with the truth, principle, and reality, as to whether black Afrikans born in captivity, had the right to return home to Mother Afrika, or not!"[29] Karudi's proposal forced African state officials to confront the real meaning of pan-African ideas and exactly how they could act on them in their capacity as state officials.

Karudi approached the Zimbabwean government in January 1983 and then the Zambian government in July. After both declined, he decided to present his case to the Tanzanian government in December 1983. Finally, the positive response he received from Tanzania represented "an effective instrument at this crucial and critical time of on-going struggle for black Afrikan liberation," and "signal[ed] amongst other things, the further coming together of Black Afrikan's [sic] both at home in Mother Afrika, and in captivity in foreign lands!"[30]

When Karudi, with Mkhululi's help, was finally allowed to stay in Tanzania in 1983, he was not only benefiting from Tanzania's propensity to accommodate Africans from around the world but from the connections that Mkhululi had made in Tanzania up to that point. By then Mkhululi had become prominent at the University of Dar es Salaam as dean of the Department of Commerce and Management and the chairperson of the Liberation Support Committee on campus. In addition, he had already discussed his desire to bring about the repatriation of other Jamaican Rastafarians to Tanzania with President Nyerere. Mkhululi had petitioned the Tanzanian government for citizenship status and land for himself and for future repatriates, and Karudi joined him in these efforts when he arrived in 1983.

The Right to Return

In 1984, a year after Karudi arrived in Tanzania, Mkhululi sent a letter to Nyerere in which he documented the request he had made in his meeting with Nyerere in 1979.[31] Fundamentally, the letter pursued the "right for the Afrikans born in the West to return to Afrika as residents." What he sought from the Tanzanian state was the understanding that the immigration laws that typically applied to visitors were not appropriate for Africans who were "returning home out of captivity," as opposed to "visiting." Mkhululi explained the plight of Rastafarians and other Africans in the diaspora, outlining the neocolonial threats that Nyerere had publicly and passionately assailed as a prominent supporter of anticolonial activism.

For Mkhululi it made perfect sense that Africans from the West returning to Tanzania be given "resident" status, which could "lead to citizenship," because of the historical context. He explained that Africans in the West had been "taken captive to the Western World" and that the desire to return to Africa began at the point of captivity. The fact that many of these captured Africans "jumped from the slave ships into the Atlantic" was proof of this strong desire to return to Africa. Indeed, the Rastafarian emphasis on repatriation emerged from this tradition of resistance, which defined the experience of Africans in the West. Mkhululi maintained that "Rastafari continue[d] to be at the forefront of the struggle to return home to Mother Africa."[32]

Mkhululi pleaded with Nyerere to consider the plight of diasporic Africans who were forced to return to the oppressive West. He argued that the idea of a Tanzanian rejecting a fellow African wreaked havoc on African unity. Yet Mkhululi understood that in order to return home to Africa, he had to be real about the fact that he was requesting permission to gain citizenship in a state that was invested in defining citizenship and sovereignty. His language shifted from "Africa" and "continent" to "Tanzania," as was the case when he explained that Rastafarians were not visitors and should not be given the type of visa that can expire as they were home and "should not be seen as different from any other *Tanzanian*." His letter went on to add, "When the visa expires, the one who is at home and who should not be seen as different from any other Tanzanian, is being forced to leave. Leave? To go where? Back to the West from which we have escaped? When people are sent back in such a manner, consider the negative effect on the unity of Africans in their liberation struggle."[33] Mkhululi made it clear that to classify returning Africans as visitors was to cling to an erroneous and detrimental paradigm. Plus, he emphasized how dangerous the West was for Rastafarians and other Africa-centered people in the west, who were "beaten, imprisoned, harassed and refused even employment because of our struggle for the African cause from our places in the West."[34] Mkhululi stressed the failure of decolonization to ensure better living conditions for diasporic Africans in the West Indies.

In keeping with the Rastafarian notion that the circumstances of the African in the West were inherently oppressive and that the postcolonial world represented neocolonial realities, Mkhululi stressed that Africans in Jamaica continued to live in danger. Here he replicated arguments that had been made by Jamaican Rastafarians in the 1940s. On the heels of the 1930s rebellions, Rastas had petitioned the government, expressing the desire to go home to Africa and making it clear that only through this physical move could they accomplish real change and freedom.[35]. Repatriation was necessary to free diasporic Africans from "Western Capitalism, imperialism [and] racism." Mkhululi assured Nyerere that Africa was the "only secure base for Africans," who were constantly under threat in the West, especially if they embraced their African roots. In order to highlight examples of neocolonialism in the diaspora, Mkhululi mentioned "President [Ronald] Reagan's invasion of Grenada" and the leadership of the Jamaica Labour Party (JLP) under Edward Seaga in Jamaica, which was "backed by United States imperialism" and was now committed to "extreme capitalism."[36]

Mkhululi's intention was to place the U.S. invasion of Grenada in 1983 within the context of the Cold War and the role of the United States in creating neo-colonial realities. Anticolonialists everywhere had kept abreast of the activities of Grenada's Maurice Bishop, who led the New Jewel Movement in its attempt at a socialist revolution in Grenada. When the revolutionary government disintegrated and the U.S. government under Reagan invaded Grenada, many anticolonialists, including Jamaica's Michael Manley, saw this as an infringement upon Caribbean sovereignty. Manley, who had developed a close personal and political relationship with Bishop, condemned U.S. intervention into Grenada's domestic affairs and insisted that such intervention had to be seen within the context of the struggle "between neocolonialism and independence." Having observed U.S. activities in Latin America since the dawn of the Cold War era, Manley feared that America's so-called rescue mission in Grenada had set a dangerous precedent for the Caribbean. He was certain that "the genuine political agenda has got to be traced back to the Monroe doctrine; has got to be traced back to perceptions of U.S. foreign policy and what it ought to do in this hemisphere."[37]

Manley even took the time to write to his friend Julius Nyerere to express his outrage over the U.S. invasion.[38]

Mkhululi presented the neocolonial ideas and actions of the JLP under Edward Seaga as another example of oppressive forces in Babylon. Having defeated Michael Manley and the People's National Party (PNP) in the 1980 elections, the JLP represented the antithesis of Manley's democratic socialism platform. Within the context of the Cold War, the JLP was able to gain the support of the United States through its embrace of capitalism and its rejection of nonalignment and communism.[39] As further proof of the ideological distance between the two leaders, Seaga's enthusiastic support for the U.S. invasion in Grenada was matched by Manley's unmitigated disapproval and outrage. These were developments in Jamaica to which Nyerere would certainly have been privy. Apart from the fact that he maintained contact with Manley, it was common for those like Nyerere who were engaged with African liberation and anticolonialism to stay abreast of such events in every corner of the world.

In a pragmatic move, Mkhululi appealed directly to Nyerere's particular approach to building the Tanzanian nation. Having established that the postcolonial period had ushered in new colonial forces, Mkhululi went on to assure Nyerere that if allowed to settle permanently in Tanzania, Rastafarians would undoubtedly contribute to nation building as it had been conceptualized by the Tanzanian state.[40] Here Mkhululi demonstrated that, like the African American black power advocates before him, he was all too aware of Tanzania's politics. He was eager to show that not only was the philosophy of the Rastafarian movement compatible with Tanzania's anticolonial philosophy but Rastafarians would aid in the development of the Tanzanian nation. To demonstrate this, Mkhululi had taken the initiative to visit an *ujamaa* cooperative village in Tanzania. He detailed the visit to Hurui Village, Kondoa District, in the Dodoma region, on March 7, 1984, where he and Karudi were hosted by village members Mzee Issa A. Dello and Ndugo Athumani Irove.

On this visit to the village Mkhululi and Karudi aimed to "look at land for the purpose of agricultural production," and some members of the village willingly showed them an appropriate area of land. The tour of Hurui village was followed by a meeting, where Mkhululi and Karudi shared their plans and received constructive advice. The group itself represented a moment of pan-African unity as Karudi and Mkhululi shared their ideas and received constructive advice from Tanzanians. Along with Mkhululi, Karudi, Dello, and Ntuve were other Tanzanians from the village. Donald Davidson, another Jamaican Rastafarian who had gone to Tanzania via England, was also present. Davidson had not been recruited by Karudi or Mkhululi and had gone to Tanzania independently, but he now joined them in their efforts to gain the support of the Tanzanian government. As Mkhululi put it, his intention was to "use a core of Africans born abroad and returning home to Africa, and Tanzanians committed to the assistance of brothers and sisters returning from slavery, from bondage, from death threats and experiences of death, to launch a multi-purpose cooperative project . . . those returning in selected numbers would come into this Production Cooperative Unit and would expand its base and output, in preparation for others to come." In a show of solidarity with Tanzanian politics, Mkhululi assured Nyerere that "the Project/Cooperative would be governed by the Cooperative Laws and Acts of Tanzania, and the principles embodied in its constitution would reflect the practical development aspirations of Tanzania." The cooperative was only one of the ways in which the brothers and sisters from the West could contribute to Tanzanian society because they had gained other expertise in the West, where they were "doctors, nurses, engineers, teachers, planters and other nation builders." Mkhululi had also prepared a book titled *Cooperative and Management,* available in Kiswahili and in English. The book was meant to educate potential repatriates about the realities of life in Tanzania prior to their arrival. In addition, Mkhululi stressed that "the fundamental principles and philosophy of the movement of Rastafari is cooperative" in order to link Tanzanian politics and the Rastafarian movement and to remind Nyerere that it would not be difficult to make this transition due to the ideological links between the two philosophies.[41] Mkhululi explained that Rastafari sanctioned a utopian life that was strikingly similar to Nyerere's *ujamaa.* While this socialist vision served to generally alienate Rastafarians from the Jamaican state and society, the opportunity to practice this way of life in Africa came in the form of support for a state project.

In keeping with his efforts to affirm the Tanzanian nation-state, Mkhululi also used the nation's history of activism and its contributions to liberation struggles, along with Nyerere's work on behalf of Africans globally, to reinforce the idea that to accommodate Rastafarian repatriation was indeed the natural progression for Tanzania and for Nyerere. According to Mkhululi, "history records the excellent contribution/performance of Tanzania in this process of freedom and in respect of human dignity." In light of this history, he anticipated "consistency in a very urgent and positive response to our request for freedom from captivity." Furthermore, to Nyerere, Mkhululi asserted that "this is an accomplishment that fits your time, that fits your comprehension, that fits your wisdom."[42] He used Tanzania's reputation to explain to Nyerere why Tanzania was the perfect place to undertake this task and then used Nyerere's specific experience with Jamaica to enhance his argument. Mkhululi relied on previous linkages that were formed between Tanzania and Jamaica by making a specific reference to Nyerere's visits to Jamaica. In 1974, two years before Mkhululi repatriated to Tanzania, Nyerere had been greeted by thousands of enthusiastic supporters during his tour of Jamaica.[43] Mkhululi reminded Nyerere that "the respect and reception you, your ministers, and other Africans visiting Jamaica have received from the masses is proof of that true spirit of brotherhood, which exists between people of the same roots, found on different soils."[44]

Zion Train: Get on Board

On December 12, 1985, the president's office in Tanzania issued a letter regarding "Africans in the West." It declared that Nyerere "agreed with the principle of black Africans returning to Africa." More specifically, the letter confirmed that with regard to black Africans living in Jamaica, the president was agreeable with their coming to live in Tanzania.[45] The letter was signed by minister Mizengo Kayanza Peter Pinda, who served as the personal assistant to Nyerere's private secretary, Joseph Butiku. It marked the official state response to the requests of the Rastafarians, which began with the meeting between Mkhululi and Nyerere in 1979.

While the letter served to document Nyerere's official response to the Rastafarians, it stated that Nyerere would take the issue to "the attention of the party for further deliberations" and that the Rastafarians were being asked to consult the office of the prime minister for future assistance. Though the letter did not provide details as to what Nyerere would discuss with the party, the absence of specific details concerning whether or not they would be offered resident status or awarded land suggested that those were the issues that would receive future attention. The letter also marked the beginning of a relationship between several government officials and the Rastafarian community. As they continued to help Rastafarians for years after the letter was issued, it was clear that they shared Nyerere's commitment to pan-Africanism. Pinda became a trusted ally of the community, as did ministers Paul Rupia and Gertrude Mongella, who has held several positions in the government, including that of minister for tourism and natural resources.

Pinda argued that Nyerere had "made it clear that it was going to be a special case for Africans from the West" and that meant that though there were "laws governing immigration" there would be "no rigidity" if Africans from the West sought to settle in Tanzania.[46] Nyerere and the officials who worked with the Rastafarians were willing to circumvent the rule of law in order to accommodate them. On one hand, this represented the practice of a black (inter)nationalism that defied the Western notions of the nation-state. The state's decision to accept Jamaican Rastafarians as returning Africans upheld the concept of a transnational African identity that challenged the pervasive idea of Westphalian sovereignty.

On the other hand, this made for an unpredictable and unstable situation. Though Nyerere was no longer president, the letter that initiated the process by which the Rastafarians gained future assistance from the government clearly stated that Nyerere had authorized the support they received. In addition, the "special case" status meant the offers that were extended by the government would not be codified in law. Instead, they relied on executive intervention to ensure that there was "no rigidity" with regard to the law. The advantages and the disadvantages of such a flexible arrangement became clear when Karudi and Mkhululi, encouraged by the letter of 1985, began to recruit other diasporic Africans to repatriate to Tanzania.

The letter marked a pivotal point in the relationship between Rastafarians and the Tanzanian state in that it represented a victory for Mkhululi and Karudi, who both envisioned Tanzania as the future home of their Rastafarian brothers and sisters in the West. Though they had both walked away from the Twelve Tribes of Israel's community-based approach to repatriation, they hoped to share their good fortune with other Rastafarians. The Tanzanian government's commitment to repatriation encouraged Mkhululi and Karudi to not only recruit more Rastafarians to repatriate but to prepare Tanzania for their arrival. As they continued to petition the government for land upon which to "resettle," Karudi left Tanzania in search of Africa-bound Rastafarians. The letter marked a point at which the ideas of African unity as espoused by Jamaican Rastafarians and by Tanzanian pan-Africanists could be realized through concrete action. This was tangible support for their project, and it encouraged them to proceed with their ambitious plans to "set up Jah Kingdom" based on an *ujamaa*-type community model.

Having received the "right of entry," Karudi set out to "secure the necessary finance" to establish a Rastafarian community in Tanzania. As chair of URIA, Karudi worked on behalf of Rastafarians generally, yet, he also thought about his personal journey, noting that he had worked tirelessly and at "this crucial point" he urgently needed to "consolidate the gains which he had made." In keeping with his and Mkhululi's propensity to frame the mission in biblical terms, Karudi proclaimed that "what was sown in tears must now be reaped in joy."[47]

Karudi estimated that his short-term goals to set up Jah Kingdom would total £45,568.00. This included the funds needed to construct a house in Dar es Salaam as well as airline tickets for him to do the "organizational work and fundraising."[48] He envisioned an itinerary that would take him from Dar es Salaam to London, and from London to Jamaica, New York, and Toronto before returning to Dar es Salaam via London. Upon receiving the "right of entry" from Nyerere's office in December 1985, Karudi planned to leave Dar es Salaam in May 1986. Included in his financial estimate was the cost of airline tickets for seven Rastafarian "experts/elders" from whom he would seek help to "select land and to effect re-settlement." Karudi's thinking was in keeping with the notion that elders acted as spiritual leaders in the decentralized movement of Rastafari.[49] For the elders he sought one-way tickets from Kingston to Dar es Salaam with a projected departure date of July 1986. He anticipated a cost of £1500.00 per elder.

In 1986 Karudi arrived in England (en route to Jamaica) and began heavy recruitment among the Rastafarian community there, which included people from Jamaica and other Caribbean islands. This is when he encountered Iman Mani, originally from Dominica. Other members of the community had recommended Mani, who identified with the Nyabingi order at the time and was preparing to repatriate to Ghana. Mani had been active in what he called "liberation work," which included antiapartheid activism. He had been to Ghana and had established meaningful connections there, but was encouraged by Karudi's description of the opportunities Tanzania offered to returning Rastafarians.[50]

Mani arrived in Tanzania on August 30, 1986, and his experience at the airport in Dar es Salaam reflected both the promise of the welcome issued by President Nyerere's office, and its limitations. Relying solely on Karudi's assurance that Nyerere's office had agreed to the principle of diasporic Africans returning to Tanzania, Mani failed to present the Tanzanian immigration officers with the appropriate documents required for entry. As a result, the immigration officers detained Mani with the intention of sending him back to England on the next available flight.[51] Twenty hours later, Pinda, who had been informed of Mani's plight by Mkhululi, sent a letter from Nyerere's office demanding that Mani be allowed to enter the country immediately. Though the department of immigration complied with the demands of the letter, it confiscated Mani's passport for a period of nine months, during which time he was expected to report to the department quite frequently.[52]

Mani's experience at the airport foreshadowed the experiences of the other Rastafarians who subsequently arrived in Tanzania. The "special case" status they received allowed them to live there, and later to gain land, but the process by which they claimed the opportunities offered to them was by no means smooth. Still, Mkhululi and Karudi continued to recruit Rastafarians for repatriation to Tanzania. While Mani stayed with Karudi's family and began to adjust to life in his new surroundings, Karudi continued his mission to help others return home to Zion.

In August 1986 Karudi arrived in Jamaica, where he "canvassed a wide range of Rastafari . . . which included, among other esteemed elders, Ras Mortimo Planno"[53] and Sangi Davis, a member of the executive body of the Twelve Tribes of Israel. Mkhululi, who had also been a member of the Twelve Tribes, tried to convince Davis and others to repatriate to Tanzania. Davis refused the offer because, "as a Rastaman," he remained focused on Ethiopia. Though members of the Twelve Tribes rarely imagined repatriation outside of the framework of its well-organized system of return to Ethiopia, Davis was convinced that the group's leader, Brother Gad, would not have prevented him from choosing to go to Tanzania. Still, though he subsequently "grew and realize[d] certain things" that led to a more expansive idea of Africa, he admits that "back at that time," he thought he "could just go to Ethiopia," which had a "special place" in his heart.[54] Undeterred, Karudi continued to seek returnees.

On September 6, 1986, Karudi reported to C. L. R. James that the work of "establishing the Provisional Elder Council" was "going well."[55] This had much to do with his efforts to recruit Ras Daniel Heartman. Heartman was indeed a suitable candidate, as he had been "treated as an elder by many" by the time he was a mere twenty years old due to his "incredible presence and spiritual depth." Heartman, formerly known as Lloyd George Roberts, was born in Kingston on January 7, 1942. A brilliant artist, his absence from the Jamaican and Caribbean "canon" belies the undeniable popularity of his distinct and captivating pieces. He worked "primarily in pencil, sometimes in pen and ink, and dabbled in painting."[56] Rastafari has made its unmistakable mark in the realm of the visual arts, and Ras Daniel Heartman has been at the forefront of the powerful expressions of the Rastafarian ethos and sensibilities through art. Even in instances when he was not known by name, his widely recognizable pieces were known for the ways in which they captured the dignity of the Rastafarian, who was at once human and divine, consistently Africa-bound, thoughtful and pensive, yet hauntingly alive.

One of the important features of his self-portrait *Not Far Away* was its engagement with the prominent Rastafarian theme of repatriation to Africa. Karudi and Mkhululi were happy that the famed artist, whose images were treasured masterpieces within the Rastafarian community, had seized the opportunity to make the move to Tanzania. Heartman enthusiastically absorbed Karudi's description of the opportunities that were being provided by the Tanzanian state. Though he had nurtured a commitment to repatriation for many years, Heartman's alacrity was intensified by the dire circumstances in which he and his son, Ato Kidani Roberts, found themselves. For about seven years prior to Karudi's arrival they had been homeless, venturing from one place to the next and depending on the kindness of others. Karudi's assurance that he would receive land and a house in Tanzania was particularly exciting for Heartman in light of the penury that had plagued him for much too long. According to his son Ato, "he [Karudi] told us that the government [of Tanzania] had accepted us already and he told us that there was a house prepared there and that was exciting because my old man was excited about being in his own place after being homeless for almost seven years."[57] Like most Rastafarians, Heartman had initially thought about going to Ethiopia, but was in no way conflicted about going to Tanzania, as for him "Africa was Africa" and if Jah had decided that he should enter through Tanzania, he was open to that revelation. Invigorated by Heartman's eagerness to join him in Tanzania, Karudi assured him that he would raise the funds for him and his son to make the trip.

Approximately two years later, with the support of the Bristol-based URIA, Karudi had raised enough money to purchase airline tickets for Heartman and Roberts. At that point, the only remaining obstacle was that Heartman was "totally conflicted" about having to apply for a Jamaican passport in order to travel. This was consistent with the Rastafarian rejection of Jamaican nationality and identity. It also underscored the fact that many Rastafarians were yet to ponder the actualities of repatriation. In an attempt to live his life in a way that was consistent with his philosophies, and in honor of the identity he consciously embraced, Heartman even pleaded with the Jamaican authorities to allow him to board the aircraft without a passport, explaining that he was going home to Africa. Heartman

Left to right: Ras Daniel Heartman, Ras Ato Kidani Roberts, and Joshua Mkhululi shortly after Mkhululi welcomed them to Tanzania. Courtesy of Ato Kidani Roberts.

must have assumed that Tanzania (and other African nations) did not abide by immigration laws, or that if they did, such laws did not apply to Rastafarians. In order to begin his journey, he finally applied for a passport and left Jamaica for Tanzania in October 1988.

The trip to Tanzania was punctuated by a three-day stay in Bristol among the Rastafarians from whom Karudi continued to receive moral and economic support. The "fabulous welcome" Heartman and Roberts received from the community when they arrived at Heathrow Airport warmed their hearts and prolonged their diaspora-fertilized expectations of how the process of return would unfold. But as they learned four days later at the airport in Dar es Salaam, England was also a part of the African diaspora and the response they received came from fellow travelers, for whom Africa also remained a mythic construction. Ras Bupe Karudi and Mkhululi met them at the airport in Dar, receiving them eagerly. Yet, Heartman was terribly disappointed. According to Roberts, "My daddy was surprised . . . because he expected this big welcome from the people, like the prodigal son . . .

return[ing] home. He was expecting drums a beat and people a dance just to welcome their brothers and sisters . . . but that wasn't there."[58]

The presence of both Mkhululi and Karudi ensured that immigration officers were furnished with the documentation necessary to prove that Nyerere's office had authorized the entrance of Heartman and his son. Yet, Heartman and Roberts had not met the vaccination requirements, and the immigration officers were reluctant to allow them into Tanzania without the proper immunization for diseases such as yellow fever. They were both detained for a few hours at the airport while Mkhululi explained to the immigration officers that, as a Rastafarian, Heartman was strongly opposed to the use of conventional medicines. The immigration officers eventually accepted this explanation and they were allowed to enter Tanzania.

Pan-Africanism, Race, and Citizenship

When the Tanzanian state documented its offer of permanent residency with the option for citizenship to Rastafarians, it specifically extended the invitation to *wajamaika weusi* (black Jamaicans). In both Kiswahili and in English, the first letter, as well as subsequent letters concerning land allotments to Rastafarians, repeatedly underscored that race was central to the pan-African negotiation that was taking place between Rastafarians and the Tanzanian state; that those Jamaicans who sought to permanently reside in Tanzania had to be black in order to belong to the nation.

Race had been a major issue of contention in Tanzania since the colonial period. The British had initiated and maintained a social hierarchy that was inextricably bound to race. Indeed, "The creation of the African colonial state coincided with the historical zenith of virulent racism. The colonial construction of the African as savage other permeated all spheres of policy thought."[59] By the late 1940s, as the British and the Tanganyika African National Union (TANU) jostled for political power in colonial Tanganyika, race emerged not only as a prominent social issue but also as a central topic for government regulation. Through a policy of multiracialism, the British sought to secure the privileges of the minority races (whites and Indians) and to prevent a transfer of power to the African majority. Under the guise of a deceptive notion of "racial parity," the British colonial authorities had begun to make institutional changes to further that end. This meant that though Africans constituted the vast majority of the population, each existing race in Tanganyika would have equal representation in the legislature, creating a gross imbalance. As early as 1952, while still a student in the United Kingdom, Nyerere saw through this ruse and declared that racial parity was "a principle which in spite of its deceptive name assumes the principle of racial superiority."[60]

At a meeting in 1954, when the Tanganyika African Association was transformed into TANU, the party officially rejected the colonial government's tripartite arrangement and opted for a system whereby Africans outnumbered other races, reflecting the actual makeup of the population. Though colonial officials vacillated in terms of their opinion of Nyerere during this period, lauding him as wonderfully moderate at points, his resistance to multiracialism frustrated them, and Governor Edward Twining accused him of "black racialism," which he found to be "contrary to the principles of the Trusteeship Agreement and to the policy of the British Government."[61]

But TANU was home to members who were far more strident in their critique of multiracialism. In 1957 Zuberi Mtemvu and others who broke with TANU to form the African National Congress offered a more biting analysis of the United Tanganyika Party, referring to the organization as a "paternalistic" one and accusing its members of seeing "TANU as a danger to the Europeans and Asians in Tanganyika and this makes its multiracialism and even its paternalism a mockery." As James Brennan has argued, the focus on race obscured other important points of contention within the party. But, there is no denying that in the final analysis, race was indeed the hot-button issue within TANU and ultimately defined the terms for the divisions within the party during this period. In seeking to secure a system in which each person was allowed a vote, Nyerere and other nationalists sought to level the playing field, end white supremacy, and provide the African majority with the basic guarantees of a democracy. The shameless efforts of imperial apologists to derail this change by accusing them of "racialism" represented a dramatic instance of irony.

In keeping with the notion of racial parity and the effort to maintain white supremacy, the colonial government joined forces with the United Tanganyika Party, which was funded by European and Asian business interests. Together they proposed a multiracial "tripartite" election in 1958. That year, at a game-changing meeting in Tabora, TANU had to decide whether to participate in the tripartite/racial parity elections designed by the British or boycott the entire process. Having initially opposed participation in such elections, Nyerere changed course amid an ebullient and contentious debate that saw many party members passionately favor a boycott. Within the party, this put Nyerere at odds with more militant members who championed Africanization as a means of overturning the colonial denigration of Africans. Much to the shock and chagrin of the British officials, Nyerere's gamble paid off, and TANU emerged victorious, having acquired supporters among the two-thirds of the non-African elected representation. This surprising turn of events resulted in the formation of a competing political party. Mtemvu broke from the party to form the African National Congress with the slogan "Africa for Africans," while others who also favored Africanization, such as Oscar Kambona and Bibi Titi Mohammed, remained in the party and represented its more radical contingent.

TANU's victory also marked the point at which its constitutional path to independence was guaranteed, but race remained a thorny issue as Nyerere and TANU made the transition to a postcolonial government. In terms of the role of race in nation building in Tanzania, Nyerere had clearly stated his commitment to a policy of nonracialism for the new nation. In other words, he declared that "loyalty to the country," and not race, would "be the basis of determining the citizenship of the country." Nyerere argued, "if we begin now in Tanganyika saying that all people in Tanganyika are equal except the Indians, and the Arabs and the Europeans, and the Chinamen, who happen to live in Tanganyika, we shall have broken a principle. It won't let us stop there. If we in Tanganyika are going to divorce citizenship from loyalty and marry it to colour, we won't stop there, sir. We will go on breaking that principle." He insisted that to base citizenship on color would be to "commit a crime . . . discrimination against human beings because of their colour is exactly what we have been fighting against."[62]

In theory, Nyerere's rejection of "racial thinking" also extended to his conceptualization of pan-African politics. He explained his position and defined pan-Africanism at the Sixth Pan-African Congress, which was held in Tanzania in 1974: "Let us make it clear. We oppose racial thinking. But as long as black people anywhere continue to be oppressed on the grounds of their colour, black people everywhere will stand together in opposition to that oppression, in the future as in the past. . . . For although this Congress movement was made necessary by racialism, and was itself originally confined to black people, our particular struggle for dignity has always been one aspect of the worldwide struggle for human liberation." He made the point that if black people continue to defend their position as different from the rest of humankind, "we shall weaken ourselves, and the racialists of the world will have scored their biggest triumph."[63] Nyerere's ideas represented those of a person who understood that race was both a social construct and a social reality. This meant that though race was not rooted in biology, pan-African solidarity was born in response to race-based oppression. As such, he understood that unity based on race was justified and necessary for liberation. Yet, he suggested that this was different from buying into race as an immutable category.

Nyerere's offer of the right to return to "black Jamaicans" in particular had much to do with his understanding of how race functioned in the Jamaican national context. On a visit to Jamaica in September 1974, he revealed more about his thinking on the complexity of race in different local contexts within the pan-African struggle. As he thanked Jamaica for its support of African liberation movements and encouraged the nation to "even intensify" its support for "these matters," he outlined his perception of a racial norm in Jamaica that differed markedly from the situation in Tanzania. According to Nyerere,

> it is obvious to the meanest intelligence that the people of this country can trace their ancestry to many different parts of the world—to Europe, to Africa, and to Asia. Your national motto "out of many, one people" proclaims your past, and your future. That past, and that future, however, involve you directly in the conflict I have been talking about. The vast majority of Tanzanians—something like 98% of them—could react to South African racialism by a counter racialism. They could proclaim the superiority of blackness. This would be equally evil, and equally destructive of world peace and development. But they could do it and remain a nation. The countries of the Caribbean cannot do that. You are natural participants in the struggle against racialism of any kind, because its acceptance would not only divide Jamaican from Jamaican; it would also demand that a very large number of Jamaicans try to deny one part of themselves—one part of their ancestry.[64]

Nyerere saw a fundamental difference between Tanzania and Jamaica: Tanzania qualified as a black country, but Jamaica did not. Though he never wavered in his assertion that if Tanzanians reacted to South African racialism with "a counter racialism," it would be "equally evil, and equally destructive," the important point is his argument that they could do so "and remain a nation." Nyerere's argument extended not only to Jamaica, but to all the "countries of the Caribbean" as well. Here he demonstrated the reality that just as diasporic Africans nurtured uncomplicated assumptions about Africa, continental Africans also fell victim to one-dimensional ideas of the Caribbean.[65] While the large percentage of South Asians in Caribbean nations like Guyana and Trinidad would have made such an assessment more acceptable in those local contexts, Jamaica was actually a nation with a black majority (over 90 percent). Not only did he gloss over local differences within the Caribbean, but his assertion that Jamaica's motto "out of one, many people" represented the country's past and its future was exactly the interpretation of Jamaican identity that was rejected by Rastafarians.

This general association of multiracialism with the West Indies was not limited to Nyerere. On the eve of independence, as the Tanganyika Citizenship Bill was debated in the national assembly, prominent railway trade unionist Christopher Tumbo accused the bill of using the "language of multiracialism" in its reference to "several different races in Tanganyika." He strongly rejected this usage because it gave the impression that "Tanganyika is a multi-racial state and similar to the West Indies where the native people of those islands have lost identity."[66] He proposed that the language be changed to "immigrant races" in order to demonstrate that "we the natives have not lost identity." In suggesting that the people of the West Indies had "lost identity," Tumbo brought to the fore a crucial difference between continental Africans and those in the diaspora: the fact that the continental Africans engaged with anticolonial politics did not share the diasporic experience of having been physically uprooted from the continent. Yet, Rastafari posited a direct link to African roots, seeing slavery and colonialism as a powerful but ultimately unsuccessful attempt to obliterate their African cultural heritage.

The black internationalist politics that had led Michael Manley to invite Nyerere to Jamaica in the first place had ushered in a serious rejection of the motto, which functioned as a problematic framework of multiracialism, and replaced it with the idea of Africa as the root of Jamaican identity. Similar to its sojourn in Tanzania, multiracialism had a tortured past in Jamaica. When Manley's father Norman campaigned for independence from Britain, and during his time as leader of the PNP, he promoted multiracialism as the model for Jamaican society. Notably, Nyerere's visit to Jamaica in 1974, under the auspices of the PNP, with Michael Manley's pan-African politics at its helm, saw Nyerere express sentiments more in line with Norman Manley, from whose racial politics Michael had made a serious departure. Beyond the actual demographical realities of Jamaica, Nyerere's comments must have seemed both wrong and anachronistic to Manley and others in his cabinet who saw Jamaica as a black nation and Africa as its root. By the time Nyerere visited Jamaica, "multiracialism" had become a dirty word for Rastafarians and other Jamaicans with black nationalist sensibilities.

As Rex Nettleford has argued, "Jamaica's multi-racial nationalism . . . met its fiercest and most positive antagonism from the black activist Rastafari movement." Reflecting a widespread embrace of multiracialism across class and racial lines in Jamaica, Rastafari was "regarded by most Jamaicans as nothing more than a bizarre aberration or at best an inverted version of intolerable 'racialism.'"[67] Like African nationalists who were also accused of racialism, Rastafarians were blamed for introducing ideas about racial difference into a society that did not have a racial problem. They were fully aware that this was a ploy to maintain a stratified society that relegated those of African descent to the very bottom of the socioeconomic ladder. The government's duplicitous use of the term "racialism" to deny the existence of the very racism it created represented yet another example of the "trickery" used to repress and oppress those of African descent who fought for justice. Rastafarians were the "first in the new Jamaica to question the society's identity in terms of its racial and cultural antecedents," and many within Jamaica were unprepared not only for their rejection of the subterfuge but the "Jamaican perception of itself as an extension of Europe."[68]

In the midst of a spurious national platform of multiracialism, which was grounded in widespread denial of race as a fundamental organizing principle in Jamaican society, Rastafarians put the spotlight on race and the reality of racism. Race had been central to Rastafarian philosophy since its emergence in the early 1930s, and the polarities that structured foundational Rastafarian concepts assumed racial absolutes. The idea of Haile Selassie as a black (and therefore, affirming) god was a crucial corrective to the white, oppressive god of colonial Christianity. It recognized the Anglican Church's role in creating and maintaining white supremacy in Britain's West Indian colonies through economic investments, a white image of Christ, and a biblical interpretation that justified slavery. Similarly, Babylon has been associated with whiteness just as Africa was associated with blackness.

In light of the diversity within Rastafari, however, some Rastafarians adopted more rigid understandings of the role of race than did others. For instance, while some members of the Bobo Shanti have expressed black "supremacy" as the group's focus, the Twelve Tribes of Israel has long welcomed white members into its fold. Some Rastafarians see the Twelve Tribes as a group that caused much confusion with its acceptance of white members. With salvation as the ultimate goal for this group, it welcomed whites who embraced an African-centered biblical hermeneutic that venerated Haile Selassie. It is also true that a rigid understanding of race is sometimes undermined by the Rastafarian notion of peace and love, which sees it affirming human life generally.

Just as Nyerere and other Tanzanian state officials were accused of racialism when they tried to pursue democracy, Rastafarians have also been so accused. But, as the white Jesuit priest Joseph Owens has argued, this is "perhaps the most widely misunderstood aspect of Rastafarian teaching." Owens accurately argues that "a pronounced race-consciousness most certainly exists among the Rastafarian brethren [and sistren], but it belongs . . . to an altogether different category from the aberrations of prejudice built into the social relations of Western society."[69] In other words, the Rastafarian engagement does not constitute a case of reverse racism because it is not an "equally perverse" use of race practiced by those with power. As Nettleford astutely concludes, "Rastafarians are not that unsophisticated to be racist but they are by no means foolish enough not to be race conscious."[70]

As is the case with Rastafari more broadly, thinking on race has evolved within the movement. The period of decolonization had made it abundantly clear that, as Frantz Fanon had warned, black elites could be complicit in upholding structures that oppressed other black people based on factors such as class. As such, the term "Nyabingi" evolved from "death to white oppressors" to mean "death to white *and black* oppressors." Ever aware of global shifts and current affairs, Rastafarians understood that the age of decolonization had allowed certain gains such as political independence. But they also understood that decolonization was unfinished. Some Africans remained under the yoke of colonial rule, and others were threatened by new forms of oppression that continued to discriminate against Africans based on race.

Racial politics remained relevant in this period. Rastafarians who went to Tanzania were very conscious of race. An issue of URIA's monthly publication was devoted to the issue of racism. It established that Rastafarians were "not a race of haters" and URIA did not seek to promote "the evils of racism," which it saw as the "propaganda of Europeans." Instead it understood racism to be "systemic," with social, political, and economic impact, and as such URIA acknowledged "the fullness of the existence and the need for the natural and unmolested progression of I-n-I noble, regal and divine Afrikan race without the hindrance and obstacle of neo-colonization and destabilization."[71] Like the Tanzanian state officials with whom they collaborated, the members of URIA walked a tightrope: they recognized the absurdity of race and racial discrimination as constructed by British colonial rule while also confronting the reality of continued racial discrimination in the so-called postcolonial period. Though not used in a way that alienated more expansive visions of pan-Africanism, race remained an important part of solidarity politics.

Not Visitors

As *wajamaika weusi* (black Jamaicans), Rastafarians were allowed to resettle in Tanzania, and according to the "special case" provision granted them, they received the resident permit class A, which had to be renewed every two years. Drastically reduced in cost, they paid the equivalent of US$15 for a permit that was typically about US$1600. Citizenship was available to them all through the normal channels, including the cost of US$1500.[72] The critical distinction between repatriation and migration (or visiting) turned on the Rastafarian pursuit of citizenship.[73] Though citizenship was the ultimate goal, Rastafarians interpreted the state's incremental offerings as important steps in the right direction. The initial letter of 1985 was vague in its broad assertion that black Africans living in Jamaica could come to live in Tanzania. But the absence of firm stipulations at that point, coupled with the promise that this first letter represented an attempt to expedite the process "in its early stages pending other formalities," allowed Karudi and Mkhululi enough room to pursue the realization of all that they had dreamed. They were also encouraged by the exceptionality of their permanent residency arrangement, which saw them renew residency every two years with the Immigration Department of the Ministry of Home Affairs.[74] In the meantime, Rastas continued to ask the government to allow them to gain citizenship without having to pay the standard fees.

As frustrating a process as this became, citizenship was available to them (through normal channels) in Tanzania, an opportunity that was unavailable to Rastafarian repatriates in Ethiopia. As Erin MacLeod has argued, for the Rastafarians who repatriated to Ethiopia citizenship was "an emotional issue . . . one that holds great weight in terms of legal status and symbolic belonging."[75] Yet, unlike the situation in Tanzania, the Rastafarian population in Ethiopia "remains deprived of land, rights and nationality."[76] Those who repatriated to Tanzania were aware of the ongoing struggles for legal status in Ethiopia, and were buoyed by the generosity of the Tanzanian state. Though the process was not seamless, the actual provision of the right of entry guaranteed permanent residency with the option for citizenship, and this boded well for the future. Karudi praised Nyerere for his vision and lauded his commitment to pan-African practice. More than a decade after the sixth Pan-African Congress brought in a seemingly rigid division between statist aims and grassroots activism, Rastafari had proven that it possessed the power to drive historical actors and effect policy at the state level. Though the desire to physically return to Africa emanated from the experiences of displaced diasporic Africans, continental Africans were also seriously engaged with the implications of return and its practical execution. They, too, were "trodding diaspora." Julius Nyerere and other state officials in Tanzania affirmed the idea of diaspora as formulated by Rastafarians. Even as Jamaican Rastafarians and Tanzanian pan-Africanists navigated the local differences that complicated their vision of African unity, they constituted diaspora in a way that solidly established Africa as the primary site of identity construction and belonging.

. . . . . .

Among the Rastafarians who repatriated to Tanzania were individuals who were initially opposed to the acquisition of travel and immigration documents—something that has a long history within Rastafari. From within Jamaica many resented the way that a passport imposed Jamaican identity upon them while simultaneously denying their African identity. Their refusal to pander to the immigration processes of the West was powerful in light of how travel documents and immigration status had been used as important tools in the process by which the Jamaican government and other governments of the West impeded the mobility of revolutionary pan-African figures. This reached a crescendo in the Jamaican context when Walter Rodney was banned from reentering the country in 1968.

The need for a visa to enter an African country represented an assault on their rights as Africans. Yet when Tanzania became the African state to officially validate their claims on African identity, they pursued its immigration documents with tenacity. From within an African state, the idea of the nation-state registered differently; it meant they would belong to both Tanzania and all of Africa. It was also a very pragmatic pursuit: legal proof of citizenship was the only way to guarantee that they would never have to return to the West. This was their goal.

Pan-Africanism was just as complex for the Tanzanian state. Nyerere had a profound understanding of what he deemed the "real dilemma" he and others faced: "on the one hand is the fact that Pan-Africanism demands an African consciousness and an African loyalty; on the other hand is the fact that each Pan-Africanist must also concern himself with the freedom and development of one of the nations of Africa." In 1966, he understood that "these [two] things" had "already conflicted."[77] The realities of the period set the terms in which he, as an African state official, practiced pan-Africanism. Still, in the midst of potential conflicts between nationalism and pan-Africanism, the postindependence period allowed African leaders with pan-African commitments to use the mechanism of the state to enact such ideals. This also showed the extent to which race was a meaningful social and political category in Tanzania, and leaders used it as a criteria for the right of entry given to Rastafarians. Nyerere and the officials who supported this initiative demonstrated the type of pan-African action that the rise of the African nation-state was able to accomplish. But like many other state-driven initiatives in Tanzania, bureaucracy sometimes impeded efficiency. The Rastafarians were elated by the official right of entry they received in 1985, approximately six years after Mkhululi first presented their case to Nyerere. The land grant they longed for would take until 1989 to become a reality. They could then begin the process of making a life in Tanzania.

5 Sow in Tears, Reap in Joy
Rastafarian Repatriation and the African Liberation Struggle

Tanzania's official welcome to Rastafarians, granted in December 1985, represented a mighty step forward on their mission to set up Jah Kingdom. They paused to acknowledge that the "battle was progressing," and had "more faith" that they would put to very good use "the right of entry, leading to citizenship, and land to effect an agriculturally based resettlement."[1] Ras Bupe Karudi returned to Tanzania from his trip to recruit additional Rastafarians on January 8, 1987, and he was pleased that the "five month mission to further the just cause" of repatriation "was accomplished." As always, all praise and gratitude went to Jah, "ever the maker of the way."[2]

From the Tanzanian government Rastas received a generous offer of land with no restrictions in terms of acreage or location. In both a symbolic and material sense, there was nothing more valuable than this. Having emerged as leaders of the effort to make Tanzania the "Zion" for many other Rastafarians, Ras Bupe Karudi and Joshua Mkhululi basked in the joy of this accomplishment. But, along with the practicalities of transporting others from the Caribbean, they would have to secure shelter, food, clothing, and medicine. Indeed, malaria threatened to derail their plans, claiming the lives of two Rastafarian elders (Ras Daniel Heartman and Ras Kwetenge Sokoni) within a few years of their arrival.

From within different family constellations, Rastafarians made the transition from dream to real life on the ground in Tanzania, and with that came the difficulties of making diaspora fit into a specific local context. As the returnees went about establishing a community in Tanzania, the group included men, women, and children. Yet, the written record of the repatriation, produced by men, was a male-centered one that affirmed a masculine interpretation of the journey and of Rastafarian activism more broadly. The challenges of writing diaspora are mapped unto issues of gender, and this becomes clear through the juxtaposition of Ras Bupe's narrative to that of his wife, Kisembo. Kisembo's perspective shows that she, like her husband, was a serious pan-Africanist. She also exposes the undeniable but often overlooked interplay among politics, religion, and family.

As the participation of Africa in creating and defining diaspora is crucial to "trodding diaspora," the Tanzanian state's role in facilitating the repatriation by providing land is a key point here. The state provided this in the midst of an already challenging process of nation building both economically and politically. The state's act of pan-African solidarity had the potential to offend locals as it clashed with preexisting tensions over land tenure in Tanzania and illuminated the contradictions at hand. But, local Tanzanians were also "trodding diaspora." As Rastafarians nurtured their religious beliefs in Tanzania, they continued to practice Rastafarian rituals of worship. Reggae music had made an impact on young Tanzanians in Dar es Salaam, who had begun to adapt their perception of a Rastafarian way of life to their local circumstances prior to the arrival of Jamaican Rastafarians. The arrival of the Rastafarians from Jamaica, however, marked the introduction of Rastafari as a religion and serious philosophy far beyond popular culture. Some Tanzanians embraced their message, including the worship of Emperor Haile Selassie I. Among those who accepted the divinity of Haile Selassie, there were some who rejected a diasporic hermeneutic for Rastafarian philosophy and origins. This brought about issues of authenticity, which invariably surface in black global projects. The debates proved Rastafarian religion to be portable and sustainable, in various ways, in a continental East African space.

Finally, the struggle to survive did not prevent the returnees from contributing to Tanzania's growth. At a time when Julius Nyerere and other African leaders welcomed diasporic help in nation building, Rastafarians made their mark in the area of education, journalism, and accounting. They also demonstrated the great extent to which they connected repatriation to a much larger struggle for African liberation by securing moral and financial support from a broad network of black activists such as Jacob Carruthers and John Henrik Clarke. Additionally, they demonstrated their commitment to supporting the freedom fighters of the liberation movements of southern Africa, making it clear that repatriation represented far more than a narrow, insular desire to escape oppression in the West.

・・・・・・

Upon returning to Tanzania from his trip to recruit Rastafarians, Karudi wrote that he was relieved to find his family doing well. He feared that he had left them without having adequately provided for their needs. Though his wife Kisembo and two children were there, Karudi made only infrequent references to his "family," never mentioning their names. As he recorded the details of the political work he did in service of repatriation, his understanding that women did not in any way contribute to this type of work was clear. From Kisembo's perspective, Karudi's depiction of himself as one who worried over the family's needs did not ring true.[3] In fact, her work to set up Jah Kingdom was unavoidably linked to his neglect of familial responsibilities. Ras Bupe, like many black male activists who saw themselves as making the ultimate manly sacrifice while disregarding and betraying their partners, also attempted to craft historical narratives that completely ignored his role in the making of such histories of problematic family dynamics.[4]

Ras Bupe's own analysis of how the demands of the repatriation intersected with his family life suggests that he embraced patriarchal ideas that were widespread within the movement. In reflecting upon the trials and tribulations of the journey to build the world he and his fellow Rastafarians imagined, Karudi admitted that his marriage suffered as a result of the "sacrifice."[5] But, this "sacrifice" served to affirm not only his devotion to Jah and the cause of repatriation but also his masculinity. Karudi explained that the work of repatriation had forced him to "become a bachelor." For him this constituted a point of pride as it allowed him to place himself within the context of Rastafarian elders who had been forced to adopt an ascetic life as a result of the struggle. Other male pan-Africanists such as Kwame Nkrumah of Ghana had made similar pronouncements in their definition of the kind of masculinity required of those who would do the work of African liberation.[6] Based on a biblical fundamentalism that arguably provides the most widely used justifications for gender inequity within Rastafari, Karudi established the political work and activism of Rasta as an inherently male undertaking. He also suggested that women served to weaken men and therefore distracted them with their wiles. As a child, Karudi had observed and learned from a "Jah-fearing, giant-like" Rastaman named Bongo Bobby who lived through the state repression of Rastafari during the early decades of the movement in Jamaica. Bongo Bobby had, "through faith in Jah," become "a bachelor without any [sexual] relations." Karudi considered it a privilege to have witnessed the journey of the "ancient Rastaman of dat blessed generation" because he could now relate to his experience. Bobby had "consciously accept[ed] to sow in tears, to reap in joy, even to the extent of becoming . . . a bachelor without any relations." Karudi explained that this state was by no means "normal or natural," but it was the price Bobby had paid for being on the "frontline of the battlefield." Most telling was Karudi's assertion that this "sacrifice," which was "demanded by Jah, could not take less than all of man's heart, mind, soul and strength, [man's] everything."[7] From Karudi's perspective, only men made sacrifices and suffered for the liberation struggle.

Karudi referred to his family only within the framework of "protecting" and providing." Yet, despite his expressions of concern for their well-being, he did very little to actually provide even basic necessities such as food and lodging for them. Before the official land grant was issued, the Karudis went "from here to there," living with different families. From his perspective, they were "living on faith." From Kisembo's, this was yet another example of his failure to "check things out knowing that he had a family."[8] As they depended upon the kindness of strangers for a place to stay, Kisembo and Ras Bupe were able to purchase land in Mbezi Beach upon which they hoped to build a house that would act as an African/Rasta reception center for returning diasporic Africans and for Tanzanians who embraced Rastafari.[9] Ras Bupe contributed a small portion of the cost, while Kisembo used some of the money she had saved from the time spent working in London to purchase what she describes as a "cheap, cheap" plot of land.[10] By 1987 Ras Bupe was overseeing the construction of the house, to be known as the House of David, which was by then promised to Ras Kwetenge Sokoni and his family, who were set to arrive from Bristol, England, upon its completion. The Sokoni family began to finance the project by sending money from Bristol.

In the meantime Ras Bupe continued to aggressively solicit money to aid in the process and for the wider effort of what he hoped would be a mass exodus of Rastafarians from the West to Tanzania. Fund-raising had also been a major concern of the Rastafarians who repatriated to Ethiopia. In 1972, Solomon Wolfe, a returnee, established the Shashamane Land Grant Development and Re-settlement Committee to "serve as a base for raising funds to develop the land on which they had settled."[11] Karudi's fund-raising efforts began with a letter he sent to pan-Africanists across the diaspora soliciting support for the mission in 1986. He identified a list of folks he believed were "Black Afrikan individuals/personalities who have professed some degree of consciousness, seriousness and so concern for the welfare of their race." Beyond their established commitment to their race, this had to be a group of people he could trust with private information. Nyerere had requested that the mission remain private, and state documents affirming support of the repatriation reflected this commitment to confidentiality as they were stamped "private."[12]

Karudi agreed that their efforts should be kept private because "one could never be too careful in an undertaking such as this, and it is therefore of extreme importance that the present stage of struggle remains confidential." This was based on his understanding that "the proved enemies of Black Afrika will not take kindly to this positive step forward in the centuries old struggle for the survival and upliftment of the exploited, downpressed and suffering one Black Afrikan, family, both at home and abroad."[13] Karudi's list of trusted individuals included black power activists, scholars, African freedom fighters from liberation movements, and musicians. This list covered a wide range of ideological orientations, including religious affiliation. This affirmed Karudi's (and Rastas') wide-ranging idea of pan-Africanism. His exchanges with these pan-African activists revealed Rastafari's entrenchment in the black networks of the period. They also demonstrate that there were those who thought Rastafarians were at the vanguard of repatriation in the modern era.

In response to Karudi's request for support, Harlem-based African American attorney Joseph R. Mack found it "very fitting" that the "task" of repatriation "should be initiated by the Rastafarian brothers from Jamaica, since it is that movement that has most identified with the spirit of repatriation in Africa, combining the consciousness of the concept of Marcus Garvey of 'Africa for Africans' with the symbolic significance of an African king in the person of His Royal Majesty Haile Selassie."[14] Similarly, Conrad W. Worrill of the National Black United Front (NBUF), based in Chicago, saw the prominence of Rastafari and declared that "return to Africa may take on many forms, but we must give undying support to those in the vanguard of the repatriation movement that is so important to the ultimate dignity of those African people removed from the motherland by the brutality of the Europeans." Worrill pledged the support of the NBUF to Karudi and the Universal Rastafari Improvement Association (URIA) for its effort "to raise the question of repatriation at the highest level that has at the root of its mission African people throughout the world becoming whole again."[15]

Al Hajj Anas M. Luqman, the founder and president of the Chicago-based Organization for African-American Unity, assured Karudi that the "nobility of the cause you and the group you represent is the answer to the prayers, blood and tears of centuries of past, present, and future Afrikans born in captivity." As a Muslim, Luqman was as strong and devoted to Allah as Karudi was to Jah, greeting him in "the name of ALLAH, the Beneficent, the Merciful" and ending with the proclamation that Allah was "the one God." But, like Karudi, he was committed to a pan-African ideology that stretched to accommodate various religious affiliations. In the final analysis, Luqman understood that Africans were "part of a global struggle, and although we speak many different languages, we all owe our allegiances to certain historical values that bind us together as a Nation." He also believed that Africans "must adopt a multi-strategy approach and give everybody the opportunity to do what he or she can do to make a contribution to the struggle of total liberation with our dignity and humanity intact," adding that he found Karudi's contribution to this effort "praiseworthy."[16]

Jacob Carruthers, a founding member of the Kemetic Institute of Chicago, enthusiastically endorsed Karudi's project, agreeing that "black people need to know that we can also come back to the blackland [sic] to stay." Carruthers added that "those of us in the diaspora need to know that we can come back home, because our security and safety in these alien lands of our captivity are not guaranteed." Much like the Rastafarian understanding of Babylon, he understood that "indeed many of us are perishing in captivity" and needed to return to "the land that gave birth and nurture to our foreparents."[17] Other individuals who pledged support included L. E. Mitchell from Detroit, who declared that the repatriation deserved "all moral, financial, and educational support mustered on its behalf," and respected African American historian John Henrik Clarke, who placed the repatriation within its (diasporic) historical context and pledged his support.[18]

In Karudi's letter to "Black Afrikan individuals" he had sought both financial and moral support. He received fervent affirmation of the validity of the mission, its historical significance, and the pioneering role of Rastafari.[19] There is documented evidence that a Caribbean Reggae Band based in England, Misty in Roots, made good on its pledge when its members held a concert to raise funds for Karudi and donated two thousand pounds in proceeds from the event.[20] Clarke contributed eighty dollars toward the cost of Karudi's travels to recruit elders,[21] and Karudi also received the sum of five hundred pounds from a few "brethren in Bristol" to aid with the construction of the house in Dar es Salaam. It is likely that these brethren were affiliated with URIA, which was based in Bristol and acted as a center for fund-raising.

The most detailed record of monetary support emerged from Karudi's sustained correspondence with noted West Indian scholar, activist, political theorist, and historian C. L. R. James. More than any other figure, Karudi kept James abreast of developments in Tanzania and during his trips abroad to seek repatriates. On August 15, 1986, Karudi acknowledged the receipt of two hundred pounds from James to help with Iman Mani's travel expenses from England to Tanzania.[22] Four days later he sent another receipt to James documenting another contribution of one thousand pounds, which he divided into six hundred pounds for his own living expenses and the remaining four hundred for "working expenses of [the] mission to England, Jamaica and America."[23]

Joshua Mkhululi also attempted to raise funds by encouraging reggae artists he knew to donate their proceeds to the cause of repatriation and resettlement, and later he founded the Ras Daniel Heartman Foundation with the same goal in mind. Based on his belief that "there is no business like show business," he hoped to invite prominent reggae artists such as Buju Banton, Luciano, Sizzla, and Richie Spice to Tanzania. After the land grants, he was able to announce that land was indeed available for returning Africans and for the reggae artists, who would be given "first choice." Mkhululi explained that "because the land is free, anyone who comes at this time can get a plot freely and non-financial assistance to build a house of quality—red bricks, wood, stones, concrete block, or a combination of these."[24]

Karudi and Mkhululi disagreed on how much assistance they should expect to receive from the Tanzanian government. Mkhululi had petitioned the government for the right to reside in Tanzania, and for land, but he knew that Tanzania could not afford to finance the establishment of the Rastafarian community. When Karudi and Mkhululi began to recruit Rastafarians to repatriate in the mid-1980s, Tanzania was already experiencing great economic hardship. The government, which could barely keep food stocked on store shelves throughout the country, could not afford to provide the repatriates with substantial financial resources. Similarly, though Karudi found other Rastafarians in Jamaica who were willing to repatriate to Tanzania, most could not afford the airfare.

Though Karudi praised Nyerere and Tanzania for allowing him and others to return home, he demanded that the government provide the "promised principled material support" that was necessary for the repatriation to succeed. There was precedence for this Rastafarian pursuit of state help with repatriation. On the heels of the 1938 rebellions in Jamaica, Rastafarians had petitioned the colonial government demanding that the state facilitate their desire to return "home" to get their "riches once more."[25] Of course, requesting that the British colonial government help them to return to Africa took on a different meaning and could be interpreted as a form of reparations for slavery and colonialism. Making the request of an African state functioned more as soliciting help from fellow Africans who were equally committed to the cause of liberation, and in this period there were Africans with state power to supply assistance for pan-African projects.

As they engaged in fund-raising activities, they worked hard to make the House of David hospitable. Along with the money from the Sokoni family, Mkhululi has written that along with Karudi, Juma Ntuve (a Tanzanian who had joined them), and Iman Mani, he helped with the initial phase of construction. Ras Kwetenge Sokoni, his three wives, and their fourteen children arrived from Bristol in 1987 to occupy the house.[26]

Sokoni was prominent within URIA. Polygyny constituted one of the main ways in which Sokoni and his wives attempted to live their perception of a precolonial African cultural lifestyle. The wives' understanding of their relationship is crucial to any analysis of such family arrangements within Rastafari. In the absence of their voices, assessment of polygyny runs the risk of denying their agency through the imposition of theoretical frameworks that may not apply to their experience or historical context. References to polygyny appeared in European accounts of family life among enslaved Africans in the Caribbean. For Jamaica in particular, Lucille Mathurin Mair notes the widespread occurrence of polygyny across the areas of Africa from which enslaved Africans in Jamaica were taken in the seventeenth and eighteenth centuries. Indeed, "polygyny became a strong factor in external assessments of man/woman relationships in Africa and a vital measuring rod of the status of the continent." From the vantage point of Europeans convinced of the superiority of the legal monogamy in which they became invested in the eighteenth century, polygyny was further evidence of the barbarism of African societies and peoples. Though monogamy was not absent from Caribbean plantation life, polygyny, which Europeans saw as a "repulsive institution," was key to how Europeans constructed notions of "black masculine oppression" and "black female debasement."[27] Many Europeans assumed that enslaved Africans were prone to polygamous family structures, but they did not seek a profound understanding of the political, social, cultural, and economic contexts out of which they were born and in which they often thrived.[28] In keeping with Europeans' wholesale repugnance toward and dismissal of African cultures, the regulation, construction and control of family became a crucial component of the civilizing mission of empires.

As Emily Burrill acknowledges about the French in colonial Mali, concern over marriage became a central component of the civilizing mission and she notes that "throughout the colonial period, the institution of marriage played a central role in how empires defined their colonial subjects as gendered persons with particular rights and privileges."²⁹ Indeed, marriage became an essential tool in colonial state making across the British colonies in the Caribbean as well. This was certainly the case in postemancipation Jamaica, where, "issues of sex and marriage were placed at the very heart of the agenda of the British civilizing mission." Civil authorities and Christian missionaries joined hands to impose the "ideal of legal Christian monogamous marriage," which was a foundational part of "an entire ideology of what constituted morality and civility" in Jamaica. Sure of the civilizing power of Victorian Christianity, "both the missionaries and the civil authorities exhibited a virtually obsessive interest in the sexual proclivities of the Jamaican people, and sought to bring them under moral control." Afro-Jamaicans resisted this form of British cultural imperialism by avoiding marriage and establishing their own rules for family, love, life, and household arrangements.³⁰ This widespread decision by both men and women to eschew marriage in favor of cohabitation or other nonlegal relationships, identified in the colonial histories as "concubinage," produced children marked as "bastards" or "illegitimate" by colonial observers. Moore and Johnson argue that the Jamaican concept of marriage, "shaped largely by conditions of life on the slave plantations, was simply *different* from the slave model."³¹ As the decision to forgo marriage continued long into postcolonial Jamaica, the arrangements that defied English definitions of family were widespread within the movement. But unlike the wider Jamaican society, Rastafarians' assertion that their cultural heritage lies in Africa and not on the plantations of Jamaica led some to see polygyny (and not just "concubinage") as a part of their expression of African identity. While diversity within the movement prevents an analysis that applies to every Rastafarian who champions polygyny and/or chooses to live such a lifestyle, many Rastas lacked the details of the complex ways in which polygamous societies functioned across west and west central Africa. As such, their sketchy notions often reproduced some of the stereotypes about Africa that were nurtured by colonial writers. Still, the decision to live this way, particularly by women, represented a resistive lifestyle that was incomprehensible and frowned upon not only by state elites but by ordinary Jamaicans.

The history of family dynamics within the repatriation offers another angle of the freedom struggle that ventures into how the public battle was intertwined with the intimate lives of the repatriates. Ras Kwetenge fell gravely ill after only a few years in Tanzania. As his condition worsened, his first wife accompanied him on a flight from Dar es Salaam to England for medical treatment. Sokoni took his final breath on the flight, and his wife was distraught. In that moment, her beloved husband had died, and with him their hopes for a joyful life in Tanzania. For his family, Sokoni's demise encapsulated the worst of the transition to life in Tanzania. Though it is not clear whether or not the structure of the house was completed before the Sokoni family arrived in Tanzania, it is clear that the infrastructure for plumbing had not been installed. They had lived quite comfortably in England, which made the reality of a house without proper plumbing even more difficult to withstand.

Tanzania's gift to Rastafarians was life affirming, and Sokoni's horrifying death anathema to the mission at hand. For him and his wives, Tanzania's inspiring open-door policy had been enough to repeatedly resuscitate hope, even as hardship stifled its air supply. This changed after his death, and his wives and children returned to England. The remaining returnees mourned the loss of Sokoni, who had become a trusted leader of spiritual instruction and had made a meaningful impact on Tanzanians who embraced Rastafari.

Karudi had lamented the epidemiological reality of life in Tanzania. During a period of two months in 1987, the members of his family had succumbed to malaria twice, though it spared him both times. Karudi wrote that "malaria fever has again been causing problems, as since returning home, the entire family apart from I-man, have twice gone down with the dreaded fever."[32] But he had not managed to escape the sneaky disease a year earlier. During April 1986 he had suffered through "two attacks" of malaria and was convinced that the intractable disease was "nothing short of an epidemic" in Dar es Salaam. He thought its impact was worsening due to "increasing resistance to the Western drug used to treat the disease." True to the general Rastafarian approach to illness, he had "successfully use[d] traditional Afrikan medicine," which he described as "roots and herbs," to treat malaria. He accused most Tanzanians who suffered through bouts of malaria of having been "indoctrinated into believing that Western medicine is better than Afrikan medicine to treat the disease" and claimed to have been "often frowned at" for taking "Afrikan medicine." As Karudi commented, "such continues to be the extent of the effects of white domination on Black Afrikan minds in Mother Afrika and abroad."[33] The emphasis on consciousness and the religious aspect of Rastafari sometimes led to a judgmental attitude among Rastafarians. It would be wrong, however, to equate this with the nineteenth-century variant of diasporic notions of superiority over continental Africans. Rastafarians exhibited this tendency across the diaspora as much as they did in Africa. The members of

URIA in particular had learned so much about Africa by the 1980s that the only firm distinction they made between Africa and its diaspora pertained to the continent's status as their ancestral home. They knew that Africans on the continent and the diaspora were engaged in the same struggle, as colonialism had caused a lingering "downpression" across Africa as well.[34] That continental Africans were also brainwashed by colonial ideas was greater evidence of the global reach of white supremacy on African people, even in the area of health care choices. Malaria posed a real threat to Rastafarians and could be counted as a serious portion of the "price of liberty," just as it had been for African Americans who settled in Liberia in the nineteenth century.[35] And yet the struggle continued.

How Can We Sing Jah's Song in a Strange Land?

While the Tanzanian government granted Rastafarians the right to resettle in 1985, it did not issue a land grant until September 15, 1989, when the Ministry of Lands, Natural Resources and Tourism issued a letter addressed to Mkhululi titled "Repatriation of Africans from Jamaica to Africa—Land for Resettlement."[36] The letter documented the offer of land that had been made in a meeting on August 1 of that year, and detailed the process by which repatriates could acquire land. The Rastafarians were allowed the freedom to select land from any area of Tanzania. They had to have the prime minister's office get in touch with the "relevant regional and district authorities in the regions or districts" where the land was located. The prime minister's office provided an introduction of sorts.

Rastafarians received a generous offer of land with no restrictions in terms of acreage or location. If the land did not exceed one hundred acres in size, the village governments would allocate the land; if it exceeded one hundred acres but was smaller than three thousand acres, it had to be approved by the district authorities. Land that exceeded three thousand acres but was smaller than five thousand acres had to be approved by the regional authorities, while plots of land that exceeded five thousand acres had to be approved by the minister in charge of lands. Finally, the letter advised that for all cases, "recommendations of Land Advisory Committees at District and Regional levels will have to be sought prior to submission to the relevant approving authority."[37] Though the government offered the official land grant in 1989, the actual process of allocating land was not expedited until 1991, after the Rastafarians met with Minister Paul Rupia and decided to select land as individuals in different areas of Tanzania.

The Rastafarian community had suffered a major setback with the passing of Ras Kwetenge Sokoni and Ras Daniel Heartman, who as learned elders represented a unifying force and were respected as teachers for the community they hoped to build. Still, the land grant marked a significant accomplishment. It legitimized their act of repatriation and boosted their ability to attract other Africans in the West to Tanzania. Notably, the offer of land from the Tanzanian state affirmed the Rastafarian conceptualization of the relationship between Africa and its diaspora. It was not insignificant that the subject of the letter they received saw them as "Africans from Jamaica" and offered them land for "resettlement" as opposed to "settlement." Through the language employed in the letter, the Tanzanian state demonstrated its embrace of the Rastafarian paradigm of African identity and represented an expression of pan-African solidarity between continental Africans and those of the diaspora, whereby the notion of diaspora was constituted as a territorialized identity rooted in Africa.

The process by which Karudi gained access to the land he chose in Kigoma was similar to the experiences of the other Rastafarians who received land. On Karudi's behalf, a letter was sent from the office of the prime minister and the vice president to J. K. Kileo, the development manager in Kigoma.[38] The letter informed Kileo that the government had made the decision to allow the "Black Jamaicans" in Tanzania to live in the country as a "special case" and introduced Kileo to Karudi, who had chosen land in Kigoma.[39] In addition, the letter asked Kileo to ensure that Karudi was given one thousand acres of land plus an extra 321 acres (to be granted immediately for farming) in a speedy manner.[40] The following year, the regional commissioner wrote a similar letter to the district commissioner reinforcing the ideas from the letter of 1991 but adding that Karudi should be given the title deed for the land (per the office of the prime minister and the vice president), as well as further assistance with all that was needed to settle on the land.[41]

The 1991 meeting, which set the recognition of the individual land grants in motion, came at a time when land tenure reform emerged as an important issue in Tanzania's national politics. In January of that same year, the president of Tanzania, Ali Hassan Mwinyi, had created the Commission of Inquiry into Land Matters, which was asked to "review laws and policies concerning the allocation, tenure, use, and development of land, and to make recommendations for reform," and also "to examine the nature of disputes that had arisen, and to propose measures for their solution."[42] This was in response to internal and external pressures on the government to tend to matters of land tenure.[43] Internally, the grievances of citizens—mostly from rural areas—concerning what they perceived to be the mishandling of land tenure matters under Nyerere's policy of "villagization" had become a serious issue for the government to address. In addition, as Tanzania was in the process of making the transition from a one-party system to a multiparty system, politicians were eager to convince the population that they were willing to place land matters on the national agenda.[44] In terms of external factors, Tanzania had already embarked upon the road to liberalization and had come under pressure from the International Monetary Fund (IMF) and the World Bank to make reforms in this area.

Under the leadership of Issa Shivji of the faculty of law at the University of Dar es Salaam, the Commission of Inquiry into Land Matters presented its findings in a two-volume report after traveling around Tanzania and venturing to other countries like Kenya and Zimbabwe to examine their land policies. The commission aimed to properly represent the sentiments of the population, and recommended people-centered policy changes. The report, which was completed in November 1992, outlined the inadequacies of Tanzania's land tenure policies and made recommendations for changes. The commission found that the state's policy of establishing villages was not accompanied by a legal framework. The government had thus far placed very little emphasis on land rights, which caused grave problems when villagization caused people to be displaced in an ad hoc manner from land over which they previously had customary rights. In the vast majority of the complaints that the commission received from the rural areas, the villagers stressed that they were not allowed to participate in decisions that the government made regarding land.[45] Though villagization was obviously tied to land tenure issues, it was "not conceived in light of a coherent land tenure policy."[46]

Though much of the rhetoric of policy statements like *Arusha Declaration* had stressed the participation of the people as a central aspect of the democratic process, the government's efforts to establish *ujamaa* villages failed to rely upon the input of the Tanzanian people. In the final analysis, despite the best of intentions, villagization had become a state-driven process, with the state as the "primary pro-active agent."[47] What existed was a flawed system whereby "rules were made and enforced, and disputes settled, largely by executive action."[48] The general failure of the government to incorporate the input of the people in decision making about land tenure had much to do with its failure to fully appreciate the importance of female labor in the villages. The system was fundamentally flawed because the "whole thrust of ujamaa did not address the issue of who commanded the labour power of women and children in the villages."[49] Furthermore, *ujamaa* and the *Arusha Declaration* had not employed the indigenous knowledge of Tanzanian women into their agricultural policies. Though Nyerere acknowledged discrimination against women among his own ethnic group, the Zanaki,[50] and also implemented policies to ensure female involvement in government agencies,[51] the government failed to address the biases against women in the realm of land tenure rights. For example, customary tenure prevented women from owning and controlling land, and customary laws of inheritance did not cater to the needs or interests of widows and daughters.[52]

The report found that the rallying cry of the disgruntled villagers was *hatukushirikishwa*, an expression of anger over not having been allowed to participate in issues related to the administration of land.[53] One prominent point of contention, which pertained to the land grants that the Rastafarians received was the alienation of land by the government to "outsiders." By the time President Mwinyi appointed the land commission in 1991, fears of what the villagers perceived to be the arbitrary alienation of land by government officials to nonvillagers had reached a boiling point. In truth, this frustration had roots in the colonial period. European powers were motivated by the desire to exploit African peoples and acquire resources when they divided the continent among themselves at the historic Berlin Conference of 1884. The Germans acquired Tanganyika in 1885 and encouraged the settlement of Germans and the establishment of plantation agriculture for crops such as sisal and coffee. In 1895 they established an imperial decree that "merged sovereignty and property in one entity by providing that all land, whether occupied or not, was treated as unowned Crown land and vested in the Empire."[54] This allowed the colonial government to alienate large tracts of fertile land to European settlers—at the expense of the indigenous people of Tanganyika. The German colonizers ensured that while the peasants worked the land, the colonial state secured the right to alienate land. This was carried out through sale or lease and tied to the commodification of land, which was new to Tanganyikan society.[55]

Tanganyika became a British mandate in 1919, and then a UN Trusteeship Territory administered by Britain in 1946. The British passed the Land Ordinance of 1923, which established a legal framework for alienating land. While it acknowledged customary tenure, it did so without "securing and statutorily entrenching customary titles and rights."[56] In addition, the ordinance declared all lands public lands that were "placed under the control of the governor for the benefit of the inhabitants."[57] The governor gained the authority to issue grants of land, called "rights of occupancy," for a period of no more than ninety-nine years.[58] In practice, this allowed the colonial state to alienate lands to foreigners, including individuals and companies. Though the British policies with regards to land tenure were not identical to those of the Germans, both policies were based on the idea that Africans did not and should not have legally enshrined rights to the land.

Even before Tanganyika won its independence from Britain, Nyerere declared a philosophical challenge to colonial approaches to land issues. In 1958 he emphatically rejected the East Africa Royal Commission's encouragement of a "freehold" system of land tenure. This system of individual titling was detailed in Government Paper No. 6, titled *Review and Land Tenure Policy*, which proposed a form of land tenure that was "individual, exclusive, secure, unlimited in time and negotiable."[59] In an article titled "Mali ya Taifa" (Wealth of the nation), Nyerere argued,

> If people are given land to use as their property, then they have a right to sell it. It will not be difficult to predict who, in fifty years time, will be the landlords and who the tenants. In a country such as this, where, generally speaking, the Africans are poor and the foreigners are rich, it is quite possible that, within eighty or a hundred years, if the poor African were allowed to sell his land, all the land in Tanganyika would belong to wealthy immigrants, and the local people would be tenants. But even if there were no rich foreigners in this country, there would emerge rich and clever Tanganyikans. If we allow land to be sold like a robe, within a short period there would be only a few Africans possessing land in Tanganyika and all others would be tenants. . . .
>
> If two groups emerge—a small group of landlords and a large group of tenants—we would be faced with a problem which has created antagonism among peoples and led to bloodshed in many countries of the world. Our forefathers saved themselves from this danger by refusing to distribute land on a freehold basis.[60]

Nyerere worried about the inequity that the freehold system would create while also acknowledging the advantages that had been given to foreigners. In keeping with the philosophical approach of *ujamaa*, Nyerere and the postindependence government were deeply concerned with the welfare and rights of the people in ways that were unknown to the German and British colonizers.

Yet when Tanganyika gained independence in 1961, the government continued to use the land ordinance that had been enacted by the British in 1923. Public lands were now vested in the president as opposed to the governor. The postindependence government did not declare a clear land tenure policy "except the abolition of both freehold titles, the semi-feudal system called *nyarubanja* and the passing of legislation against absentee landlordism."[61] As detailed by the report of the land commission, the postindependence government had made grave mistakes in the area of land tenure.

Rastafarians received a generous offer of land in the midst of the national crisis over land tenure rights. Though members of the Rastafarian community had formed meaningful relationships with the Tanzanian people, their decision to select land in different parts of Tanzania meant that they chose to enter new communities. Iman Mani, who chose and received land in Mbeya, recognized the implications of the fact that the decision to grant land to Rastafarians occurred solely at the state level. Though his obvious poverty and lack of resources ensured that the villagers in Mbeya did not associate him with the wealthy entrepreneurs or other enterprising foreigners who had historically benefited from land alienation in Tanzania, he was still an outsider who received land without the input of the people in the area. He understood this when his personal items were stolen and his farmland set on fire after he planted his food crops.[62]

Though Mani did not have a full grasp of the history of land tenure disputes in Tanzania, he understood that they were responding to what they considered to be the intrusion of a stranger who appeared without explanation and was able to acquire land. He insisted that the government should have consulted the people and prepared them for his arrival. Still, Mani's experience in Mbeya highlighted an important irony: as the Tanzanian state practiced a form of pan-Africanism that allowed it to engage grassroots diasporic Africans, its actions had the power to alienate the grassroots in Tanzania. This was also an important lesson for the Rastafarians about the ways in which their repatriation clashed with the historical, cultural, and social realities of continental Africans in their communities.

When Karudi selected land in Kigoma, a largely underdeveloped region of Tanzania, he still nurtured the dream of constructing a self-sufficient, cooperative community for future repatriates. In preparation for the move he sought further help from the government to develop the land. Minister Mizengo Kayanza Peter Pinda arranged for Karudi to obtain a truck through the Corporate Rural Development Bank (CRDB) on the understanding that he would make payments to the bank after he settled in Kigoma. When Karudi defaulted on these payments, the CRDB repossessed the truck. Pinda had encouraged Karudi to stick to the agreement by making payments, yet Karudi insisted that his mission "was spiritual and not commercial," and Pinda concluded that Karudi's commitment to a spiritual life was bordering on fanatical.[63] Kisembo Karudi agreed wholeheartedly with Pinda's assessment of her husband. In her view, Ras Bupe had failed to appreciate a very kind gesture from the Tanzanian state. Much to her disappointment, Ras Bupe's assertion that the mission was spiritual and not commercial also accommodated his thoughts on work. He maintained that Rastafarians should "live by faith." Not only was this unlike the ethos of the other Rastafarians in Tanzania but was also contrary to the Tanzanian state's ideas about the role of work in nation building. In his classic definition of *ujamaa*, Nyerere was clear that "in traditional African society everybody was a worker" and that there was "no other way of earning a living for the community."[64] In this area, Ras Bupe's attitude was incompatible with an idea that was at the heart of the Tanzanian nation as defined by Nyerere, who had even put work within the context of what he called the African "tradition of hospitality": "Treat your guest as a guest for two days; on the third day give him a hoe!" This meant that even those who visited the homes of others should not be allowed to sit idly as their hosts worked. His point was that "working was part and parcel, was indeed the very basis and justification, of the socialist achievement of which we are so justly proud."[65] This may explain why, according to Kisembo Karudi, after staying with multiple Tanzanian families during the early years, their hosts became annoyed and "started to act funny" after a while.[66] The emphasis on work in socialist Tanzania may have led to a heightened sense of outrage on the part of wonderfully hospitable Tanzanians when they recognized that the Karudi family was not in search of work.

Nevertheless, the Karudi family continued to benefit from the kindness of strangers when they, unable to handle the challenges of life in Kigoma, returned to Dar es Salaam. Desperate for help, Kisembo had written to her mother and sister in Jamaica asking for financial assistance. Her family obliged, and the Karudis subsequently rented a house in the Karakata neighborhood of Dar es Salaam from a landlord who was unusually lenient in response to missed payments and broken promises about missed payments. But Kisembo had grown tired of worrying about her family's survival. Having observed the work of a Tanzanian woman who fashioned jewelry from colorful, diminutive beads, she started a business of her own. Her amazingly rapid rise to success belied the reality of the clandestine operation she led with the help of her children: she hid this enterprise from her husband Ras Bupe. Before long Kisembo had earned enough money to feed her family, pay the rent, purchase furniture, and more. Even as Ras Bupe ate the meals she prepared, and sat in the sofa soaked with her sweat, he never asked how she had come by the food that fed him and seemed oblivious to the tedious labor that sustained him.[67]

Kisembo began to resent Ras Bupe's efforts to control many aspects of their lives, including diet and clothing. Many Rastafarian men of his generation fostered similar ideas of a man's role. As they saw it, it was their duty to "grow a daughta" by introducing her to Rastafari as a religion, and to oversee her "livity" with a watchful, paternalistic eye. In hindsight, Kisembo sees him not as a typical Rastaman, but as an extreme version of a pious one. She had initially accepted the common Twelve Tribes of Israel teaching that "man was the head of woman," and as a result, her own religious commitments prevented her from questioning him for almost fifteen years into their marriage. But this refrain, most often related to the patriarchal expectations of men, also came with the expectations of women. For Kisembo, accepting this as a theological standard meant that a man would only be allowed to secure his status as "head" if he acted as such, and she expected the head of the family to be faithful to her, to maintain a job, and to consistently provide for her and their children.[68]

There was also a religious component. In "growing a daughta," Rastafarian men often presented themselves not only as enlightened souls but also as righteous and godly human beings. Kisembo admired and respected Ras Bupe, to whom she was eternally grateful for introducing her to Jah. Even deeper than her disappointment over his unwillingness and/or inability to provide for his family was the devastation that came with recognizing that he failed to live up to the religious persona he wielded like a badge of honor. In accepting man as the head of woman, Kisembo's spirituality was intertwined with Ras Bupe's. In a sense, he represented God's divine authority on earth, and this rendered the decision to leave the marriage a very difficult one as it pertained to her spiritual life. Through this relationship, she had, in her own words, "come to the awareness of God." To further complicate matters, Rastafari also empowered her to live as a black woman "without having to conform to society" in a way that denigrated her blackness.[69] The decision to become a Rasta woman through the teachings of a Rastaman meant that her political consciousness, spirituality, and intimate relationship were inseparable. This was the very foundation of their union. It was a partnership sanctified by such a pact.

But Ras Bupe broke that pact. Much to Kisembo's chagrin, he had separated the political work of the repatriation from his family life and had neglected his wife and children in the process. Love and youthful naïveté had sustained Kisembo's admiration and respect for Ras Bupe, but his overbearing directives had become wildly impractical and hurtful. Kisembo began to see him as "selfish," as a husband who had forgotten that she also had "wants, needs and feelings." For her, his elevation of "the struggle" over his family life devalued her, their union, their children, their mission, and Rastafari more broadly. From Kisembo's perspective, the separation between the struggle and the family had never really existed, and her understanding was always that "yes, the struggle is important but your family is also important. You can't neglect your family and expect everything to be okay."[70]

As the chasm between her expectations and their actual "livity" widened, one point of contention proved the clincher that led Kisembo to leave the marriage: the issue of her children's education. In 1983, when Ras Bupe proposed that they homeschool the children, Kisembo had agreed, and they both took turns with this important task. Ras Bupe had insisted that this was the appropriate course of action based on his fears that public schools in the city of Dar es Salaam would not provide the children with the true African values of the village. Kisembo did not initially quarrel with this romanticized notion of the authenticity of rural Tanzania, which had also been encouraged by Nyerere's policies. But as the children entered their teenage years, she was convinced that she and Ras Bupe had exhausted their capabilities as teachers. She argued that their children needed to enroll in school in order to meet their potential and to become self-sufficient adults. Ras Bupe vehemently refused. Just as he eschewed work in his own life, he was unconcerned with whether or not his children would secure a vocation. It became clear to Kisembo that her husband's desire to control their lives and the restrictions he imposed were unacceptable. Yet though she argues that Rastafarian men have historically dictated too many "writs and rites," she maintains that Ras Bupe's particular brand of control was "not a general thing because not every Rastaman was that extreme."[71] She reinforces the diversity within Rastafari and highlights the role of individual personalities in Rasta histories. Ras Bupe's intractability became an obstacle as his family and others made the transition to life in Tanzania. This was the case even as his dogged, awe-inspiring determination forged extraordinary pan-African linkages and opened doors that others would never have tried to pry open.

Repatriation and African Liberation

As early as 1935, shortly after the movement was founded, Rastafarians were mobilized, along with other diasporic Africans, in response to the Italian invasion of Ethiopia. Rather than solely being a concern for Emperor Haile Selassie, it reflected a wider engagement with contemporary issues on the continent, and the concern continued into the period of decolonization. Rastafarian communities, ever abreast of current affairs across Africa, organized demonstrations protesting the counterrevolutionary actions of Ian Smith in Southern Rhodesia and in opposition to apartheid in South Africa. Activists such as Samuel Clayton, Ras Historian, and Sister Farika Birham Selassie participated in a regional planning conference for the Sixth Pan-African Conference held in Kingston, Jamaica, in 1973; Sister Farika went on to attend the actual conference in Dar es Salaam in 1974.[72] Further evidence of sustained interest in African liberation existed in *Rasta Voice*, the publication of the Rastafari Movement Association, which had been founded in 1968.

In Tanzania the Rastafarians were much closer to the action of liberation movements and took advantage of the opportunity to support them. Joshua Mkhululi helped to strengthen the relationship between the University of Dar es Salaam and the liberation movements of southern Africa, becoming the first chairperson of the Liberation and Support Committee established at the university in 1979.[73] Under his leadership, the committee set about mobilizing support for the liberation struggles in Namibia, South Africa, and Zimbabwe. In this role, Mkhululi forged deeper linkages with the people of Tanzania while extending the nation's commitment to pan-African politics into the 1980s. He also recruited others from the diaspora, such as the Jamaican scholar and activist Horace Campbell, who worked with Mkhululi on the committee and helped to raise Tanzania's profile as a hub of black internationalist ideas and action. Beyond the imperative to leave Babylon, Rastafarian repatriation has always been "linked to a commitment to African liberation."[74]

Ras Bupe Karudi had also considered the liberation struggles of southern Africa to be of great interest and significance. The presence of many liberation movements in exile in Dar es Salaam facilitated alliances. An exchange between Karudi and Thobile Gola, chief representative of the external headquarters of the Pan Africanist Congress of Azania (PAC) in Tanzania, provides evidence of such an alliance. In response to a note Karudi sent expressing condolences after the passing of the PAC's chairman

John Nyati Pokela in 1985, Gola thanked him, encouraged him and other diasporic Africans to "contribute concretely to the great cause" of liberation, and assured him of the PAC's "appreciation and cooperation at all times."[75] Karudi met with Johnson Mlambo, then the chairman of the PAC, in Dar es Salaam in September of that same year, and in his capacity as secretary general of URIA, he accepted "the invitation to close ranks in struggle with the PAC."[76] Pledging support for liberation movements was so important to Karudi that he included this alliance in his list of objectives after receiving the right of entry into Tanzania.[77] On this list he also declared his support of the Sudan People's Liberation Movement (SPLM) as it waged its "righteous and just struggle." In 1983, as Karudi and Mkhululi waited for the Tanzanian government to officially respond to their request to repatriate, Karudi had presented his case to the SPLM, a group he regarded as the "guardians and true custodians of the long exploited, downpressed, distressed and dispossessed Southern Sudanese people."[78]

Further proof that Karudi and other members of URIA were engaged with African liberation struggles and with the conflicts within the movement can be found in URIA's monthly publication out of Bristol, *URIA Voice*. One issue carried an extensive treatment of the Frente de Libertação de Moçambique (FRELIMO). While generally supportive of FRELIMO, the article went on to criticize Samora Machel, whom it described as "once a hero" but who had betrayed the movement in 1984 when he signed the Nkomati Accord.[79] It was clear that URIA's engagement with African liberation movements was by no means a superficial one.

As they struggled to set up Jah Kingdom, Rastafarians also worked hard to contribute to Tanzania's development, and education was an area in which they sought to do so. By the time Mkhululi arrived in Tanzania in 1976, the intellectual vibrancy at the University of Dar es Salaam had already been established. In fact, it had probably reached its peak in the years immediately following the release of the *Arusha Declaration* of 1967. By 1976 some of the optimism of the 1960s had waned as the challenges and contradictions of *ujamaa na kujitegemea* (African socialism and self-reliance) and the failures of Nyerere's government became palpable. In this sense, during his tenure at the university, Mkhululi benefited from the legacy of those like Walter Rodney who had created a radical atmosphere, and he built on it by extending the tradition of radical engagement with both Tanzania's national politics and pan-African politics into the 1970s and 1980s. Mkhululi was instrumental in establishing the master of business administration program at the university, and he became the first dean of the faculty of commerce and management in 1979.[80] As Tanzania struggled to live up to its ideals of self-reliance and to stave off the machinations of neocolonial international threats, Mkhululi served the nation by increasing the number of faculty and by training numerous students in the area of commerce and management. In this capacity, his activities in Tanzania intersected with those of other diasporic Africans who aimed to contribute to the nation-building effort by providing much-needed knowledge and expertise to the newly independent African nation. As dean Mkhululi encouraged his faculty to work closely with the people of Tanzania far beyond the confines of the university and to "strengthen the spirit of sharing and cooperation" within communities.[81]

Like Rodney, Mkhululi was committed to bridging the distance between the university and the wider community as he tried to make *ujamaa* a workable idea. He attempted to enforce *ujamaa*'s spirit of sharing by establishing a cooperative at the university that tried to distribute goods for the people of Tanzania in an equitable fashion. He also worked as a community activist in Kunduchi, in the Kinondoni District, where he established bonds with the people of the community.

Upon resigning from the university in 1985, Mkhululi relocated to Arusha, which had a climate that was better for his respiratory problems, but he continued to contribute to Tanzania's nation building in meaningful ways. In September 1987 he was instrumental in establishing the Institute of Accountancy Arusha (IAA) and served as its first principal. The Tanzanian government, through its Ministry of Finance, aimed to meet the nation's growing demand for trained accountants, and C. D. Msuya, then the minister of finance, economic affairs, and planning, hailed the opening as "yet another milestone by Tanzania in her efforts to promote trained and qualified manpower in accountancy and auditing" and noted that "with the expansion of national economy, the demand for the professional accounting cadre is increasing."[82] As principal, Mkhululi was responsible for the "day to day running of the Institute."[83] His work marked an important contribution to the nation's goal of self-reliance, considering that when Tanzania gained independence from Britain in 1961, it "did not have one single qualified accountant," and the government had to recruit expatriate staff as a short term solution."[84] In subsequent years, Mkhululi worked as a government consultant on a contractual basis with the Tanzanian Public Service College, which oversaw the training of government employees. Meanwhile, he continued to nurture his dream of an "Africa Teacher's Training College" in Arusha to "prepare teachers for all levels of education and training."[85]

Education was an area in which Karudi also contributed to African liberation. Karudi became a beloved member of his community in Kipawa, Dar es Salaam, where he ran a free school for the children in the area out of his own meager resources. When he noticed that many of the children in his neighborhood were not attending school due to financial woes, Karudi decided to use a room in his house as a school, and enlisted the help of two Tanzanian friends to help him with the task of "teaching the beautiful likkle [sic] children of Zion." With "blessing from Jah," Karudi "simply began with the teaching of two children," but soon the number of children grew to sometimes more than fifty in a single year. It was not his intention to start a school while they were still struggling to set up Jah Kingdom but, as he noted, "when Jah gets ready, things will, and must move accordingly!" Karudi's school accommodated the children free of charge "in the foothills of Zion, despite the economic hardships of having to survive."[86]

In keeping with the Rastafarian understanding that "the first stage in the liberation of any downpressed people is the liberation of the mind," Karudi tried to establish a book project. After a few years in Africa, he observed that there existed a "pressing need for Afrikans at home (in Mother Afrika) and not only abroad in (in captivity), to know much about who they are, and where they are coming from." In recognizing knowledge production as an integral component of colonial rule, he hoped to correct the efforts of "those who control" to use "the thing called propaganda." As the struggle for freedom continued in Africa and across the diaspora, Karudi's book project was envisioned as a means to address the fact that black people were, in his estimation, suffering from mental enslavement more than any other group in the world. He put together a list of "selected Afrikan writers with required skills, commitment and dedication" who had been "positively inspired by the God of Afrika to begin the crucial and most significant task of bringing to light the true account of Black Afrikan civilization." His list included such stalwarts of the black intellectual tradition as Yusuf Ben-Jochannan, Edward Blyden, Frantz Fanon, Amy Jacques Garvey, C. L. R. James, and George James.[87]

Karudi understood that selecting the necessary books was only a part of the process and that "without distribution, there will be a continued failure to make the long overdue and much needed contribution." As such, he met with Walter Bgoya, the managing director of the Tanzanian Publishing House, a government-owned company also committed to African socialism. Bgoya, who had worked with Tanzania's foreign Ministry, began a new position in 1972 as the manager of the publishing house,[88] and shortly thereafter, African Americans who traveled to Tanzania made contact with him. This led Bgoya to work with the Drum and Spear Press, founded by former members of the Student Nonviolent Coordinating Committee.

At a time when black activists debated the merits of armed struggle, "picking up the book was figuratively equivalent to picking up the gun," but for the Rastafarians of URIA there was no conflict: they advocated for both armed struggle and mental emancipation through books. The link between African liberation/consciousness, independent education, and the pursuit of power emphasized the point that knowledge production constituted yet another battlefield upon which the colonizers and the colonized met. The Drum and Spear Press aimed to publish texts relevant to Africa and its diaspora. Inspired by *ujamaa* and employing it as a pan-African ideology, the goal was to promote cultural nationalism and consciousness among black people.[89]

Though agricultural work was definitely the focus of Nyerere's scheme for nation building, he had also recognized the value of reading and the importance of controlling the content of books used to educate the population through publishing "within the country."[90] Once again, Rastafarians were in the midst of important currents within black radical politics. On a visit to London, Karudi had discussed the prospect of his book project with C. L. R. James and followed up in September 1986 in a letter. James expressed a desire to "play a leading role in the setting up of a printing and publishing establishment in Tanzania," which inspired and emboldened Karudi.[91] James died in 1989, and the plans did not come to fruition, but Rastafarians certainly had an impact on the consciousness of local Tanzanians who learned about Rastafari through contact with them.

Jamaican Rasta or Tanzanian Rasta?

Beginning in the mid-1980s, reggae music—and Bob Marley, in particular—had led to a noticeable presence of Rastafarian images and language across different parts of Tanzania. Yet unlike Jamaican Rastafarians and the Tanzanians who gathered around them in Mbezi Beach, the Tanzanians who had been introduced to Rastafari through reggae music rejected the idea that Haile Selassie was divine. Limiting her study to a specific street corner in Dar es Salaam, Eileen Moyer conducted ethnographic research in response to the "increasing popularity of Rastafari-inspired discourses among young men living and working in the streets." She found that these young men had adapted Rastafari to their local concerns and circumstances, using their understanding of Marley's lyrics and image to critique and exercise control over the local hardships they faced. This was commonly framed within the Rastafarian discourse of "peace and love." In discussing what she sees as the Tanzanian interpretation of Rastafari, Moyer argues that "Marley could be understood as a global symbol, a floating signifier waiting to be taken up by oppressed people throughout the world" and that the youth of Tanzania "cannibalize" Rastafari to "meet their own needs." She suggests that there were also "real Rastafari communities" in Dar es Salaam, defining "real" Rastas as those who follow a Rastafari belief system and adhere to its tenets. She notes that many of these people are "linked to foreigners who had repatriated to Tanzania in search of Zion." Based on what she perceives to be an "almost universal distrust of outsiders," Moyer never gained access to these "real" communities despite the efforts of one Rastaman who "valiantly tried to convince the brethren of his church" to allow her into their space. Using the perspectives of the young Tanzanian men with whom she spoke, Moyer reports that Tanzanians learned about Haile Selassie, food restrictions, and the religious significance of ganja from the "real" Rastas. Her binary relies solely upon her interaction with one group, and thus ignores important gray areas. Nonetheless, she correctly refers to significant debates over authenticity that emerged in Tanzania after repatriation introduced a diasporic Rastafarian philosophy and "livity" that was different from the Rastafari that had traveled to Tanzania through reggae music.[92]

The groups of local Tanzanians who embraced Rastafari in some way or another extended beyond Moyer's street corner in Dar es Salaam; such groups existed in other areas, including Mbeya, Morogoro, and Tanga.[93] Research conducted by Miho Ishii, along with the records of the repatriates, speaks to the conflicts that arose through the particular debates between the group in Morogoro and the repatriates.[94] Following Ras Kwetenge Sokoni's death in 1994, Ato Kidani Roberts and his wife, Angelina Belinda Tyhoye, moved into the house in Mbezi Beach and assumed leadership of the camp associated with it. A Tanzanian of the Sukuma ethnic group, Tyhoye had embraced Rastafari, and along with Roberts sought to revive the religious practices of Rastafari. They organized necessary documents and prepared the room in the House of David that was used as a tabernacle before each *bingi* (worship service). Meetings were held on Saturdays from 10:00 A.M. to 6:00 P.M. and included Nyabingi songs, Bible readings, and the ritual discourse known as reasoning.[95] Sokoni, who had been widely recognized as a committed, knowledgeable, orthodox elder and teacher,

Sow in Tears, Reap in Joy 159

had commanded great respect and maintained a high level of cohesion within the group. Roberts, heartbroken by Sokoni's death on a personal level, worked hard to run the camp according to Sokoni's model, which followed the Nyabingi creed. Generally, the group was committed to the worship of Haile Selassie as the Almighty God and practiced a "livity" that included an ital diet, the exclusion of whites from membership and from entering the tabernacle, and the seclusion of women during the menstrual cycle. In this sense, the Jamaican Rastafarians in Tanzania reproduced patriarchal norms that were prevalent in the movement.

In response to a rift that emerged after Sokoni's death, unification became a major focus for Roberts and Tyhoye. During Sokoni's tenure as spiritual guide, biblical readings, the Ethiopian anthem, chants, and songs had been expressed as they were in Jamaica, using the Jamaican nation language, heavily influenced by Rastafari's unique lexicon. A family known as the Katondo brothers departed from Sokoni's approach when they decided that Kiswahili should now be the language of the bingis. While they argued that Kiswahili was more suitable because it was an African language, Roberts maintained that Kiswahili was no more African or "pure" than English because of its Arabic influences. He was not only eager to "uphold Sokoni's way of doing things" but also insisted that Rastafari had to be constituted from within the lexicon that gave it expression.[96] Yet, the Jamaican nation language connected Ras Ato to a specific cultural milieu, where Rastafari was illuminated within the syntax, vocabulary, mechanics, and cadence of the language that constituted it in Jamaica. This was not a local history to which the Katondo brothers were connected. They chose to remain with the Mbezi Beach group, but the issue remained unresolved.

The repatriates nurtured the idea that they, and not those in Morogoro, were the "authentic" Rastafarians. Ishii argues that both groups accused each other of being "heretical." The major fault line pertained to Haile Selassie's divinity. Though most Rastafarians would not claim proselytization as a typical feature of the movement, the repatriates saw themselves as teachers of the faith. As was the case within the wider movement, this religiosity sometimes pushed Rastafarians to present themselves as the "enlightened" ones with the knowledge to show Tanzanians the "right way." Two Tanzanian Rastafarian sisters reportedly argued that the group at Mbezi Beach "was a higher class since they worship Haile Selassie as god."[97] This suggests that some Tanzanians also saw the returnees as more "authentic." Still, there were also Tanzanians who had embraced Rastafari as a religion and accepted the divinity of Haile Selassie but who broke with the House of David in order to practice their perception of a purer and more faithful form of the Nyabingi branch of Rastafari. Among these was a group that broke from the Mbezi Beach group under the leadership of Ras Tekla, a South African who had migrated to Tanzania.[98] One of the members of this group, calling himself Ras Mabondo Mekonnen, saw himself and Tekla as Rastafarians representing the Emperor Haile Selassie I Rainbow Royal Circle Throne Ancient Mystical Order of Nyabingi, Tanzania.[99] Ras Mekonnen referred to their group as a "theocratic administration." In a way that duplicated the profound religious framework through which Karudi and Mkhululi understood their path as Rastafarians, Mekonnen began his correspondence with others in the "omnific name of the Most High Haile Selassie I, the first" and closed with "glory be to the Most High Haile Selassie the first and Empress Menen." Notably, Mekonnen's group challenged the male-centered outlook of the Jamaican repatriates when they acknowledged and praised the empress. This was particularly poignant because some diasporic Rastafarian men had been known to justify patriarchal attitudes by claiming that such attitudes were common in African societies. In addition, these continental Africans saw themselves as the "sons and daughters of Zion in Zion" who had established the "first [Rastafarian] churchical order devoid of the influence of the Rastafari elders who are already established in Tanzania."[100] In this case, continental Africans left the Mbezi house to form their own because of their belief that the repatriates were not "dealing with the Churchical order of Nyabingi." They insisted that they were a group of men and women who "accepted supreme responsibility of the Nyabingi order and its international programme." In an utter rejection of the notion that the Jamaican repatriates were the "real" and "authentic" Rastafarians, they considered it their duty to "raise up the order of Nyabingi from where it originate[d]" and they established linkages with the "East African community" in order to achieve that goal. This was a direct reference to and reclamation of the term "Nyabingi," which, as was detailed in chapter 1, originated in East Africa. Furthermore, they were "practicing [the] highest form of discipline, moral integrity and ital livity."[101]

The repatriates who believed that they were indeed the "authentic" Rastas expected Tanzanians to embrace all aspects of the Rastafarian philosophy and practice they presented, including the worship of Haile Selassie and their understanding of the ways in which Western powers had assaulted a "pure" Africa during colonial rule and continued to do so through contemporary neoliberal policies. While the geopolitical landscape meant that both Tanzania and Jamaica were subjected to similarly oppressive

Signature Rasta colors: Men carrying the version of the Ethiopian flag commonly associated with the reign of Haile Selassie I. The flag also bears an image of the Lion of Judah, a prominent Rasta symbol. Members of the Emperor Haile Selassie I Rainbow Circle Throne Ancient Mystical Order of Nyabingi, Tanzania. Courtesy of the National Anthropological Archives, Smithsonian Institution, Carole Yawney Papers, series 6, box 606, "Tanzania."

IMF policies and structural adjustment programs, Tanzanians had never imagined a pure and uncorrupted Tanzania. The repatriates accused Tanzanians of falling prey to colonial thinking by wearing Western clothing instead of the traditional Kanga. Rastafarians certainly waged similar critiques at those of African descent in Jamaica and beyond, but in Tanzania it was tied to their frustration over not being immediately and seamlessly understood.

Men and women of the Emperor Haile Selassie I Rainbow Circle Throne Ancient Mystical Order of Nyabingi, Tanzania, displaying the "upside-down trinity" symbol common across the different houses of Rastafari. The gesture, popularized by Haile Selassie I, is often used to represent oneness of purpose, spiritual continuity, and shared commitment. Courtesy of the National Anthropological Archives, Smithsonian Institution, Carole Yawney Papers, series 6, box 606, "Tanzania."

The repatriates expected all Tanzanians to immediately embrace them as Africans and not Jamaicans. Roberts complained that many local Tanzanians had continued to identify the repatriate Rastafarians as *wajamaika* (Jamaicans). He noted that Tanzanians who had become a part of the Rastafarian community in Mbezi Beach after Sokoni had started the first bingi had "of course learn[ed] certain things" and saw him as an African returning home. But, he experienced a "whole heap of tribulations" when he arrived in Tanzania and came to the "realization that the people [were] not thinking of I-n-I as being African." According to Roberts, "I wish I had known a lot more before I left [Jamaica] so that my hopes would not have been that high, so we would know what to expect. That was a real disappointment for me." Roberts's frequent trips to England also separated him from the average Tanzanian citizen. Every time he returned to Tanzania from his trips abroad, some people responded in a way that stressed the extent to which he was a

Sow in Tears, Reap in Joy

Beyond reggae and "peace and love": Members of the Emperor Haile Selassie I Rainbow Circle Throne Ancient Mystical Order of Nyabingi expressing their religious identity through clothing, images of Haile Selassie I (medallions), and rods. Courtesy of the National Anthropological Archives, Smithsonian Institution, Carole Yawney Papers, series 6, box 606, "Tanzania."

"different youth," an outsider: "I would return with things and they would throw words that I am not African anyway because I didn't give them what I had."[102]

From his vantage point, Roberts failed to see that his continued link to the diaspora allowed him certain privileges that marked him as an *mzungu* (foreigner) in Tanzania. In their studies of Rastafari in Tanzania, both Moyer and Ishii refer to this tension, which suggests that it was indeed a percep-

Nyabingi drumming session held by members of the Emperor Haile Selassie I Rainbow Circle Throne Ancient Mystical Order of Nyabingi, Tanzania. In a tribute to orality, djembe drums accompany a larger bass drum inscribed with Word, Sound, Power, a popular Rasta phrase describing positive vibrations in words and sounds. Rastafarians typically use the bass drum along with the kete and funde, not the djembe, which is associated with West Africa. Courtesy of the National Anthropological Archives, Smithsonian Institution, Carole Yawney Papers, series 6, box 606, "Tanzania."

tion held by some Tanzanians. Moyer reports that one complaint of the young Tanzanian men she interviewed was that the Jamaican Rastafarians did not acknowledge their "relative power and wealth."[103] From the perspectives of poor Tanzanians who did not travel, Roberts appeared privileged. He had experienced real poverty in Jamaica, but in connecting with the Rastafarians in England and making trips to visit them he had joined a very cosmopolitan Rasta network. Ras Bupe's travels to recruit Rastafarians had also made him into an itinerant Rastaman. Ishii astutely observes the contradiction inherent in Babylon simultaneously being the place from which to escape and "an important hub for the movement."[104] England was a source of moral and financial support, a veritable lifeline as Rastas faced the uncertainties of life in Tanzania.

This contradiction was not new within the black radical tradition. In his monumental study *Black Marxism*, Cedric Robinson examined the role of the British metropole in developing the radicalism of black intellectuals like George Padmore and T. Ras Makonnen during the 1930s. Robinson ponders the reality that someone like Padmore could vehemently oppose British imperialism while also maintaining "enthusiasm for the metropole." Yet, in the end, he notes, perhaps they "understood that the project of anti-imperialism had to be centered in the metropole. After their time and because of their work, decolonization and Black liberation would return to their native lands."[105] Rastafarian rhetoric has never suffered under the weight of "enthusiasm for the metropole," but as it did for their black intellectual forebears, England became a nurturing space for Rastas' antiracist, anti-imperialist radicalism. Unlike the Caribbean, it also provided opportunities to generate resources for repatriation. England and other parts of the diaspora acted as a safety net for the repatriates, and this was an option that Tanzanians lacked. When diasporic sensibilities failed to gain traction among some Tanzanians, the repatriates' connections to the diaspora affirmed and validated them. But England was not their home and, unlike many Jamaicans who identified as British subjects, they knew it. Theirs was a liminal space. But, they never lost the notion of Africa as home, or the desire to remain there, even when they complained that the Tanzanian government moved slowly.

The Tanzanian government's response to the Rastafarians was, in some ways, as protracted as decolonization itself. Karudi showed his frustration with what he deemed to be not only a slow bureaucratic process but the unwillingness of government officials to efficiently implement the "just decisions" of Nyerere, the "proved visionary and world statesman."[106] One might argue that this was inevitable, for though Mkhululi first approached Nyerere in the late 1970s, the right of entry for Rastafarians was not secured until December 1985, the same year that Nyerere left the presidency, and Tanzania (and the entire Third World project) had changed by then. The nation had begun to head in the direction of liberalization.[107] The economic crisis had begun in the 1970s, and by the mid-1980s the pressures and demands of structural adjustment programs forced African and Caribbean governments to alter their priorities. As Vijay Prashad demonstrates, the Third World "went into a tailspin" as a result of the "enforced debt crisis."[108] This was indeed an economic problem, but it was much larger than mere economics and deeply affected the "sovereign decision-making right of the African nations."[109] Within a climate that left these nations increasingly dependent on foreign aid, repression in universities became a harsh reality. This stifled creative thinking about nation building and had an impact far beyond academia. Pan-Africanism did not fit neatly into a neoliberal world agenda. Yet Nyerere remained active, retaining considerable influence in Tanzania, and the Rastafarians continued to exchange letters with government officials well into the 1990s. For instance, in 1992, the Ministry of Finance granted Mkhululi's request for an exemption from duty and sales tax on a vehicle and household furniture.[110]

By 1991, however, the language of the Tanzanian government had generally changed. Its first letter regarding repatriation, which documented the "right of entry" to "Black Africans living in Jamaica" in 1985, placed no restrictions on the number of Rastafarians that would be allowed to enter the country. But in 1991, a letter sent from the prime minister and vice president's office to the development manager in Kigoma on Ras Bupe's behalf focused clearly on "wajamaika weusi ambao tayari wako hapa nchini" (black Jamaicans already in the country). Furthermore, it stated unequivocally that all other Jamaicans who wished to live in Tanzania in the future "itabidi kufuata taratibu zote za uhamiaji nchini kwa mujibu sharia" (would be free to follow the country's immigration rules as stipulated by law).[111] The right of entry was no longer available to other Rastafarians in the diaspora.

・・・・・・

The Tanzanian state tried to facilitate the repatriation of Rastafarians amid the already challenging internal and external pressures the state faced in the 1980s. For Rastafarians, the land grant represented far more than a symbolic act; it signaled permanence and greater stability at home in Zion. The repatriation offers a unique prism for the evolution of Rastafari in the African context: the Rastafarians had negotiated difference within other multifaceted black communities, but had done so in diasporic sites like the United Kingdom and the United States. As an African hub of pan-African activity, Tanzania raised different questions and inspired different forms of negotiation. Tanzanians juggled multiple identities, including the cultural realities of ethnicity that were not a part of African diasporic experiences. Furthermore, though many black people across the diaspora had pursued an authentic experience of "Africanness," continental Africans could make claims to authenticity in ways that registered powerfully—and differently—from within Africa.

Beyond the daily struggles to conquer disease, acquire material resources, and adapt to local realities, repatriation became a window into how the religiosity, radical politics, and gender trouble of Rastafari traveled with Rastafarians from Babylon to Zion. The great extent to which Kisembo Karudi's memory of the journey contradicts that of her husband Ras Bupe Karudi serves as a cautionary tale to those who ignore the ways that masculinist renderings of Rastafari histories overshadow the presence and activism of Rastafarian women. Kisembo's story shows that women were not only present in the radical history of repatriation to Africa but also sacrificed for the revolution—and at great cost.

The religiosity and radical politics of Rastafari traveled with the repatriates and shaped the lives they led in Tanzania. Their connection to "black Afrikan individuals/personalities who have professed some degree of consciousness, seriousness and so concern for the welfare of their race" shows Rastafari's entrenchment in a far-reaching black network.[112] Many of the individuals who pledged their support for the repatriation, such as Al Hajj Anas M. Luqman and Jacob Carruthers, drew from the same intellectual genealogy that connected Rastafari to expressions of black cultural nationalism: a common thread that ran through Garveyism, the Nation of Islam, and the Moorish Science Temple. Yet as chapter 6 will show, Rastafari's connections were not limited to this circle. The repatriation's most reliable supporter was none other than C. L. R. James, a major thinker of the radical Left, who diverged ideologically from the other "individuals/personalities."

6 Strange Bedfellows

Rastafari, C. L. R. James, and the "Africa" in Pan-Africanism

On April 24, 1986, Ras Bupe Karudi wrote to C. L. R. James from Tanzania. Karudi greeted James in "the precious name" of Emperor Haile Selassie I and extended his sincere hope that James had "remained safe and well protected within the caring wings of the Almighty."[1] James emerged as a consistent and dedicated supporter of the repatriation, and Karudi regularly provided him with updates about the ongoing mission. In a subsequent note to James, Karudi continued to assert his sacred worldview, greeting James with "praises" to the "maker of heaven and earth, and all that therein dwells—Jah Rastafari!" Karudi provided constant reminders that Jah was "good" and "great" to the elderly and ailing James.[2] On several occasions, James had acknowledged the importance and power of religion in his writings. Still, as a Marxist, he remained ambivalent about religion, and it is not likely that he suffered Karudi's religious platitudes gladly. Received wisdom concerning the relationship between Marxist thought and religion would certainly propose that Karudi and James made for strange bedfellows.

The undeniable religiosity of the Rastafarians did not prevent them from forging useful and beneficial relationships with a wide cross section of black intellectuals and activists. Though James consistently supported African freedom from imperialism, he remained conflicted about African identity. He never fully accepted Africa as the cultural root of the West Indies, and never destabilized a Eurocentric notion of modernity. Unlike Rastafarians, in James's thinking, precolonial Africa did not oust Greece from its position as the bearer of civilization. After having established contact with James in December of 1985, Karudi secured James' full support of the repatriation. They corresponded frequently as Karudi acknowledged receipt of various monetary gifts from James, visited him whenever he traveled to England, and provided periodic updates about the process of setting up Jah Kingdom in Tanzania. Rastafari was a force that black intellectuals could not ignore.

• • • • • •

The relationship between religion and black radical thought changed in the era of independence. The African leaders who set the terms of pan-African politics did not bash religion, as did the elites of the early twentieth century. During those years, as black intellectuals sought to define the relationship between black people and various forms of Marxist thought, their embrace of Marxism eschewed religion. As a result, the important scholarship on the black intelligentsia in the early twentieth century has not, following the lead of the intellectuals themselves, centered religious discourses.[3]

But black internationalism during the interwar years was not devoid of religion. Lara Putnam has looked beyond the realm of educated elites to find evidence of religion's ubiquitous presence. Putnam has made it clear that religion was alive and thriving in black internationalist circles between the 1900s and 1930s. She rightfully locates religion among the "common people" and their "popular beliefs," noting the agency of laypeople to whom religion "mattered deeply." Putnam juxtaposes the religiosity of the people in the "British Caribbean migratory stream" with the secularism and downright disdain for religion among many of the black intellectual radicals in Harlem, such as Richard B. Moore.[4] This division between the intellectuals actively engaged with decrying religion as the "opium of the people" and the religiosity of common people works well for the interwar years, but the period of independence defies this inflexible division between religious people and irreligious elites.

This comfortable coexistence of religion and various iterations of Marxist concepts reflects one aspect of a larger shift from one historical period to another. Kwame Nkrumah and Julius Nyerere, unlike their intellectual forebears, did not seek to build pan-African connections through the institutional support of the Comintern. This is not to say that Nyerere seriously engaged Rastafarian religion. In fact, he informed Joshua Mkhululi and Ras Bupe Karudi that the religious interpretation of their mission was a matter with which they (and not the Tanzanian government) had to reckon. With great pragmatism they obliged, and left all religious references out of their interactions with Nyerere. That he was Catholic and Rastafari reserved its most venomous vilification of Eurocentric Christianity for the Catholic Church and the pope never came up in discussions. The point here is that, within the motley crew of black radicals who were at the forefront of pan-Africanism in the period of decolonization, religion was not solely the domain of the common people and did not stand in the way of alliances.

The Rastafarian mission to return to Africa happened in a specific historical moment and context. Nyerere and other African socialist leaders were inheritors of the intellectual labors of the internationally connected black intelligentsia of the first half of the twentieth century. They had been influenced by the different yet coexisting strands of black radicalism including the Pan-African Congresses and the Universal Negro Improvement Association as well as black intellectuals who "plotted their internationalism through the corridors of International Communism."[5] But the age of independence brought about considerable changes and allowed developments in each strand that had not been possible in earlier periods. For example, political independence created the conditions for a series of new developments: for the first time a Pan-African Congress was held in Africa, African state leaders could at least attempt to put into action some Garveyite ideas of self-determination that had been curtailed by the global politics of the interwar years, and these leaders did not seek to build networks through the institutional apparatus of the white radical left. Overall, with independence came an enormous change in attitude. In 1973, in preparation for the Sixth Pan-African Congress (6th PAC), to be held in Tanzania in 1974, James underscored this shift in his explanation of how the 5th PAC—held in Manchester, England, in 1945—differed markedly from the Sixth. "At the time of the 5th PAC," James recalled, "the issue for the African world was the fact that we were not only subordinate in ideas and in actual life to Western society, to those who led the world at the time, but we didn't have much prospects of emerging from that subordinate position." By contrast, he noted, the concerns at the sixth PAC were different because "since World War II and into the present time [1973], the attitude of blacks to Western civilization has changed immensely. In addition many positions have been won. For instance, in Africa and in the Caribbean, political independence has been won."[6]

James did not gloss over the extent to which political independence was an imperfect revolution. He did, however, fail to mention one of the key ways in which the African-centered leadership of socialists as the architects of pan-African politics in the era of independence did not resonate fully with some prominent black radicals from the English-speaking Caribbean, including himself. In the history of the dialogue between Africa and its diaspora in the West Indies, the intellectual intervention of African socialists like Nyerere represented a generative and revealing moment. As independent nations in Africa and the West Indies set about defining the postindependence path forward, the issue of national cultural identity was unavoidable. Continental Africans emerging from colonial rule had no choice but to contend with the long and complex cultures to which they remained undeniably connected. Neither the European education of African leaders nor their efforts to force different cultures into a composite "African" culture served to distance them from their known root cultures, which were altered to varying degrees, but never eliminated, under colonial rule. For African leaders and other continental Africans, even if they preferred to identify with a particular ethnic group instead of a homogenizing national identity, it was clear that their roots were on the continent.

This was not the case in the West Indies. Some diasporic Africans, including those in the Caribbean, had celebrated precolonial Africa as a source of black pride and inspiration in previous periods. But prominent black thinkers engaged with defining freedom in the decolonizing West Indies often saw Africa as one choice among others when constructing identity. Unlike continental Africans, West Indians of African descent in this period had been born in the West Indies, and many chose to see this as an opportunity for them to seek their cultural heritage in Europe. To a degree this represented a crisis of the colonial condition buttressed by the prevailing idea of the West Indies as a creolizing space disconnected from Old World roots. Yet ambivalent black West Indians could reject old Africa while claiming old Europe. James, who emerged as *the* West Indian figure to express the "great[est] interest" in the repatriation, epitomized such ambivalence toward Africa. He was a liminal figure in the larger shift from the pan-Africanism of the first half of the twentieth century to the later phase that found him donating time, support, and substantial sums of money to Rastafarian repatriation in the 1980s.

James was a black intellectual who was not religious, and certainly had a critique of Christianity. In 1985 he maintained the view that Christianity had been used to "justify the spread of slavery" and that worldwide progress depended on the pursuit of the goodness that had "hitherto been rejected under the name of Christianity."[7] Yet, Karudi repeatedly used religious references in his letters to James. Such references went beyond his typical framing of the repatriation in religious terms to offer direct religious instruction and benedictions to James. At a time when James was ill, Karudi frequently enquired about his health and reminded him to "do the exercise ... eat properly [and] try to forget the gin." He also suggested that James should keep his room "well ventilated and warm," but, "above all," he urged him to read Psalm 51 of the Holy Bible. In his deep appreciation for the fact that James repeatedly found the time to be "a physical and moral support,"

Karudi offered religious pronouncements such as "May Jah always be with you."⁸

More than any other figure, Karudi kept James abreast of developments in Tanzania and during his trips abroad to seek repatriates. Karudi visited James in England when he stopped there en route to Jamaica, and twelve days after arriving in Jamaica he wrote to James with an update on his efforts to recruit elders. He also thanked James for his first installment of "material support" in the amount of twelve hundred pounds, even enclosing a receipt for James's records.⁹ It was clear that James demanded accountability in the form of timely reports from Karudi regarding the use of the money, and Karudi continued to update James at every step of the journey. Karudi promised to visit with James in England on his way back to Tanzania and assured him that the "report on the period in Tanzania" from February to July 1986 (since the receipt of the "right of entry" from the Tanzanian government until Karudi's departure to recruit returnees) would be "forthcoming."¹⁰

In a letter to Karudi on December 27, 1985, which proved that Karudi had reached out to James before the Tanzanian government officially offered the right of entry, James stated that he had "listened with great interest" to Karudi's proposal for the future of the people of Africa and of African descent.¹¹ James expressed admiration for Karudi's mission while directly establishing ideological distance from Rastafarian "doctrines" about which James claimed to be ignorant: "I am particularly struck by your idea of the transfer of population from the Caribbean to Africa. I am impressed by the work you have done and I want here to publicly recognize while I cannot embrace your doctrines in general (because I do not know them) I would like in particular to express my admiration and concern for the future of your work in regard to populations of the Caribbean and of Africa."¹²

One can assume that, as a Marxist, James had very little patience for religion. Even so, he acknowledged its importance. Based on James's treatment of vodou in his seminal work *The Black Jacobins* and his treatment of millenarian movements in *The History of Negro Revolt*, Robin Kelley has argued that James "insisted that revolutionary mass movements take forms that are often cultural and religious rather than explicitly political."¹³ James saw value in the religious expressions of the rank and file, especially when religion acted as the fulcrum of resistance to oppressive forces. In a review of Orlando Patterson's novel *The Children of Sisyphus*, which dealt with the meaning of the Rastafarian presence in newly independent Jamaica, James addressed the Rastafarian movement in particular. He identified Rastafari as "the sect of Jamaican Negroes who reject the bastardized version of British society which official and educated Jamaica seeks to foist upon them." In addition, he explained that "they have created for themselves a new world in which the Emperor of Ethiopia, Haile Selassie, is God on earth. His kingdom in Africa is the promised Heaven to which all the Rastafari elect to go, not when they die but when they can raise the money for the passage." It is doubtful that when James penned this review in 1964 he would have seen himself as one who would be instrumental in helping a group of Rastafarians "raise the money for the passage." His comment on the practical side of repatriation was likely to have carried a hint of sarcasm. Up to that point, Rastafarian repatriation had been widely associated with an impractical religiosity that spurred on delusional Rastas to abandon their belongings and wait for the Black Star Line. James confirmed such assumptions when he referred to the "colossal stupidities" and "the insanities of the Rastafari" who nurtured "imaginative fantasies to escape to Africa."[14]

The condescending tone of such remarks notwithstanding, James provided a justification for these "fantasies," explaining that they resulted from Rastafarians' "conscious refusal to accept the fictions that pour in upon them from every side" and that repatriation came out of their "determination to get out of it." Additionally, his assessment of and attention to the dire circumstances of colonial and postcolonial Jamaica that provided the conditions for the emergence of Rastafari were indeed congruous with his long-standing belief in the efficacy and necessity of "revolution from below."[15]

It is also likely that James's support of Rastafarian repatriation to Tanzania was tied to his perception of Tanzania as a revolutionary state that was people-centered. In 1969 James bemoaned the fall of African states, noting that "as rapidly as it came, Africa began to descend . . . African state after African state falling apart and becoming decayed and degenerate."[16] Having been an active participant in the black internationalist formations that generated and contributed to the process by which African decolonization unfolded, James had been a key observer of key phases in the history of African liberation, noting the shifts and developments from one era to the next.

Following the coup in Ghana that ousted Kwame Nkrumah, James argued that the hope for the continent rested on Tanzania. In particular, he praised the efforts of Julius Nyerere, who, in James's estimation was "building not only a new economy, he's building a new government society and he's linking the mass of the people to those who are being educated."[17] In particular, James lauded the *Arusha Declaration*, Nyerere's policy document released in 1967, highlighting its leadership code and Tanzania's education policy as a truly revolutionary undertaking and what Africa needed. As James saw it, Nyerere was "ushering in something so entirely new that it ought to be a matter of great satisfaction to black people everywhere." Nyerere's approach was necessary "in order to get out of the rut of degeneration and degradation in which they have been declining ever since the victory of independence."[18] James seemed most impressed with what he perceived to be Nyerere's attempts to use the leadership code and the educational policy to ensure that an elite class would not be created and that leadership and education did not mean separation from the masses.[19]

As James highlighted the revolutionary position of the Tanzanian state—and in particular, its leader, Nyerere—he was really lauding what he perceived to be the state's attempts to privilege the people. Importantly, James's love affair with Tanzania seemed to endure even into the mid-1980s, long after Nyerere and the Tanzanian state more broadly had been critiqued for a top-down approach to governance and to the implementation of "villagization" in particular.[20] James was fiercely critical of the Sixth PAC, declaring it a failure, but did not seem to hold the Tanzanian government responsible for its role in the decision to exclude nonstate actors from the conference.[21] Though John McClendon has argued that James discussed and distributed copies of Issa Shivji's revealing critique of Nyerere in the 1970s, James did not publicly chastise Nyerere as he had Nkrumah.[22] This, along with unpublished writings that referred to Tanzania many years after the Sixth PAC, suggests that when Karudi reached out to James in 1985, James still held Tanzania in high esteem.

James praised Nyerere's education policy because it turned on his understanding that Nyerere was addressing the problem of nationalism that had plunged the continent into disarray and that Nyerere was trying to avoid the class separation between a formally schooled elite and the wider population. While this is undeniably true of Nyerere's intent, it did not represent the entirety of his platform. James appeared to be less concerned with Tanzania's efforts to craft a decidedly African-centered path—a point of connection between Nyerere and Rastafarian philosophy. As a crucial aspect of the liberatory project, Nyerere rejected colonial European education. In keeping with the basis of *ujamaa* (African socialism), Nyerere's "Education for Self-Reliance" was deeply concerned with not only an education that was rooted in precolonial Tanzanian ideas about education but one that freed Tanzanians from the oppressive nature of European education. Colonial education, Nyerere posited, was "motivated by a desire to inculcate the values of the colonial society and to train individuals for the service of the colonial state." In addition, he went on to juxtapose the "formalized" colonial European educational systems to "informal" African educational systems, noting that "they are different because the societies providing the education are different, and because education, whether it be formal or informal has a purpose."[23]

The anticolonialism of the Rastafarian movement and Tanzanian state officials, the latter led by Nyerere, saw the liberation of the mind as a central component of its struggles. In keeping with their emphasis on the reclamation of the dignity of the African, Rastafarians and these Tanzanian state officials aimed to affirm an African identity. As Tanzania and Jamaica had both experienced British colonialism, they identified the British colonial educational system as an integral part of a knowledge regime that was designed to miseducate African people.[24] Within such a context, colonial education was inextricably tied to the efficacy of colonialism as a system of knowledge production. Education was used to further disconnect Africans on the continent and across the diaspora from their African selves. Walter Rodney has concluded that "in the colonial system, it was not the people themselves, not the colonized, who set the terms and goals of their education." The colonizer's purpose "was to create or recreate them [colonized Africans] in his own image, to mutilate and transform the very sense of their African identity."[25]

Seven years after "Education for Self-Reliance" was published, Nyerere decided to expand his thoughts on the matter. This resulted in "Education for Self-Liberation," a document that reflected his radicalism and deep entrenchment in the ongoing liberation struggles in which education played such an important role.[26] Regretting that education in Tanzania had thus far been failing to cater to the specific needs of Tanzanians and turning them into "Black Europeans," he declared that "the primary purpose of education is the liberation of man." Underscoring the significance of mental emancipation, he added that "a man can be physically free from restraint and still be unfree if his mind is restricted by habits and attitudes which limit his humanity." Nyerere argued that mental emancipation was crucial if Tanzanians were going to see themselves as equal members of the human race "with the rights and duties of humanity." He demonstrated the primacy of one's state of mind in the liberation struggle in his assertion that "indeed it is only after men have been to some degree liberated mentally that the struggle for physical liberation can be waged with a hope of success."[27] This was a powerful assertion about the mental and psychological impact of colonialism and reflected Nyerere's general emphasis on mental liberation.

This pursuit of liberation loomed large in Rastafarian philosophy. The act of freeing oneself from mental enslavement had everything to do with the enlightenment that made the Rastafarian critique of colonialism possible. That colonialism constituted a powerful knowledge regime, and that "Babylon" had purposely distorted many truths in service of this regime demanded the skepticism that was the trademark of Rastas' interaction with the system. Indeed, Babylon "specialize[d] in obfuscating the truth and teaching the people 'misphilosophy.'"[28] Both Joshua Mkhululi and Ras Bupe Karudi agreed that under colonial rule in Jamaica they were "taught lies about Afrika in what was supposed to be the respectable school system." Rastafarians had always seen the colonial educational system as one of Babylon's most vicious tools, one that forced them to "sing praises to the queens and kings of England and other pirates who were knighted for their outstanding contribution to [the] capture and enslavement of black humanity."[29] The colonial educational system was particularly oppressive because it assumed, in the words of Paulo Freire, that "knowledge is a gift bestowed by those who consider themselves knowledgeable upon those who they consider to know nothing." Additionally, such a system "negate[d] education and knowledge as processes of enquiry" and projected an "absolute ignorance" unto the colonized.[30] The Rastafarian rejection of colonial values is rooted in a profound understanding of the characteristics of this system and the Rastafarian consciousness represents a pointed challenge to its premise. When Karudi revealed the process by which he came to understand the nature of his oppression in the West, he explained that "as a youth, by the rivers of Babylon (Jamaica)," he questioned and rebelled against Babylon's "miseducational system."[31] For Rastafarians, in the same way that the Christian churches of the West interpreted scripture in a way that justified the enslavement of Africans, the educational institutions of the colonial system deliberately constructed false truths about Africa and Africans. Rastafarian reggae singer Bob Marley demanded that Babylon "tell the children the truth" in light of the fact that the colonizers were "building church[es] and universit[ies]" and "deceiving the people continually."[32]

In contrast to the Rastafarian position, James did not emphatically reject colonial education. Rather than a form of indoctrination, James lauded the colonial education he had received in Trinidad as "first-class." He declared: "nobody that I know anywhere [was] getting a better education than

I was getting in the Caribbean between the years of 1901 and 1918."[33] In fact, he took pride in his mastery of European history and literature.

James's view of colonial education was consistent with his conception of Caribbean identity. He argued that the only thing that made Caribbean black people African was their black skin and that the effort of some to "make us all African" constituted merely "a defense against the European imperialism." Dismissing this as reactionary, he "did not think that the way to build against European imperialism [was] to build up the native." Yet, he was certain that Caribbean people "had to form what is in reality an extension of European civilization in the tropical Caribbean." James maintained that he had gone to Africa many times and knew a lot about it, "but the average man in the Caribbean belongs to western civilization not to Africa."[34]

Even so, by the 1980s James was a well-respected and prolific scholar-activist from whom black radicals sought support. His interactions with freedom fighters of African liberation movements demonstrate the seriousness with which he engaged African liberation. Ten months before he first established contact with Karudi, he agreed to allow the Namibia Support Committee to use his name as a sponsor for a conference that was held to commemorate Namibia's struggle against foreign domination in September 1984.[35] Only five months before he started to contribute to the Rastafarian repatriation efforts, a representative of the Pan-Africanist Congress of Azania wrote to James to thank him for a donation of thirty pounds toward its struggle.[36]

As a well-respected giant of the black intellectual tradition, James forged relationships with black radicals including African freedom fighters, Caribbean intellectuals, and African American black power advocates. Much of the reverence that such radicals felt toward James was generated by his groundbreaking text *The Black Jacobins*. James explained that he was motivated to write this book, which represented an onslaught on Western historiography, because he had grown tired of reading English and French sources about how black people "were born miserable" and "how they died miserable." He decided to "write something where the blacks do something. And the only place where I had read that the blacks had done something was in Haiti."[37] Hailed as a radical offering when it emerged in 1938, *The Black Jacobins* was an account of the Haitian Revolution that made black people the subjects and solidified James's place in the black intellectual tradition as a "black heretic."[38] Yet, his idea that Haiti represented the "only place" where "blacks had done something" suggests that for him, New

World blackness was not necessarily rooted in Africa. And while he was critical of Western education in terms of the class divisions it created between the elites and the populace, he remained firmly in its framework and never rejected it as the standard by which one became educated.

In reference to James's construction of Caribbean identity, Paget Henry and Paul Buhle have argued that because of the "colonial context in which this identity emerged, it was rather ambivalent."[39] They explain that this "ambivalence" comes from "the fact that colonial cultures tend to be hybrid formations—the results of processes of cultural penetration and control." James advanced this notion of hybridity when he argued that the "African . . . had to adapt what he brought with him to develop a philosophy and religion. His philosophy and religion proved to be a combination of what he brought with him to the particular circumstances that he found in his environment."[40] Yet discussion of the African component of Caribbean hybridity received very little attention from James; instead he emphasized the European nature of Caribbean identity.

Crucial to that identity was what James saw as its inherent connection to European languages. Beyond his sense of the facility that this connection gave to the populations of the Caribbean on the world stage, it spoke volumes about James's level of comfort with and acceptance of colonial society and the European languages that became the languages of Caribbean peoples. Whereas many Africans on the continent and in the Caribbean were at least conflicted about the impact of European languages on the colonized, James celebrated this as greater evidence of the ways in which Caribbean people were linked to Western civilization. As George Lamming notes, "James never abandoned the idea that the supreme good fortune of the Caribbean was its link to European civilization . . . and its link to what he would regard as the major languages." For Lamming this is the problem of the "Euro-centered James."

Though James remained ambivalent about Africa throughout his life, it is worth noting that his engagement with the continent did evolve over time. Italy's invasion of Ethiopia in 1935, which initiated the process by which the continent became the fulcrum for diasporic activism in the pan-African world, turned James's attention more intently to Africa. It also demonstrated the complexity within each period of pan-Africanism and cautioned against imposing intransigent ideological labels on black radicals like George Padmore and James. Between 1964, when he wrote the review of *The Children of Sisyphus,* and 1985, when he began to contribute to Rastafarian repatriation to Tanzania, James had been involved with the black radical activities centered on Africa. His work with the Center for Black Education, which was based in Washington DC, attests to this. Upon returning to the United States in 1968, James worked with black radicals including Charlie Cobb, Courtland Cox, and Jean Smiley, who formed the Center for Black Education. This organization reflected the eagerness of black radicals to return to Africa during this period and fostered ideological commitments that were similar to those of Rastafarians. The center's goal was "the total independence, sovereignty, and unification of all African people on the African continent and the Afro-Caribbean and the transportation of our people from European states to successful integration into Africa."[41] It also aimed to facilitate travel to Africa for individuals who wished to support the continent. This organization had also created the Drum and Spear Press initiative that was a precursor to the book project initiated by Karudi.[42] James's work with this organization over the course of five years contributed to his thinking and evolution in the area of pan-Africanism and connects him to the particular activism of this period.[43]

The major difference between James's ideas and those of Rastafarians turned on the matter of identity: while James embraced and celebrated a European basis for Caribbean identity, Rastafarians rejected Europe and saw Africa as the root of the Caribbean. Rastafarians advanced a rigid dichotomy between Babylon (the Western world, as created by Europe) and Zion (Africa). At the center of Rastafarian philosophy was the idea of the African in the Caribbean existing in a state of anomie, dispossession, and exile. The creation of a Rastafarian lexicon demonstrates the emphasis Rastafarians placed on epistemological questions. Beyond Rastafari, Caribbean literary figures such as George Lamming and African literary figures such as Ngugi wa Thiong'o have also examined the impact of the colonial experience in terms of language and have struggled with the implications of expressing themselves in what they perceived to be "languages of exile."[44] Nyerere had similar ideas in mind when he made Kiswahili the national language of Tanzania; it was indeed an important part of his decolonization project. Yet James never experienced English as a language of exile and, unlike Rastafarians, did not reject European culture and influence.[45] Where James saw European colonialism as the basis for a modern and therefore potentially revolutionary Caribbean, Rastafarians saw the evils of a capitalist, oppressive influence that Africans in the Caribbean must reject in order to assert their subjectivity and core African identity. Where they saw brainwash, James saw an opportunity for progress. Rastafarians deconstructed the European modernity that evolved in opposition to the notion of African barbarism, primitivity, and traditionalism. Therefore, Rastafarians saw nothing positive in Europe's influence. In fact, in order to be civilized and humane, European mores had to be thrown off. This was the nature of their pan-Africanism and anticolonialism.

· · · · · ·

Despite such ideological differences, James maintained an enduring interest in Rastafarian repatriation and was a constant source of both moral and material support. In the final analysis, the interactions between James and Karudi reinforced the reality of the pan-African agenda as one that was broadly defined and encompassed a multiplicity of subjectivities and viewpoints. James, like others from whom the Rastafarians sought support, did not agree with all aspects of Rastafarian thought, but he understood the historic context of repatriation to Africa and lauded the attempts of Rastafarians to create their world anew, based on the anti-imperialist, anticolonial posture to which James remained committed.

Epilogue

Kisembo Karudi left Tanzania for England in 1998. She was no longer willing to tolerate Ras Bupe Karudi's worsening efforts to exercise complete control over her life, and she was determined to protect and to educate her children. But she was not willing to leave Tanzania for good. Though the marriage was seriously strained, she returned to Tanzania frequently with the intention to retire there. She also continued to support Ras Bupe financially, and she eventually purchased the house they had rented in Karakata with the money she earned working in England.

Kisembo's role in the repatriation underscores the need to venture beyond the male-centered narratives that have dominated histories of Rastafari and of pan-Africanism more broadly.[1] The present volume has focused on her experience while also demonstrating the great extent to which pan-African politics were deeply informed and shaped by women's own understanding of their activism, as well as the relationships between Rastafarian men and women. Rather than an easily classified, one-dimensional position, Kisembo's pan-Africanism included both acceptance of and resistance to male dominance. In the specific case of Rastafarian repatriation, the move to Africa as a family magnified and clarified her husband's gendered interpretation of the struggle and created the circumstances under which she pondered her own interpretation.

As a Rastafarian woman, Kisembo's particular brand of pan-Africanism could not be severed from her religious commitments. The way she defined and redefined her pan-Africanism in Zion reinforced what Ras Bupe Karudi and Joshua Mkhululi had established in their writings: that their struggle to return home to Africa was "of [both] spiritual and historical significance."[2] As *Jah Kingdom* details, their explanation of the religiosity of Rastafari inspired analysis of how Tanzanian Rastafarians as continental Africans have either accepted or rejected the idea of Emperor Haile Selassie I as God. Outside of the written documentation of both men, Kisembo's religiosity corroborated their understanding of the role of religion in the repatriation. But her experience demands a more expansive treatment of the role of religion in pan-African movements. In particular, within Rastafari, religion, gender, and pan-African activism are inseparable.

The mission to "set up Jah Kingdom," which began in the 1970s, has left a legacy yet to be explored. Future studies will build on the fieldwork conducted by Miho Ishii in 1998, which rightly underscored Tanzania (and Africa more broadly) as a rich site that "demands new investigation" of Rastafari. The repatriates became the "center of the Rastafarian movement" in Tanzania and have been "influential to the ideas and activities of Rastas in and around" the country. Several Rastafarian groups emerged in the 1990s, and among them was the Mbigiri commune, which gained the status of a nongovernmental organization in 1995. This marked a turning point, as Rastafari moved from a street corner phenomenon to a movement that gained recognition through its efforts to establish communes. This development connected a group of Tanzanian Rastafarians to Rastafari's established engagement with communal living. In the case of Mbigiri, the commune represented a desire to leave the crisis of urban life in Dar es Salaam and to return to the *shamba* (farm).[3] In this sense, Rastafari, formed in the diaspora, became the vehicle by which local Tanzanians connected with *ujamaa*, the national socialist platform that originated in Tanzania. Along with the quest for a better life that seemed to evade them in the urban space of Dar es Salaam, the return to the *shamba* also represented the fact that Rastafari's celebration of African "tradition" and "roots" also resonated with Tanzanian Rastas.[4]

Alongside the Mbigiri commune, the growth of Rastafarian groups in Tanzania gained the attention of several local newspapers in Tanzania in the late 1990s.[5] Rastafari in Tanzania, like the larger movement that had started in Jamaica, was a diverse one, yet the content of that diversity featured elements that reflected the African context. Those who claimed Rastafari included some who followed the teachings of the repatriates closely. Others seemed to easily combine Rastafari with their identity as Muslims. Future work could also explore whether or not Rastafarian practice in Tanzania has been combined with indigenous African religions, thereby reconciling the contradiction inherent in the propensity of many Rastafarians to frown upon such religions.

The growth of Rastafari in the late 1990s also had implications for the relationship between Rastafari and the Tanzanian state. With Rastafari came dreadlocks and the use of *bangi* (ganja/marijuana), also known as *dawa* (medicine). Some Tanzanian Rastafarians reported having been targeted for *bangi* use and being shaven while in police custody. Marijuana had been a separate local issue in Tanzania,[6] but because of its use as a Rasta sacrament, locals and law enforcement personnel came to associate it with Rastafarians.[7] As Ishii reports, some Tanzanian Rastafarians began to see the state's response to this as repressive and representative of a "Babylon system." Future works might also discern whether or not this idea was pervasive, as it stands to substantiate a clear irony: the same state that Jamaican repatriates salute for the pan-African practice that made their return home from Babylon to Africa possible was later perceived to be the Babylon of Tanzanians who embraced Rastafari.

Jah Kingdom also offered a methodological imperative to the study of pan-Africanism. The history of Rastafari's entrenchment in a far-reaching pan-African network calls for a particular approach to the histories of black radicals who lived and thought about the freedom struggle in transnational terms. Instead of a framework that privileges the nation-state and the national archive, "trodding diaspora" offers an analytical (and archival) approach that is transnational, multisited, and sometimes multilingual. This grounds the transnational dimensions of pan-Africanism, tying the pursuit to uncover such histories to the issue of historical evidence and the whereabouts of the archives necessary to write pan-African histories. This methodology translates into a much more capacious framing and understanding of the interplay between Africa and its diaspora.

・・・・・・

On May 20, 2016, Ras Bupe Karudi died in the Muhimbili National Hospital in Dar es Salaam, having succumbed to the injuries he sustained in a car accident. He was laid to rest ten days later. Along with Kisembo and her children Kiyende and Nyamekye, the Rastafarian men and women of Tanzania celebrated Ras Bupe's life with the respect paid to a much loved leader and pioneer. Joshua Mkhululi had garnered a similar outpouring of respect and affection when he was buried in Arusha in 2009. Of the twenty-six original repatriates, only two remain. Kisembo and her son Nyamekye have decided to keep the house she owns and will leave England permanently in the near future.

No one could have predicted that a once ostracized movement on the fringes of Jamaican society would get an African government to validate its philosophy and grant its followers the opportunity to realize arguably the most elusive of Rastafarian dreams. The Rasta men and women who mustered the courage to actualize the dream of repatriation to Africa created the unique pan-African history detailed in the preceding pages. Movement in search of a better life has featured prominently in the history of those of African descent in the Caribbean and across the diaspora more broadly. Jamaican history in particular has seen migration to places like Cuba and Panama in search of work and opportunities in the nineteenth century, and to the United States and England in the twentieth century.[8] The move to Africa, however, was very different. Embedded in repatriation to Africa was something much greater than a quest for a different material reality. The Rastafarians were not immigrants; they were returning Africans, *repatriates*, and analyses and assessments of their journey must take this distinction into account. At its core is a renewal of self: the physical act of a spiritual, psychological, and epistemological shift from what Rastafarians see as an imposed diasporic identity to one that affirms their dignity as black people and human beings.

In terms of their personal lives, there was indeed a great deal at stake. They were leaving the only reality they had ever known, and they were leaving loved ones behind. Like their ancestors who fled New World plantations with little real knowledge of life beyond their gates, Rastafarians stepped out on faith, convinced that freedom and self-determination would undoubtedly be better than the life they had been forced to endure. They certainly gained. They proved to the world that they strived to bring Rastafarian philosophy and action together. Additionally, they benefited from being closer to the front line of the African liberation struggle, which allowed them to act as Africans, thereby putting into action Rastafari's core objective. Their individual sacrifices, when put together, had an impact on Tanzania's growth, which constituted their contributions to Africa's development. For example, Mkhululi made his mark in university education by training Tanzanians in the areas of accounting and finance. His contribution came at a time when the country's dependence on foreign personnel for basic governmental offices undermined its commitment to self-reliance.

Despite the obstacles he and the other Rastafarians endured, Iman Mani remained grateful for what he accomplished in Tanzania. He was employed as a journalist by the *Daily News*, Tanzania's oldest English-language newspaper, and decided to live in Dar es Salaam with his Tanzanian wife and their two children. In addition, as a result of Karudi's school for the "likkle [sic] children of Zion," a number of Tanzanian adults will connect a Rastaman to the memories of their formative years. Children from different ethnic groups and religious traditions performed a daily ritual that signified the coming together of Africa and its diaspora in Karudi's school. Upon arrival each morning the children greeted Karudi with the obligatory salutation of respect for an elder, "Shikamoo," to which he would answer "Marahaba," the typical response of the elder. This exchange in Kiswahili was followed by a Rastafarian exchange: the children said "Selassie I," and Karudi responded with the usual "Rastafari."[9] The final repatriate, Saburi Omega, arrived in Tanzania in 1989. He still lives there and has successfully established a "food therapy program," which encourages the use of food as medicine, and recommends healthy food choices to a loyal following.[10]

When the Tanzanian government revoked its open invitation to "black Jamaicans" in 1991, Mkhululi and Karudi had not managed to bring about a mass exodus of Rastafarians from Babylon to Tanzania. Yet Rastafarians the world over benefited from their efforts to actually live a dream that they, along with many others across the African diaspora, had fostered in pursuit of freedom. The repatriation may inspire many to ponder whether or not this group of Rastafarians accomplished their aims. Were they better off for having left the Caribbean for Africa? Did the hardship they faced in Tanzania pale in comparison to that which they had known in Jamaica? What, in the end, did they gain? What, if anything, did they lose?

Rastafari's assertion of African identity forced Jamaica to contend with a portion of the population that could not, by choice, be included in the nation. Ironically, the Jamaican state's foreign policy under Michael Manley helped to facilitate the actual departure of the Rastafarians in this study through sustained linkages with Julius Nyerere and Tanzania. The Rastafarian threat to Jamaican nationhood forced the state into a dialogue with Africa, and by extension, repatriation centered the great extent to which the histories of the Caribbean and Africa were closely intertwined. The return reinforced what Rastas always knew: national borders within the black world were arbitrary and more porous than nationalism and its advocates cared to admit.

As such, pan-Africanism remained alive and well, even after nationalism triumphed as the route to independence. Analyses of its continued resonance have only just begun in earnest, having disappeared into the shadows of a robust investigation of nationalism and its discontents. Furthermore, the missteps of black elites and the rise of neoliberalism foreclosed discussion of the radical, alternative visions that persisted in a so-called postcolonial world. In effect, it foreclosed an engagement with hope. Proof of this lies in the language of crisis that has come to dominate scholarly and popular interpretations of the state of Africa and the Caribbean since the 1980s. This approach to African affairs has been captured by the term "Afro-pessimism," while political theorists of the Caribbean have captured the general tone of disillusionment with terms such as Obika Gray's "predation politics," Brian Meeks's "hegemonic dissolution," Louis Lindsey's "myth of independence," and Anthony Bogues's "postcolony."[11] Along with the early observations of Frantz Fanon, C. L. R. James, and Walter Rodney, fictional engagement with Africa and the Caribbean had signaled the anxieties since the early years of independence. For example, Orlando Patterson's *The Children of Sisyphus* offered a raw, unrelenting look at life for black people in an impoverished Jamaican community.[12] With Rastafarians as leading characters, it also established their importance in the postindependence moment. Chinua Achebe's *A Man of the People* accomplished something similar for Nigeria, focusing on the misdeeds of the elite class.[13] These insightful observers saw the challenges of the postindependence moment and rightfully critiqued newly installed black governments for their role in perpetuating inequalities of various forms.

In 1990, a year after the Rastafarians received land in Tanzania, Julius Nyerere underscored the grave situation in which the people of the world who inhabited what he referred to as the Global South lived. As chairman of the South Commission, Nyerere concluded that the north was comprised of the "rich, industrialized and powerful," countries that had control over the International Monetary Fund and other "powerful institutions." By contrast, the south was made up of countries that were underdeveloped, powerless, and poverty-stricken. Thirty years after the euphoria of independence in 1960's Africa, Nyerere was clear that the north still had "dominance in all fields," which it fiercely protected for its own selfish needs. Indeed, he condemned the north for instituting and maintaining financial and political "structures and practices" that "help[ed] to perpetuate the underdevelopment of the south and its off-shoots: poverty, ignorance, malnutrition and disease."[14] This was the harsh reality in which Rastafarians tried to make a life in Tanzania. African states and African people within them were as deeply affected by the inequities of a capital-driven world as were those of African descent across the diaspora.

The kind of collaboration depicted in this volume represents both a continuation of a tradition that preceded independence from colonial rule and a pan-Africanism that adapted to the failures of nationalism. This took into account the variances within the global black community and the geopolitical landscape that lionized a racial hierarchy and capitalism. Africans at the state and nonstate levels understood that along with racism, they were dealing with capitalism and its attendant dismissal of true equality for all. They also knew that some black people sought to define freedom within capitalism's web. Capitalism's reach rendered alternative visions wildly utopian. Rastafari, with its critique of both racism and capitalism, fit perfectly within the orbit of the pan-African agenda that made a valiant effort to stave off the machinations of international capital and to secure real freedom for black people in the process. Furthermore, Rastafarians certainly defied the expectations of the British colonial official who declared in 1959 that "the Rastafarite cult is not likely to attract intellectuals and the majority of the members of the cult are of low mentality."[15]

Yet the movement has fallen prey to the reductionist and sanitized narratives that strip oppositional movements of their radicalism. Rastafari's dynamic and ever-poignant critiques of racism and capitalism throughout the 1970s and beyond have been concealed by the focus on Rastafari as popular culture. The movement has been subjected to the same hegemonic structures that have frozen Martin Luther King Jr. in his "I Have a Dream" speech, extracted only "one love" from Bob Marley and converted Nelson Mandela the freedom fighter into Mandela, the lovable voice of reconciliation. This incomplete memory of social movements and black radicals has consequences for the history of the radical tradition by marginalizing more nuanced renderings of that history. It also ignores the fact that, in the face of an oppressive geopolitical landscape, people have continued to struggle and to define themselves against and outside oppressive structures.

The focus on culture reproduces the claim that the radical pan-African politics of Rastafarians was no longer relevant after independence from colonial rule. It has also encouraged a paradigm that shifts ownership of Rastafarian evolution and meaning away from Rastafarians. Beyond their personal stories was what their repatriation to Tanzania exposed about the dialogue between Africa and its diaspora, and about Rastafari's capacity to enhance this dialogue in meaningful ways. It is through the framework of the "trod" that we most effectively explore the meaning and purpose of Rastafari's enduring presence in the world.

By introducing Rastafarian philosophy and practice to Tanzanian locals, Ras Ato Kidani Roberts and Ras Kwetenge Sokoni instigated profound conversations about the relevance of Rastafari to continental Africans other than state officials. Most poignant was the revelation that Africans in an East African space could accept Emperor Haile Selassie as God, which destroyed the assumption that the Rastafarian veneration of an actual (continental African) man could only manifest in a place of exile where exilic yearning was far removed from local realities. This, along with the struggle over authenticity between Jamaican and Tanzanian Rastafarians, demands that studies of the evolution of Rastafari as a religion take seriously how Africa has talked back to its diaspora. Most powerfully, the conflict over authenticity, common in global black histories, shows that Rasta did indeed expand to include continental Africans. Founded in the diaspora, Rastafari has called out to Africa, and through local Tanzanians who embraced Rastafari and claimed it as their own, Africa answered. What greater validation and justification for continuing to study Africa and its diaspora in tandem?

From scholars to colonial actors, Jamaican state officials, and citizens, Rastafarian repatriation has not been given the serious attention it deserves. Beyond the notion that repatriation constituted an unrealistic, escapist approach to New World problems, the common Rastafarian belief that repatriation would unfold according to providential design further relegated it to the realm of the fanciful. The history of Rastafarian investment in such an approach—made palpable by numerous examples of them ignoring the need for travel documents and waiting for Marcus Garvey's Black Star Line—has overshadowed the actual history of repatriation and its meaning, particularly after the site of inquiry shifted to Africa. This has much to do with the religious aspects of Rastafari, which saw its followers ground political claims in the moral and sometimes cosmic language of religion. This was not an anomaly in the long history of black diasporic movement, as the widespread reliance upon the exodus narrative attests.[16] Yet while Rastafari owes much to Christianity, the veneration of Haile Selassie has added another layer of cynicism and ridicule to the scrutiny of those who dismiss repatriation. Repatriation, however, is more than just the stuff of dreams and unbridled optimism. Sometimes dreams become real.

Rastafarians lived the negotiation between Africa and its diaspora, and learned about the ways in which diasporic creations did not always neatly fit on the continent. Aspects of their repatriation dreams were romanticized and problematic. This is indeed typical of any effort to plug a global imaginary into a local space. They also learned about the strength of their global perspective and the importance of their intellectual contributions to pan-Africanism. Nyerere, the officials who worked with the Rastafarians, and some Tanzanian locals understood and shared their political orientation. This showed the wider movement what was possible through repatriation beyond Ethiopia. And they demonstrated the power of Rastafari not only to evolve, grow, and adapt to different geopolitics and still remain relevant, but to also remain an enduring path to freedom.

Notes

Introduction

1. For Ras Bupe Karudi, naming was an important expression of his commitment to black radical thought and to repatriation in particular. He rejected the name given to him by his parents (Sydney Headley) and chose Ras Bupe Karudi. "Karudi" comes from the Kiswahili verb "Kurudi," which means "to return," and demonstrates the extent to which he identified as "the one who returned." As the endnotes in chapter 5 show, in some of the primary documents Karudi penned during the late 1980s, he also referred to himself as "Jah Bupe Akiiki Karudi."

2. Kisembo Karudi, interview with the author, July 16, 2016, London, UK.

3. I will use "Rastafarian movement," "Rastafari," and "Rasta" interchangeably to refer to the movement at large.

4. Gebrekidan, *Bond without Blood*; Price, "Cultural Production of a Black Messiah."

5. For excellent examples, see Sterling, *Babylon East*; Hansin, *Rasta, Race and Revolution*; Middleton, *Rastafari and the Arts*.

6. On Rastafarian repatriation to Ethiopia, see Bonacci, *Exodus!*; for a study of Ethiopian responses to Rastafarian repatriation, see MacLeod, *Visions of Zion*.

7. Bones, "Repatriation: The Way Forward," *Voice of Rasta* 33 (October–November 1981): 5.

8. The coexistence of transnationalism/movement and the investment in rootedness rejects a dichotomy established between the two in the literature on the African diaspora. See Gilroy, *Black Atlantic*. For an illuminating discussion of this tension see Campt, *Other Germans*, chap. 5.

9. While the present project focuses on the African diaspora located in the Caribbean, I recognize that the African diaspora is a more global idea that goes far beyond the Atlantic world. Works that examine the African diaspora as it pertains to the Asia, Europe, the Indian Ocean, and the Mediterranean include Alpers and Caitlin-Jairazbhoy, *Sidis and Scholars*; Hunwick, "African Slaves in the Mediterranean World,"; Harris, *Global Dimensions of the African Diaspora*; Jayasuriya, *African Diaspora*; and Jayasuriya, *African Identity in Asia*.

10. Gilroy, *Black Atlantic*; Hall, "Cultural Identity and Diaspora"; Appiah, *In My Father's House*.

11. See, for example, Gilroy, *Black Atlantic*.

12. Exceptions include Gomez, *Exchanging Our Country Marks*; Warner-Lewis, *Guinea's Other Suns*; and Warner-Lewis, *Central Africa in the Caribbean*.

13. Pierre, *Predicament of Blackness*, 4.
14. Chude-Sokei, "Roots, Diaspora and Possible Africas," 227.
15. See Hartman, *Lose Your Mother*.
16. Tanzania (formerly Tanganyika) was colonized by Germany in 1891, but was formally mandated to Britain by the United Nations in 1919, after World War I. In 1946 Tanganyika was administered as a UN Trusteeship Territory by Britain until it gained its independence in 1961. It merged with the island of Zanzibar to form the Republic of Tanzania in 1964.
17. Falola, *Nationalism and African Intellectuals*, 27.
18. As headquarters of the Liberation Committee of the Organization of African Unity, Tanzania was a safe haven for liberation movements including the African National Congress (South Africa), the South West Africa People's Organization (Namibia), the Frente de Libertação Moçambique (Mozambique), and the Zimbabwe African National Union and Zimbabwe African People's Union (Zimbabwe).
19. Karioki, *Tanzania's Human Revolution*, 99.
20. See, for example, Brown, *Fighting for Us*; and Rickford, *We Are an African People*.
21. Coulson, *Tanzania*; for Nyerere's own perception of the paradoxes, see Nyerere, *Arusha Declaration Ten Years After*.
22. The literature on the paradoxical history of villagization in Tanzania is rigorous. For studies that focus on the state in their critique of villagization, see Schneider, "High on Modernity?"; Schneider, "Developmentalism and Its Failings"; Jennings, "We Must Run While Others Walk"; Bender, "For More and Better Water, Choose Pipes!"; Scott, *Seeing like a State*; Finucane, *Rural Development and Bureaucracy in Tanzania*; and Ingle, *From Village to State in Tanzania*. For a study that calls for a less-state-centered approach that considers other influences and realities on the ground see Lal, "Self-Reliance and the State".
23. Aminzade, *Race, Nation, and Citizenship in Post-Colonial Africa*, 12. For an excellent introduction to dissent within Tanzania, see Maddox and Giblin, *In Search of a Nation*.
24. For a more in-depth engagement with how the idea of Africa has been invented by different historical actors, see Mudimbe, *Invention of Africa*; Ferguson, *Global Shadows*.
25. Homiak, "When Goldilocks Met Dreadlocks," 60–61.
26. On the orality of Rastafari, see Pollard, *Dread Talk*; Prince Williams and Michael Kuelker, *Book of Memory*.
27. Iton, *In Search of the Black Fantastic*. Giulia Bonacci shows that some Rastas have made claims on Ethiopian nationality and are not antistatist per se. See Bonacci, *Exodus!*
28. This point has been made for the postcolonial African archive. See Allman, "Phantoms of the Archive."

29. For an insightful discussion of the difficulties some scholars of Rastafari face in attempting to gain the trust of Rastafarians, see Homiak, "When Goldilocks Met the Dreadlocks."

30. Beyond the papers that exist in the private collections of Rastafarian organizations worldwide, the National Anthropological Archives of the Smithsonian Institution, which curated an exhibition on the Rastafarian movement in 2008, is home to organizational papers that attest to this documentary trail.

31. Schneider, "Tanzania National Archives."

32. For a recent and insightful discussion of such issues, see the articles in Helton, ed., "The Question of Recovery: Slavery, Freedom, and the Archive," special issue, *Social Text* 33, no. 4 125 (2015).

33. The Bobo Shanti, a centralized group, was founded in 1958 by King Emmanuel. Its followers maintain a commune in Bull Bay, Jamaica, where they observe strict lifestyle rules such as the seclusion of women during menstruation and a holy sabbath. More on the Twelve Tribes of Israel and the Nyabingi in chapter 1. The Ethiopian World Federation and the Ethiopian Orthodox Church have also been crucial to Rasta's evolution.

34. My thanks to Jahlani Niaah for this concept of a "launch pad diaspora." I use it here to refer to England's role as not only a part of the African diaspora from where Rastafarians departed to Africa, but also its role as a space where Rastafarians from Jamaica created a Rastafarian diaspora within the wider African diaspora.

35. Campbell, *Rasta and Resistance*, 187.

36. Center for Contemporary Cultural Studies, *Empire Strikes Back*, 99, 124, 128–29, 130, 131, 290.

37. Gilroy, *There Ain't No Black in the Union Jack*, 187, 191. Campbell, *Rasta and Resistance*, 189, argues that the movement in the United Kingdom was a "relatively short phase, essentially 1975–1979." For Rasta in the UK, also see Ernest Cashmore, *Rastaman*, and Len Garrison, *Black Youth, Rastafarianism and the Identity Crisis in Britain*.

38. Gilroy, *There Ain't No Black in the Union Jack*, 192.

39. Homiak, "Rastafari," 257.

40. Kelley, *Freedom Dreams*, 16.

41. Jah Bones, "Rasta Evidence to Scarman Inquiry," *Ethiopian World Federation—Voice of Rasta* 35 (1982): 3, Black Cultural Archives, Periodicals, 116Brixton, London.

42. The Coral Gardens Affair of 1964, the most violent act of the postcolonial state against Rastafari, marked the movement's marginal status in Jamaica. See Deborah Thomas's film *Bad Friday*, which details the incident, as well as the politics of how it has been remembered. In the United States, surveillance of black radicals took the form of COINTELPRO, an acronym for Counter Intelligence Program, which referred to a series of covert operations that were used by the Federal Bureau of Investigation to destroy what the United States perceived to be revolutionary movements that posed a threat to national security. This was matched in

the Caribbean by the repression of West Indian governments that acted, in the words of Walter Rodney "within the context of anti-communist and anti-socialist hysteria." See Walter Rodney, "Contemporary Political Trends in the English Speaking Caribbean," *Black Scholar* 7, no. 1 (September, 1975): 20.

43. For more on the planning of the conference and the controversy surrounding the Tanzanian government's decision, see James Garrett, "Historical Sketch: The Sixth Pan African Congress."

44. "Caribbean Militants Denounce Pan African Congress," *Daily Gleaner*, July 1, 1974.

45. Quoted from the original call for the conference, which James himself helped to write. James, "Towards the Seventh," 13.

46. Carter to Department of State, Telegram 02167, June 29, 1974, 1974DARES03167, Central Foreign Policy Files, 1973-79/ Electronic Telegrams, RG59: General Records of the Department of State, National Archives (accessed June 9, 2015), U.S. National Archives, Washington, DC.

47. I expand upon this point in chapter 1 based on evidence from Rasta and Rasta-inspired periodicals that emerged in Jamaica in 1968–69.

48. Jah Bupe Akiiki Karudi to C. L. R. James, September 6, 1986, Box 7 Folder 192, CL.R. James Papers, Special Collections, U.W.I. Trinidad.

49. Henry, *Caliban's Reason*.

50. On the shift to liberalization in Tanzania, see Lofchie, *Political Economy of Tanzania*; and Campbell and Stein, *Tanzania and the IMF*.

51. Walter Rodney, "Africans Abroad in Jamaica," unpublished manuscript, n.d. (early 1970s), box 13, folder 11, Robert W. Woodruff Library.

52. Waters, *Race, Class and Political Symbols*, 306.

53. Cooper, "Possibility and Constraint."

54. My treatment of this is in contrast to recent historical work on race in Africa, which has shifted the focus away from European conceptions of race that lionize a black/white dichotomy to examinations of how Africans have contributed to race making in different contexts. See Glassman, *War of Words, War of Stones*; El Hamel, *Black Morocco*; and Powell, *Different Shade of Colonialism*.

Chapter One

1. For a discussion of the role of fire within Rastafari, see Chevannes, *Rastafari: Roots and Ideology*, 160.

2. Governor H. M. Foot to His Excellency Douglas Laird Busk, CMG, August 16, 1956, FO 371/138109, British National Archives.

3. Governor Blackburne to Secretary of State for the Colonies, June 10, 1959, FO 371/138109, British National Archives.

4. "Racism," *URIA Voice* 4 (1984): 12, Anthropological Archives, Smithsonian.

5. In 1981 the organization Rastafari International, which was based in London, organized a conference to discuss the "burning issue of repatriation." A report of

the conference can be found in *Voice of Rasta* 32 (1981), Periodicals, box 114-119, Black Cultural Archives, Brixton, London.

6. "Doctrine & Principles," *URIA Voice* 4 (1984): 6, Anthropological Archives, Smithsonian.

7. "Institutionalize [sic] and Systematic Racism," *URIA Voice* 2 (1984): 1-3, Anthropological Archives, Smithsonian.

8. Ibid., 2. Clergy represented the Church of England across the Caribbean, they invested in slave plantations and they employed a biblical hermeneutic that justified the enslavement of Africans; see Bennett, *Bondsmen and Bishops*. For a concise and informative summary, see Beckles, *Britain's Black Debt*.

9. Moore and Johnson, *Neither Led nor Driven*, 271.

10. For more on the cultural contributions of the Africans who arrived in Jamaica after emancipation, see Schuler, *Alas, Alas, Kongo*.

11. The British colonizers criminalized, pilloried, and dismissed Afro-Jamaican religious practices with such labels as paganism, savagery, magic, superstition and witchcraft. This was consistent with the way in which missionaries, anthropologists, and colonial administrators had characterized the indigenous religions they encountered on the African continent. Western conclusions about these religions reinforced the Hegelian notion that all forms of African culture were primitive, static, and ahistorical. Furthermore, such approaches have historically relegated African belief systems and ritual practices to the realm of "tradition" and have established a solid distinction between tradition and modernity. In contrast to this dichotomy, Jean Allman and John Parker, in *Tongnaab*, their study of the god of the Talensi people of Ghana, have convincingly argued that "African religious belief and practice is profoundly historical" and have shown how one deity underwent dramatic configuration over time. For G. W. F. Hegel's notion of primitive, ahistorical Africa, see Hegel, *Philosophy of History*, 91-99.

12. Bryson, "Art of Power."

13. Baer and Singer, *African American Religion*, 59, defines "thaumaturgical" practices as those that find the "most direct way to achieve socially desired ends . . . by engaging in various magico-religious rituals or by acquiring esoteric knowledge that provides individuals with spiritual power over themselves and others." While I would opt to omit the term "magico-religious" in favor of just "rituals," the general definition is accepted here. This element of Tacky's Rebellion has been a feature of rebellions in Africa and across the diaspora, including the Maji Maji Rebellion in German East Africa in 1905-7 and the Vesey Revolt in South Carolina in 1822.

14. On the uses and interpretations of obeah, see Paton, *Cultural Politics of Obeah*.

15. This argument has also been made for the varied processes by which Islam interacted with African religions in the western Sudan during the eighteenth and nineteenth centuries. See, for example, Miran-Guyon and Triaud, "Islam," 258.

16. Curtin, *Two Jamaicas*, 34. Schuler, *Alas, Alas Kongo*, 32-36, argues that Myalists and the Native Baptists are the same, while Stewart, *Religion and Society*, differentiates between the two.

17. Chevannes, *Rastafari: Roots and Ideology*, 20, 21.

18. Heron and Hume, "Stepping Out," 32. There are exceptions within Rastafari.

19. Chevannes, *Rastafari: Roots and Ideology*, 121–25.

20. Ibid., 154. Based on fieldwork, Homiak argues that rather than the Youth Black Faith, another group of ascetics, the Higes Knots, was actually responsible for this shift away from revivalist practices. Which group earned the credit is less important here than the general idea that the shift came about as a result of the "livity" of a new generation starting in the late 1940s. See John Homiak, "Rastafari."

21. For another perspective, see Warner-Lewis, "African Continuities."

22. For an important treatment of this paradox in Caribbean philosophy, see Henry, *Caliban's Reason*. See also Chevannes, "Ships That Will Never Sail."

23. Chevannes, *Rastafari: Roots and Ideology*, 171, argues that traces of Revivalism remain in the movement, with such linkages most visibly retained by the members of the Bobo Shanti.

24. Fredrickson, *Black Liberation*, 65.

25. Drake, *Redemption of Africa and Black Religion*, 57, 74. Blyden turned to classical literature as a source, which moved Ethiopianism beyond the scope of the Bible. He also made the argument that the Ethiopians, who were black, moved from Egypt and Nubia, southward and westward to other parts of Africa. As such, he contended that the people of the ancient kingdoms of Ghana, Mali, and Songhay were descendants of Ethiopians.

26. Hill, *Dread History*, 17.

27. Bonacci, *Exodus!*, 145.

28. Some have argued that Rastafarians were directly inspired by Garvey to see Haile Selassie as God because Garvey had purportedly said "look to Africa, when a black king shall be crowned, for the day of deliverance is near." This was presented in a seminal but controversial scholarly report on Rastafari published in 1960 (see Smith, Augier, and Nettleford, *Ras Tafari Movement*), and has also been retold by Rastafarians for decades. Hill, *Dread History*, 14–15, argues that there is no evidence that Garvey ever uttered those words.

29. Hutton and Murrell, "Rastas' Psychology and Blackness," 41–45.

30. See, for example, "The Right Hon Marcus M Garvey Speaks," *Voice of Rasta* 33 (1981): 1. The *Voice of Rasta* also honored Garvey with its slogan on the first page of each issue: "One Jah One Aim One Destiny." Another example is the article "Marcus Speaks" in the issue *Rastafari Speaks* 3 (April–May 1981): 2. Many Rastafarians commemorate Garvey's birthday with celebrations and religious rituals. Rastafarian elder Ras Negus wrote of the impact of Garvey on the "re-culturing of black people" in 1969. See Negus, *Abeng* 1, no. 11 (1969): 2, quoted in Hutton and Murrell, "Rastas' Psychology and Blackness," 53.

31. Hill, *Dread History*, 24.

32. Marcus Garvey, quoted in Hill, *Dread History*, 24.

33. Putnam, *Radical Moves*, 50.

34. For more on this point, see chapter 6.

35. Lewis, "Marcus Garvey and the Early Rastafarians."
36. *URIA Voice* 2 (June–July 1984).
37. See Pollard, *Dread Talk*.
38. For an insightful discussion of the role of orality in Afro-Jamaican history, see Johnson and Moore, *"They Do as They Please,"* chap. 4.
39. Edmonds, "Dread 'I' in-a-Babylon," 33.
40. Owens, *Dread*, 130.
41. Spencer, *Dread Jesus*, 89.
42. See Ajai Mansingh and Laxmii Mansingh, "Hindu Influences on Rastafarianism," 96–115.
43. Yawney and Homiak, "Rastafari," 263.
44. Emperor Haile Selassie had given the land to black people of the West in gratitude for the support they had given Ethiopia after it was invaded by Italy in 1935. During the invasion, which was in violation of international law and the 1928 treaty of friendship between Italy and Ethiopia, diasporic Africans were outraged and rallied in support of Ethiopia. For more on this, see Harris, *African-American Reactions to War*; Scott, "Black Nationalism and the Italo-Ethiopian Conflict"; Scott, *Sons of Sheba's Race*; and Shack, "Ethiopia and Afro-Americans."
45. For the details of this dispute, see Bonnacci, *Exodus!*, 203–4.
46. Beyond the executive body, members believe that each member belongs to a particular tribe based on the month of his/her birth. The tribes are based on the idea that each of Jacob's twelve sons was born into a tribe, which corresponds to one of the twelve months of the Hebrew/lunar calendar. As designed by Prophet Gad, through his/her tribe, each member is assigned a particular color and is perceived to have certain faculties/gifts/strengths represented by parts of the body. For example, a member born in the month of April is from the tribe of Reuben, assigned the color silver, and the human eye is his/her area of strength.
47. Angela Heron, "History," unpublished history of the organization. Private collection of Angela Heron, in author's possession. Before settling at Hope Road, meetings were held at different locations including Davis Lane, Hopeful Village, Elletson Road, Bereck Road, and Clarendon Place. The visibility of the Twelve Tribes of Israel in Jamaica and beyond grew during the 1970s and 1980s partly because the group's many activities included Reggae shows and celebrations that featured famous singers and musicians including Bob Marley, Judy Mowatt, Freddie McGregor, Dennis Brown, Sangie Davis, and Sister Carol.
48. Angela Heron, "The Twelve Tribes of Israel," unpublished document detailing the core tenets of the organization. Private collection of Angela Heron, in author's possession.
49. Giulia Bonacci, "The Return to Ethiopia of the Twelve Tribes of Israel," *New West Indian Guide* 90 (2016): 1–27; *Exodus!*, 204.
50. Angela Heron, "TTI History: Brothers and Sisters Sent to Shashamane by TTI," unpublished document, private collection of Angela Heron, in author's possession.
51. Ibid.

52. In keeping with the idea of members as "students" of the bible, the organization recommended the King Scoffield Reference Bible. Angela Heron, "The Twelve Tribes of Israel," unpublished document detailing the core tenets of the organization, private collection of Angela Heron, p. 3.

53. Naphtali, *Testimony of His Imperial Majesty*, 123.

54. For an extensive look at Rastafari as a "multiplicity of faith stances," see Spencer, *Dread Jesus*.

55. Gad Man, radio interview by Andrea Williams Green, *Running African*, Irie FM, Ocho Rios, Jamaica, July 13.

56. This point is based on more than thirty interviews with members of the Twelve Tribes conducted by the author in Jamaica in 2001. For a more in-depth treatment of the rift created by Prophet Gad's theological clarification, see Bedasse, "Rasta Evolution."

57. Angela Heron, "Twelve Tribes of Israel," 3.

58. Joshua Mkhululi, "Closing the Dispensation: A Rastafari Cultural Representation," personal journal, in author's possession.

59. Naphtali, *Testimony of His Imperial Majesty*, 72.

60. For an example of "Shiloh" as a messianic term, see Genesis 49:10. For an example of it as the name of a town, see Joshua 18:1.

61. Owens, *Dread: The Rastafarians of Jamaica*, 131.

62. Jah Bupe Karudi, "Re: Support for Ongoing Mission of Repatriation and Related," November 12, 1986, box 7, folder 192, C. L. R. James Papers, Special Collections, Alma Jordan Library.

63. Ibid.

64. Van Dijk, "Twelve Tribes of Israel."

65. Lewis, *Walter Rodney: 1968 Revisited*, 7.

66. Feierman, "Colonizers, Scholars, and the Creation of Invisible Histories," 201, notes the "invisibility" of Nyabingi mediumship.

67. Campbell, *Rasta and Resistance*, 72. As Feierman notes, other traditions place the origins of Nyabingi in northern Tanzania, Rwanda, or Zaire. See Feierman, "Colonizers, Scholars, and the Creation of Invisible Histories,"

68. Hansen, "Colonial Control of Spirit Cults," 146.

69. Among these challenges were disease, famine, and the imposition of neighboring (foreign) cultures into the area. As people from the centralized groups of the Ankole and Tutsi kingdoms moved into the area, the Bakiga sought to protect their way of life, and the practice of Nyabingi was crucial to this process. See Freedman, *Nyabingi*.

70. Hansen, "Colonial Control of Spirit Cults," 147. A woman named Muhumusa became the leader of the Nyabingi struggle against British colonial rule in particular. Under her leadership, there were raids against Bakiga who were installed in positions of power by the British, and she maintained that she would not be affected by European bullets, that they would turn to water when unleashed upon her. In 1911 the British used its military power to capture Muhumusa and to kill more than forty of her followers. See Hopkins, "Nyabingi Cult."

71. Campbell, *Rasta and Resistance*, 72.

72. Post, *Arise Ye Starvelings*.
73. Campbell, *Rasta and Resistance*, 73.
74. Barnett, "Rastafari in the New Millennium," 4.
75. Yawney and Homiak, "Rastafari," 260.
76. Homiak, "'Ancient of Days' Seated Black."
77. "Morality," *URIA Voice* 4 (1984): 36–37, Anthropological Archives, Smithsonian.
78. Ibid.
79. Mitchell, *Righteous Propagation*, 220.
80. Edmonds, *Rastafari: A Very Short Introduction*, 94. Scholars have argued that women played prominent roles in African-derived religions and that the shift away from Revivalism to an emphasis on the ritual known as reasoning was crucial to the process by which male dominance became widespread within Rasta. See Chevannes, *Rastafari: Roots and Ideology*; and Christensen, *Rastafari Reasoning*.
81. Austin-Broos, *Jamaica Genesis*, 241.
82. Tafari-Ama, "Resistance Without and Within," 193.
83. Christensen, *Rastafari Reasoning*.
84. This is based on I Corinthians 11:3.
85. This is based on 1 Timothy 1:11–15. This section relies on Ennis Edmonds's interpretation of these biblical passages; see Edmonds, *Rastafari: A Very Short Introduction*, 97.
86. Mair, *Historical Study of Women*; Shepherd and Brereton, *Engendering History*; Sheller, *Citizenship from Below*.
87. Lucille Mathurin Mair's groundbreaking work has generated important work on this; see, for example, Mair, *Historical Study of Women*.
88. Sheller, *Citizenship from Below*, 49.
89. Edmonds, *Rastafari: A Very Short Introduction*.
90. Sister Barbara, interview with the author, July 9, 2001; Sister Ann Marie, interview with the author, July 10, 2001.
91. Yawney, "Rastafarian Sistren," 73–75; Yawney, "Moving with the Dawtas of Rastafari," 67. Obiagele Lake has even argued that, compared to other Jamaican women, Rasta women are "doubly oppressed" because of Rasta's adherence to both Christian principles and the cultural norms of pre-colonial African societies. Lake, *Rastafari Women*, 93. Like Imani Tafari Ama, I disagree with this. See Tafari-Ama, "Resistance Without and Within," 94.
92. Maureen Rowe, "The Woman in Rastafari," 13–21. The debate in the literature has been tied to deeper questions concerning who can and should speak for Rasta women. For a discussion of this debate, see Yawney, "Moving with the Dawtas of Rastafari."
93. Berger, "Fertility as Power: Spirit Mediums, Priestesses and the Pre-Colonial State in Interlacustrine East Africa," 78. See also Freedman, *Nyabingi*.
94. Sister May, interview with the author, July 21, 2001.
95. "Morality," *URIA Voice* 4: 20, Anthropological Archives, Smithsonian.
96. Fanon, *Wretched of the Earth*, 123.

97. Thomas, *Exceptional Violence*, 203.

98. Hill, *Dread History*; Yawney, "Exodus."

99. Yawney, "Exodus," 171.

100. John Carradine, "The Ras Tafarites Retreat to Mountain Fastnesses of St. Catherine," *Daily Gleaner*, November 23, 1940; Hill, *Dread History*, 23.

101. "Jamaica's Great Ras Tafarite Kingdom Comes to an End," *Daily Gleaner*, October 14, 1945.

102. Governor Richards to Secretary of State for the Colonies, "Ethiopian Salvation Society," April 9, 1940, CO 137/84016, British National Archives.

103. Campbell, *Rasta and Resistance*, 96, 94.

104. See Turner, *Slaves and Missionaries*; and Hall, *Free Jamaica*.

105. Policy makers and abolitionists hoped to transform the formerly enslaved into wage laborers. According to historian Thomas Holt, this represented their strategy to deal with the "problem of freedom." See Holt, *Problem of Freedom*.

106. Hall, *Free Jamaica*; Wilmot, "Black Space/Room to Manoeuvre."

107. Smith et al., *Report on the Ras Tafari Movement*, 12.

108. Chevannes, *Rastafari: Roots and Ideology*, 122.

109. "Leonard Howell Being Tried For Sedition in Saint Thomas," *Daily Gleaner*, March 14, 1934; "Leonard Howell, on Trial Says Ras Tafari Is Messiah Returned to Earth," *Daily Gleaner*, March 15, 1934.

110. Carradine, "Ras Tafarites Retreat."

111. Lee and David, *First Rasta*, 123, 117.

112. "Jah Bones Talks to the Oxford Cultural Relations Council," *Voice of Rasta* 32 (1981): 5.

113. Hugh Foot to M. Phillips, November 19, 1956, FO 371/138109, British National Archives; Blackburne to Secretary of State. June 10, 1959, FO 371/138109, British National Archives.

114. Frank Jan Van Dijk, "Sociological Means: Colonial Reactions to the Radicalization of Rastafari in Jamaica, 1956-1959," *NWIG: New West Indian Guide/Nieuwe West Indische Gids* 69, no. 1/2 (1995): 67–101, 80.

115. Barry Chevannes, *Rastafari: Roots and Ideology*, 172, 187.

116. Bogues, "Politics, Nation and PostColony," 9, 18. Additionally, in 1959 Blackburne differentiated between Rastafari and the "agitation" of Claudius Henry. As the colonial government monitored Rastafari, Blackburne argued that there was a "definite historical background" to the Rastafarian movement, but though Henry and Rastafarians shared a "common platform" in terms of repatriation to Africa, Henry was a "charlatan . . . preying on the simple people of Jamaica." Governor Blackburne, Dispatch no. 637, P. J. Kitcatt to C. J. Audland, Colonial Office, August 31, 1959, FO 371/138109, British National Archives.

117. Chevannes, "Rastafari and the Exorcism of the Ideology," 62.

118. Ibid.

119. Smith et al., *Report on the Ras Tafari Movement*, 28.

120. For evidence that the papers were concerned with Africans in Africa and across the diaspora, see *Black Man Speaks* 1, no. 3 (1968); *Our Own* 1, no. 1 (1968). See also Lewis, *Walter Rodney: 1968 Revisited*.

121. "Literature of Black Struggle in Ja. 1968/69," *Bongo Man* 5 (1970): 1., box 39, National Library of Jamaica.

122. Rodney, *Groundings with My Brothers*, 61. Walter Rodney was born in Georgetown, Guyana, in 1942, and studied history at the University of the West Indies in Jamaica as an undergraduate, then completed a PhD in African history at the School of Oriental and African Studies in London. After completing the PhD, he went to Tanzania in 1966, to Jamaica in 1968, and then returned to Tanzania.

123. Robin "Jerry" Small, interview with the author, July 10, 2008.

124. Edmonds, "Dread 'I' in-a-Babylon," 27.

125. Joshua Mkhululi, correspondence with the author, July 10, 2007. The death of Haile Selassie led some Rastafarians to question whether he was really the second dispensation of Christ or a representative of Christ on earth. For an extensive look at Rastafari as a "multiplicity of faith stances," see Spencer, *Dread Jesus*. For a case study of how the emperor's death contributed to the evolution of the theology of one particular Rasta group, the Twelve Tribes of Israel, see Bedasse, "Rasta Evolution."

Chapter Two

1. Baraka, "Towards Pan-Africanism," 66.

2. In 1967 Kenyan scholar Ali Mazrui grappled with "Tanzaphilia," which he defined as "the romantic spell, which Tanzania casts on so many of those who have been closely associated with her." See Mazrui, "Tanzaphilia," 20.

3. Gaines, *American Africans in Ghana*, 4, 2, 6.

4. C. L. R. James, Transcript of Speech given for the African and American Teachers' Association, September 7, 1969, box 20, folder 375, C. L. R. James Papers, Special Collections, Alma Jordan Library.

5. Karioki, *Tanzania's Human Revolution*, 198.

6. For more on this, see chapter 1.

7. M. G. L. Roy to Foreign Office, November 16, 1959, The Ras Tafaris of Jamaica, FO 371/138109, British National Archives.

8. Governor Foot to the Colonial Office, August 16, 1956, The Ras Tafaris of Jamaica, FO 371/138109, British National Archives.

9. M. G. L. Roy to the Colonial Office, October 23, 1959, The Ras Tafaris of Jamaica, FO 371/138109, British National Archives.

10. Julius Nyerere, "President Nyerere's Toast to the Emperor of Ethiopia at the State Banquet," July 12, 1964, Dar es Salaam, Tanzania, Speeches and Statements, Mwalimu Nyerere Foundation, Dar es Salaam, Tanzania.

11. Pankhurst, *Ethiopians*, 263.

12. Sorenson, *Imagining Ethiopia*.
13. Thompson, *Africa and Unity*, 175.
14. Gebrekidan, *Bond without Blood*, 169.
15. Bonacci, *Exodus!*, 53, 175.
16. Lal, *African Socialism in Postcolonial Tanzania*, 37.
17. Friedland and Rosberg, *African Socialism*; Askew and Pitcher, eds., "African Socialisms and Postsocialisms," special issue, *Africa: Journal of the International African Institute* 76, no. 1 (2006).
18. Cooper, *Citizenship between Empire and Nation*; Cooper, *Decolonization and African Society*, 1.
19. For more on the need to venture beyond the national archive in order to uncover the transnational history of decolonization, see Allman, "Phantoms of the Archive."
20. West, "Seeds Are Sown," 335.
21. King, "James E. K. Aggrey."
22. Buruku, "Townsman," 101, 228, 232; Smith, *Aggrey of Africa*, 212–14.
23. Brennan, *Taifa*, 123.
24. Iliffe, *Modern History of Tanganyika*, 405.
25. For more on the content of Garveyism as it traveled across the African continent, see Ewing, *Age of Garvey*.
26. Iliffe, *Modern History of Tanganyika*, 405.
27. *Kwetu* 1–2, quoted in Westcott, "East African Radical," 92, 95.
28. Iliffe, *Modern History of Tanganyika*, 394.
29. Westcott, "East African Radical," 88.
30. Ewing, *Age of Garvey*.
31. Brennan, *Taifa*, 69, 123.
32. See Adi, *West Africans in Britain*.
33. During the early years of independence, Nkrumah and Nyerere disagreed on the approach to unity. Nkrumah argued for an immediate continental unity, while Nyerere favored a more gradual approach that saw smaller federations as the practical place to begin the process. For an insightful treatment of the debate between both leaders and its impact on pan-Africanism, see Agyeman, "Osagyefo, the Mwalimu, and Pan-Africanism."
34. Under colonial administration Kenya, Tanganyika, and Uganda had been administered as British East Africa, and in 1961 the East African Common Services Organization and Common Market was created. Nyerere and others sought this unification through a pan-African rather than an imperial paradigm. See Nye, *Pan-Africanism and East African Integration*.
35. Julius K. Nyerere, "East African Federation" in *Freedom and Unity*, 85.
36. Cooper, "Possibility and Constraint," 174–75, reminds historians of the historical importance of alternatives to nationalism.
37. Parsons, *1964 Army Mutinees*, 76, makes this point regarding East African federation. For treatments of the challenges to West Indian federation, see Palmer,

Eric Williams and Making of the Modern Caribbean, chap. 2; and Mawby, *Ordering Independence*. For a study that places federation within the context of black diaspora politics, see Duke, *Building a Nation*.

38. Gordon R. Beyer to Department of State, Telegram 03136, September 15, 1973, 1973DARES03136, Central Foreign Policy Files, 1973-1979/Electronic Telegrams, RG59: General Records of the Department of State, National Archives (accessed June 8, 2015), SDCF.

39. Julius Nyerere, "President Nyerere's Speech to the P.N.P Conference, Jamaica," September 15, 1974, Speeches and Statements, Mwalimu Nyerere Foundation.

40. Thompson, *From Kingston to Kenya*.

41. Dudley Thompson, interview with the author, July 2009, Weston, FL; Thompson, *From Kingston to Kenya*, 41.

42. Thompson, *From Kingston to Kenya*, 70.

43. Thompson interview.

44. Ibid.

45. Nyerere, "President Nyerere's Speech."

46. Azaria Mbughuni, "Tanzania and the Pan African Quest for Unity, Freedom, and Independence in East, Central, and Southern Africa," 212.

47. Ibid.

48. Pratt, *Critical Phase in Tanzania*; Hydén, "Mao and Mwalimu"; Lal, "Maoism in Tanzania"; Hydén, *Beyond Ujamaa in Tanzania*.

49. Stoger-Eising, "Ujamaa Revisited"; Hatch, *Two African Statesmen*.

50. Bunting, "Heart of Africa," 67.

51. This idea has a long history in Western thought, appearing prominently in the works of G. W. F. Hegel, David Hume, and Immanuel Kant. For examples, see Hugh Trevor Roper, *Rise of Christian Europe*; and Johnston, *History of the Colonization of Africa*.

52. For examples of this approach, see Shivji, *Class Struggles in Tanzania*; and Lofchie, "Agrarian Socialism."

53. Gaines, *American Africans in Ghana*; Cobb, *Africa Notebook*, 3; Brown, *Fighting for Us*, 10.

54. Campbell and Stein, *Tanzania and the IMF*, 3.

55. For more on Mwongozo (Guidelines), a party document that Nyerere released in 1971 in response to pressure from more militant members of TANU, see James Brennan, Taifa, 191.

56. Khadiagala, *Allies in Adversity*; Minter, *Apartheid's Contras*; Houser, *No One Can Stop the Rain*.

57. Nyerere, *Arusha Declaration Teach-In*, 1.

58. Nyerere, "Introduction," in *Freedom and Socialism*, 14.

59. Julius K. Nyerere, "*Ujamaa*–The Basis of Socialism," in *Ujamaa: Essays on Socialism*, 6–7.

60. Nyerere, *Arusha Declaration Teach-In*, 15, 16.

61. Bunting, "Heart of Africa," 67.
62. Nyerere, *Arusha Declaration Teach-In*, 1.
63. Ibid., 7.
64. "URIA Doctrine & Principles," *URIA Voice* 4 (1984): 38, National Anthropological Archives, Smithsonian Institute.
65. *Mwalimu*, the Swahili word for "teacher," was frequently used to refer to Nyerere. Salim, "Mwalimu Julius K. Nyerere," 30.
66. Salim, "Mwalimu Julius K. Nyerere," 30.
67. Nyerere, "Mwongozo," 4.
68. Julius Nyerere, "President Nyerere's Speech to the Mass Rally, Guinea-Bissau," September 19, 1976, Speeches and Statements, Mwalimu Nyerere Foundation, Dar es Salaam, Tanzania.
69. Ibid.
70. Julius Nyerere, "President Nyerere's Speech to the Liberation Committee," Dar es Salaam, Tanzania, January 8, 1975, Speeches and Statements, Mwalimu Nyerere Foundation, Dar es Salaam, Tanzania.
71. Nyerere, "President Nyerere's Speech to the Mass Rally."
72. "URIA Doctrine & Principles," *URIA Voice* 4 (1984): 6–7.
73. Mpangala, "Tanzania's Support to the Liberation Struggle," 19.
74. Brennan, *Taifa*, 2.
75. Brennan, "Blood Enemies," 404.
76. Ivaska, *Cultured States*, 17, 5.
77. "URIA Doctrine & Principles," *URIA Voice* 2 (1984): 5.
78. "URIA Doctrine & Principles," *URIA Voice* 4 (1984): 6.
79. Julius K. Nyerere, "President's Inaugural Address," in *Freedom and Unity*, 186.
80. *URIA Voice* 3.
81. Nyerere, "President's Inaugural Address," 178.
82. Julius K. Nyerere, "*Ujamaa*: The Bases of African Socialism," in *Ujamaa: Essays on Socialism*, 7.
83. Ibid., 12.
84. Chevannes, *Betwixt and Between*, 121.
85. Walter Rodney, "Africans Abroad in Jamaica," unpublished manuscript, n.d. (early 1970s), box 13, folder 11, Robert W. Woodruff Library.
86. Falola, *Nationalism and African Intellectuals*, 123.
87. Cobb, *Africa Notebook*, 3.
88. Brown, *Fighting for Us*, 10.
89. Walters, *Pan Africanism in the African Diaspora*, 66.
90. Markle, "'Book Publishers for a Pan-African World.'"
91. Du Bois, "Afro-American Militants in Africa," 4.
92. Baraka, "Towards Pan-Africanism," 67.
93. Wilkins, "In the Belly of the Beast," 58.
94. Tate, "Power of Pan-Africanism," 190.

95. Plummer, *In Search of Power*, 275.

96. Woodard, *Nation within a Nation*, 50; Malcolm X, "At the Audubon," in *Malcolm X Speaks*, ed. George, 101.

97. For an analysis of the challenges of the union, see Shivji, *Pan-Africanism or Pragmatism?*

98. Nyerere, "President's Inaugural Address," 186. For an insightful study of the role of culture in Tanzania, see Askew, *Performing the Nation*.

99. Ivaska, *Cultured States*, 71.

100. "Two from US Held after Police Find Guns and Bullets," *Daily News*, Tanzania, May 28, 1974. For an informative discussion of the Big Bust and its impact on the African American community in Tanzania, see Tate, "Power of Pan Africanism," 189–96.

101. Mwakikagile, *Relations between Africans and African Americans*, 298.

102. Sutherland and Meyer, *Guns and Gandhi in Africa*, 67.

103. Wilkins, "In the Belly of the Beast," 106.

104. See Rodney, "Black Scholar Interviews: Walter Rodney," *Black Scholar* 6, no. 3 (November 1974): 38–47.

105. Wilkins, "In the Belly of the Beast," 107.

106. Ibid., 107–8.

107. Lewis, *Walter Rodney's Intellectual and Political Thought*.

108. Rodney, *Walter Rodney Speaks*, 35.

109. Blommaert, "Intellectual and Ideological Leadership in Ujamaa Tanzania," 133.

110. Kate Quinn, "Sitting on a Volcano," in "Black Power in Burnham's Guyana," in *Black Power in the Caribbean*, ed. by Kate Quinn, 139, 144.

111. Julius K. Nyerere, "President Nyerere's Speech at the University of the West Indies (Jamaica Campus)," September 16, 1974, Speeches and Statements, Mwalimu Nyerere Foundation.

112. Julius Nyerere, "President Nyerere's Speech on Television and Radio," Trinidad, September 9, 1974, Speeches and Statements, Mwalimu Nyerere Foundation.

113. Examples of such articles include "Guyana Cuts on Imports," *Standard*, March 3, 1972; "Cuban and Tanzanian Struggle Is the Same," *Standard*, January 9, 1972; and "Thousands May Miss Jamaica Elections," *Standard*, January 15, 1972.

114. Bgoya, "From Tanzania to Kansas and Back Again," 104.

115. "Portugal's 'War in Africa' Defended," *Standard*, January 2, 1971; "Guinea Raid: 'We Were Next' Says Kawawa," *Standard*, January 3, 1971.

116. "Guinea Raid."

117. "'Help Us' Says Leader of Fight for Freedom," *Standard*, February 4, 1971.

118. "Invasions: New Strategy to Divert Africa's Attention," *Standard*, January 5, 1971.

119. For examples of the many articles that addressed this issue in Tanzanian newspapers, see "'Arms Deal a Sell-Out of Africans,' Nyerere Tells Summit,"

Nationalist, January 16, 1971; "U.K. Under Fire over Arms Sales," *Nationalist*, February, 25, 1971; and "'We Might Seek Communist Arm,' Mwalimu Warns," *Nationalist*, January 25, 1971.

120. Julius K. Nyerere, Preparatory Meeting of Non-Aligned Countries, Dar es Salaam, April 13, 1970, Speeches and Statements, Mwalimu Nyerere Foundation.

121. Ibid.

122. Fred Brooks to Walter Rodney, April 25, 1972, Walter Rodney Papers, box 2, folder 61, Robert W. Woodruff Library.

123. In 1977 Nyerere released a document titled *Arusha Declaration Ten Years After*, in which he detailed the areas where the government had failed to meet its goals. This was a stunning and rare admission of mistakes made by a government.

124. Nyerere, "President Nyerere's Speech on Television and Radio."

125. Nyerere, "President Nyerere's Speech at the University of the West Indies (Jamaica Campus)."

126. For works that contribute to our understanding of the relationship between Tanzania's nation building and various forms of Pan-Africanism, see Schroeder, *Africa after Apartheid*; and Monson, *Africa's Freedom Railway*.

127. Tanzania was divided into nineteen regions and sixty-one districts. The Kabuku Village was one of about sixty-seven villages in the Handeni district, which was in the Tanga region. In 1975, about 133,000 people occupied the district of Handeni.

128. "A Visit to Kabuku Village by Hon. Michael Manley, President of PNP and Prime Minister of Jamaica," miscellaneous party document from Tanganyika African National Union Sub Branch Office, Kabuku Ujamaa Village, Handeni, Tanzania, September 13, 1973, Bilateral Relations (Tanzania), Michael Manley Foundation.

129. Ibid.

130. "Memorandum Submitted by FRELIMO to meeting of OAU, Algiers, 1968," Tanzania National Archives.

131. Julius Nyerere, "President Nyerere's Speech at the State Banquet for President Samora Machel, Dar Es Salaam," April 28, 1982, Speeches and Statements, Mwalimu Nyerere Foundation.

132. Morrow, Maaba, and Pulumani, *Education in Exile*.

133. Sutherland and Meyer, *Guns and Gandhi in Africa*, 61.

Chapter Three

1. Michael Manley, "The Reggae Protestors," *Jamaica Observer*, February 14, 1982.

2. Manley, *Manley Memoirs*, 93, 149.

3. Michael Manley, "Statement by the Hon. Michael Manley, Prime Minister of Jamaica on the Occasion of a Special Plenary Meeting of the United Nations General Assembly Devoted to the International Anti-Apartheid Year, October 11, 1978," Bilateral Relations, Michael Manley Foundation, Kingston, Jamaica.

4. "Jamaika Iko Tayari Kusaidi Zaidi Ukombozi," *Uhuru*, September 17, 1973.

5. Bogues, *Black Heretics, Black Prophets*, 117.

6. Joshua Mkhululi, "Closing the Dispensation: A Rastafari Cultural Representation," personal journal, in the author's possession.

7. Nettleford, *Identity, Race and Protest in Jamaica*, 25–26.

8. Hintzen, "Caribbean," 477–78, makes this point effectively.

9. COINTELPRO, which is an acronym for Counter Intelligence Program, refers to a series of covert operations that were used by the FBI to destroy what the United States perceived to be revolutionary movements that posed a threat to national security.

10. In 1968, Jamaica's minister of home affairs, Roy McNeil, banned the literature of Stokely Carmichael, Malcolm X, and Elijah Mohammad. In addition, Rupert Lewis reports that the Jamaican state seized the passports of progressive intellectuals such as George Beckford, Winston Davis and Leroy Taylor. See Lewis, *Walter Rodney's Intellectual and Political Thought*, 112. Rastafarians had long been victims of state brutality, having endured beatings, the shaving of their locks, unwarranted arrests, and other forms of persecution. Many of the works on Rastafari at least mention the history of conflict between Rastafarians and the Jamaican police. These include Smith, Augier, and Nettleford, *Ras Tafari Movement in Kingston, Jamaica*; Edmonds, *Rastafari: From Outcasts to Culture Bearers*; Bishton, *Black Heart Man*; Williams, *Rastafarians*; and Yawney, "Lions in Babylon."

11. See Lewis, *Walter Rodney: 1968 Revisited*.

12. For details of the banning and the protest it engendered, which came to be known as the Rodney Affair, see Girvan, "After Rodney"; Gonsalves, "Rodney Affair"; and Payne, *Politics in Jamaica*.

13. Rodney, *Groundings with My Brothers*, 61.

14. Campbell, "Walter Rodney," 133.

15. Horace Campbell makes this point about Rodney first encountering Rastafari as a student and credits Eusi Kwayana for the suggestion that Rasta has something to do with Rodney's decision to study the upper Guinea coast for his dissertation. See Campbell, "Walter Rodney and Pan-Africanism Today."

16. For Rodney's explanation of why he chose to go to Tanzania, see chapter 2.

17. Rodney, *Walter Rodney Speaks*, 10.

18. Rodney, *Groundings with My Brothers*, 67.

19. Lewis, *Walter Rodney's Intellectual and Political Thought*, 99.

20. Rodney, *Groundings with My Brothers*, 60.

21. Rodney, *Walter Rodney Speaks*, 34.

22. Fontaine, "Rodney and the Future of Guyana," 150; Lewis, *Walter Rodney: 1968 Revisited*.

23. Waters, *Race, Class and Political Symbols*. This is not to suggest that the JLP had never engaged the African heritage of the majority of Jamaicans. The JLP was connected to another major African cultural current surrounding Revivalism, and Edward Seaga, in particular, encouraged the celebration of Afro-Jamaican religions and connected with the people he sought to represent through his emphasis on culture. See Bryan, *Edward Seaga*, 133.

24. Scott, "Dialectic of Defeat," 15. This is not to suggest that there was not a significant left movement outside of the PNP.

25. Waters, *Race, Class and Political Symbols*, 124.

26. The Rastafarian lexicon, often referred to as "dread talk," includes a preponderance of "I" words. The "I" in Rastafarian thought signifies the divine principle that is in all humanity and "I and I" is an expression of the oneness between two (or more) persons and between the speaker and God. "I-n-I" also connotes a rejection of subservience in Babylon culture and an affirmation of self as an active agent in the creation of one's own reality and identity. Edmonds, "Dread 'I' in-a-Babylon," 33.

27. Bogues, "Politics, Nation and PostColony," 18.

28. Lewis, "Jamaican Black Power in the 1960s," 71.

29. Michael Manley, "The Reggae Protestors," *Jamaica Observer*, February 14, 1982.

30. White, *Catch a Fire*, 264.

31. Michael Manley, "The Reggae Protesters." *Jamaica Observer*, February 7, 1982.

32. Michael Manley, "The Reggae Protestors," *Jamaica Observer*, February 14, 1982.

33. Ibid.

34. "Selassie as God? Zambian Says Planno is 'Talking through His Halo,'" *Daily Gleaner*, June 29, 1972.

35. For details on Dudley Thompson's time in East Africa during the 1950s, see chapter 2.

36. "Nyerere si Kiongozi wa Tanzania Pekee," *Uhuru*, September 15, 1974.

37. Yawney, "Exodus," 164.

38. Campbell, *Rasta and Resistance*, 112–15.

39. Hewitt to Department of State, Telegram 172789, August 30, 1973, 1973STATE172789, Central Foreign Policy Files, 1973–1979/Electronic Telegrams, RG 59: General Records of the Department of State, U.S. National Archives (accessed June 8, 2015).

40. Henry Kissinger to Department of State, Telegram 160546, July 2, 1974, 1974STATE160546, Central Foreign Policy Files, 1973–1979/Electronic Telegrams, RG 59: General Records of the Department of State, U.S. National Archives (accessed June 9, 2015); Gerard to Department of State, Telegram 03637, October 8, 1974, 1974KINGST03637, Central Foreign Policy Files, 1973–1979/Electronic Telegrams, RG 59: General Records of the Department of State, U.S. National Archives (accessed June 9, 2015). The Gun Court was established by the Jamaican parliament in 1974 in order to adjudicate criminal offences that included firearms.

41. Gerard to Department of State, Telegram 03059, August 29, 1974, 1974KINGST03059, Central Foreign Policy Files, 1973–1979/Electronic Telegrams, RG 59: General Records of the Department of State, U.S. National Archives (accessed June 9, 2015).

42. Campbell, *Rasta and Resistance*, 114.

43. Homiak, "Never Trade a Continent for an Island," 206.

44. Payne, *Politics in Jamaica*, 35.

45. Manley, *Politics of Change*, 25, 26.

46. Nyerere, "Democracy and the Party System," in *Freedom and Unity*, 198, 200.

47. Manley, *Politics of Change*, 28, 30.

48. Ibid., 30, 31.

49. Julius K. Nyerere, "Ujamaa—The Basis of African Socialism," in *Ujamaa: Essays on Socialism*, 1.

50. The People's National Party, Political Education Committee of the People's National Party, "Democratic Socialism: The Jamaican Model," 13, manifesto, Kingston: People's National Party, 1976.

51. Milburn, "The Fabian Society and the British Labour Party," 319.

52. This is so despite the fact that several members of the Fabian Society have written about Fabian socialism; see Shaw, *Fabian Society*; Cole, "The Fabian Society,"; Cole, "The Story of the Society"; and Pease, *History of the Fabian Society*.

53. Milburn, "The Fabian Society and the British Labour Party," 322.

54. Fabian socialism began to embrace trade union matters in the 1890s. Lewis, "Fabian Socialism," 469, argues that this was inspired by the strikes of 1889. Foreign affairs became a part of the group's agenda in the 1900s.

55. Levi, *Michael Manley*, 64.

56. Sydney Webb has been hailed as the individual who was mostly responsible for the philosophy of Fabian Socialism making it into the documents of the British Labour Party. See Milburn, "Fabian Society and the British Labour Party."

57. Milburn, "Fabian Society and the British Labour Party."

58. Michael Manley spent years trying to ensure that the worker in Jamaica had a voice; see Manley, *Voice in the Work-Place*.

59. Levi, *Michael Manley*, 153.

60. Milburn, "Fabian Society and the British Labour Party," 338.

61. Iliffe, *Modern History of Tanganyika*, 508.

62. Unlike the situation in other areas of Africa, such as neighboring Kenya, where Africans were forced to resort to violence in order to secure freedom from the savagery of colonial rule, Tanganyika gained independence from Britain through peaceful negotiations in 1961. This has led some scholars to argue that Nyerere was a moderate. Daniel R. Smith has argued that the Fabians actually developed the program of the Tanganyika African National Union, giving more credit to the society than to the African nationalists in Tanzania. Though Nyerere did indeed seek the support and advice of the Fabian Colonial Bureau, Smith underestimates the agency of Nyerere—and African nationalists, by extension—in building alliances to serve their purposes. Furthermore, though Nyerere has been influenced by Fabian socialism (or perhaps, because of it), the process to independence demonstrated a pragmatism—the situation in Tanganyika did not demand violence. That this path reflected strategy rather than a rigid rejection of violence as a tactic became clear later when Nyerere wholeheartedly supported the use of armed force by African freedom fighters in their liberation struggles.

63. Lionel Cliffe, "Joan Wicken: An Unsung Figure Who Worked alongside Julius Nyerere in the Building of Tanzania," *Guardian*, December 21, 2004.

64. Cliffe, "Joan Wicken."

65. Manley, *Politics of Change*, 17.

66. Julius K. Nyerere, "Africa's Place in the World" (1966), in "Selected Writings of Julius K. Nyerere, President of Tanzania," unpublished manuscript, Peace Corps Training Project, Syracuse University.

67. Bogues, "Michael Manley, Trade Unionism, and the Politics of Equality," 55.

68. Julius K. Nyerere, "Ujamaa: The Basis of African Socialism," in *Ujamaa—Essays on Socialism*, 6.

69. Political Education Committee of the People's National Party, "Democratic Socialism," 3.

70. Levi, *Michael Manley*, 125.

71. Ibid.

72. Michael Manley, "Speech by the Prime Minister, Honourable Michael Manley, to the Special Session of the U.N. Special Committee against Apartheid, Kingston," May 22, 1979, Human Rights and Justice File, Michael Manley Foundation.

73. Michael Manley, address at the special plenary meeting of the United Nations General Assembly Devoted to the International Anti-Apartheid Year, October 11, 1978.

74. Ibid.

75. Manley, *Jamaica: Struggle in the Periphery*.

76. Levi, *Michael Manley*, 201, 315.

77. Michael Manley, "International Conference in Support of the Peoples of Zimbabwe and Namibia," Maputo, Mozambique, May 17, 1977, Human Rights and Justice File, Michael Manley Foundation.

78. Ibid.; emphasis in Manley's original.

79. Julius K. Nyerere, "President Nyerere's Speech to the Jamaican Parliament," September 17, 1974, Speeches and Statements, Mwalimu Nyerere Foundation, Dar es Salaam.

80. Office of the Prime Minister, "Statement by PM on International Anti-Apartheid Year," press release, March 2, 1977. Human Rights and Justice File, Michael Manley Foundation.

81. Michael Manley, "International Conference in Support of the Peoples of Zimbabwe and Namibia." Maputo, Mozambique, May 17, 1977, Human Rights and Justice File, Michael Manley Foundation.

82. Hewitt to Depatment of State, Telegram 03405, October 2, 1973, 1973KINGST03405, Central Foreign Policy Files, 1973–1979/Electronic Telegrams, RG 59: General Records of the Department of State, U.S. National Archives (accessed June 8, 2015).

83. Nelson to Department of State, Telegram 01685, September 13, 1973, 1973 LUSAKA01685, Central Foreign Policy Files, 1973–1979/Electronic Telegrams, RG 59: General Records of the Department of State, U.S. National Archives (accessed December 28, 2015).

84. Hewitt to Department of State, October 2, 1973.

85. J. M. Nkomo to Michael Manley, November 23, 1979, Biography File, Michael Manley Foundation. When the Zimbabwe African People's Union, led by Joshua Nkomo, joined an alliance with the Zimbabwe African National Union, led by Robert Mugabe, they formed the Patriotic Front, which was supported by the Frontline States, including Angola, Mozambique, Tanzania, and Zambia.

86. Ibid.

87. Michael Manley to J. M. Nkomo, December 4, 1979, Biography File, Michael Manley Foundation.

88. "Michael Manley en Moçambique: Amizade que Nasce de Luta Comun," *Tempo* 462, August 8, 1979, Arquivo Histórico de Moçambique, via Aluka Digital Archive.

89. Julius K. Nyerere, "Socialism and Rural Development," in *Ujamaa—Essays on Socialism*, 106, 124.

90. Chevannes, *Rastafari: Roots and Ideology*, 242. Michael Manley, "The Prime Minister Addresses Members of the University Community," University of Dar es Salaam, Tanzania, September 12, 1973, Bilateral File, Michael Manley Foundation, Kingston, Jamaica, 4.

91. Manley, *Politics of Change*, 205.

92. Grace Pennicott-Smith, interview with the author, July 22, 2009.

93. Manley, *Politics of Change*, 205.

94. Joseph Christie, interview with the author, July 24, 2009.

95. Political Education Committee of the People's National Party, "Democratic Socialism,"

96. "At Nyerere Farm 'Just Like We Have at Home,'" *Jamaica Daily News*, September 20, 1974.

97. "President Nyerere's Visit," *Jamaica Daily News*, September 4, 1974.

98. "The Party's Controversy: President Nyerere's Visit," *Jamaica Daily News*, September 5, 1974.

99. "Sir Alex Boycotts Nyerere," *Jamaica Daily News*, September 4, 1974.

100. "JCC on Nyerere address to PNP," *Jamaica Daily News*, September 5, 1974.

101. "JCC Will Take Part in Nyerere Functions," *Jamaica Daily News*, September 13, 1974.

102. "Nyerere Booklet," *Jamaica Daily News*, September 10, 1974.

103. "Planning for Nyerere," *Jamaica Daily News*, September 11, 1974.

104. Thompson provided a human bridge between Jamaica and Tanzania. Before working with Manley's government as foreign minister in the 1970s, he had lived and worked in Moshi, a town in northern Tanzania (then Tanganyika) near the Kenyan border in the early 1950s. In 1951, Nyerere sought Thompson's help with the constitution of TANU, which had begun to campaign for Tanganyika's independence from Britain. Thompson also allowed Nyerere to use his secretary for two years, while Thompson continued to pay her.

105. "Paper on Nyerere," *Jamaica Daily News*, September 9, 1974.

106. "Make Nyerere's Visit a Milestone—PNP Youth," *Jamaica Daily News*, September 8, 1974.

107. "Crowd, Colour Greet Nyerere," *Jamaica Daily News*, September, 15, 1974.

108. E. Gordon, "The Real Fear behind President Nyerere's Visit," *Public Opinion*, September 6, 1974, quoted in Yawney, "Exodus," 165–66.

109. Yawney, "Exodus," 166.

110. Ibid., 167.

111. Carl Wint, "Mwalimu Is Here," *Jamaica Daily News*, September 15, 1974.

112. Lewis, *Walter Rodney's Intellectual and Political Thought*, 91.

113. "Welcome Nyerere," *Jamaica Daily News,* September 14, 1974.

114. Hewitt to Department of State, Telegram 03202, September 10, 1974, 1974KINGST03202, Central Foreign Policy Files, 1973–1979/Electronic Telegrams, RG 59: General Records of the Department of State, U.S. National Archives (accessed June 9, 2015).

115. Manley, *Horses in Her Hair*.

116. Manley, *In My Father's Shade*, 148–49.

117. Beverley Manley, interview with the author, July 2, 2012.

118. This is not to suggest an overly simplistic class analysis that sees all working-class black people in Jamaica as African-centered. In the words of Mervyn Alleyne, one of the outstanding features of Jamaica is the apparent contradiction between a strong "black" ethnicity on the one hand and the persistence of aspects of the pejoration of black on the other. Jamaica has always been in the forefront of struggles for the reclaiming and reappropriating of black dignity. At the same time, all the pathological expressions of marginalization persist. Alleyne makes this point in light of his observation that Jamaicans have embraced non-black Jamaicans as leaders, and that, at the level of national politics, there is an absence of successful political movements that have mobilized around race. See Alleyne, *Construction and Representation of Race*. This also relates to the fact that the critique of Rastafari has not been limited to the state or to Jamaican elites. As a result of the widespread protestant ethic in Jamaica, the veneration of Haile Selassie has been seen as blasphemy by all levels of society.

119. Beverley Manley, interview with the author, July 2, 2012.

120. Ibid.

121. Joseph Butiku, interview with the author, June 25, 2005.

Chapter Four

1. Ato Kidani Roberts, interview with the author, May 2, 2013.

2. Jah Bupe Akiiki Karudi, "Support for On-Going Mission of Repatriation and All Related," November 12, 1986, box 7, folder 192, C. L. R. James Papers, Special Collections, Alma Jordan Library.

3. As I noted in chapter 2, historically Rastafarians have not all been antistatist. Some who wanted to repatriate to Ethiopia in the 1930s and 1940s were invested in Ethiopian nationality.

4. For a discussion of the point that diaspora is oppositional to the nation-state, see Iton, *In Search of the Black Fantastic*.

5. For examples, see Edmonds, *Rastafari: From Outcasts to Culture Bearers*; Chevannes, *Rastafari: Roots and Ideology*; Owens, *Dread*; and Waters, *Race, Class and Political Symbols*.

6. Joshua Mkhululi, "Closing the Dispensation: A Rastafari Cultural Representation," personal journal, in the author's possession.

7. For an excellent discussion of the complexities embedded within this claim, see Perry, *London Is the Place for Me*.

8. Black people had been in England since the Elizabethan period, including sailors, merchants, enslaved Africans taken there by English planters from the West Indies, and black loyalists who had fought on the side of the British during the American War of Independence. For a comprehensive history of the black presence in Britain, see Fryer, *Staying Power*. See also Scobie, *Black Britannia*; and Chater, *Untold Histories*.

9. Parsons, *Second British Empire*, chapter 6.

10. "Manley Off to London," *Daily Gleaner*, September 5, 1958.

11. "One-Third of UK Colour-Prejudiced," *Daily Gleaner*, September 15, 1958.

12. "Mr. Manley's Visit to Britain," *Public Opinion*, September 20, 1958; "Thousands Book for Home," *Daily Gleaner*, September 8, 1958.

13. "Riots: Manley Flying to UK: Chief Minister Decides to Give On-the-Spot Help in Ending Racial Violence," *Daily Gleaner*, September 4, 1958; "Reports of Cultist Attacks on Policemen Draw Statement from Premier," *Daily Gleaner*, August, 40, 1960.

14. Campbell, *Rasta and Resistance*, 87.

15. Adams, *Rastafari Movement in England*, 43.

16. "Racism," *URIA Voice* 4 (1984): 27, National Anthropological Archives, Smithsonian Institute.

17. Bones, *One Love*, 38, 39.

18. Adams, *Rastafari Movement in England*, 37, 38.

19. Ibid., 10.

20. Sister Ivory Liveth Ivory to Carole Yawney, November 6, 1986, and Carole Yawney to Sister Liveth Ivory, June 8, 1986, Carole Yawney Papers, National Anthropological Archives, Smithsonian Institution.

21. "The Caribbean Focus," conference proposal, Carole Yawney Papers, National Anthropological Archives, Smithsonian Institution.

22. Adams, *Rastafari Movement in England*, 102.

23. Kisembo Karudi, interview with the author, July 16, 2016.

24. Ras Bupe Akiiki Karudi, "Every Story Has an Ending," unpublished autobiographical manuscript, 2002:17, in the author's possession.

25. Dyer, who was born in Jamaica during the 1930s, migrated to London in 1960, where he worked for more than three years. In September 1964, in response to a dream in which Haile Selassie called him, he decided to leave England with no attention to visa requirements or realistic modes of transportation. The story of Dyer's intention to get to Africa from England "on foot" has become the stuff of

legend and has made him a well-respected and famous Rastafarian. See Bishton, *Blackheart Man*, 28–29; and Campbell, *Rasta and Resistance*, 223–24.

26. Ras Bupe Akiiki Karudi, *Every Story Has an Ending*; Kisembo Karudi, interview with author, July 16, 2016, London, UK.

27. Karudi, "Support for On-Going Mission of Repatriation."

28. Kisembo Karudi, interview with the author, July 16, 2016.

29. Jah Bupe Akiiki Karudi, "Support for On-Going Mission of Repatriation and All Related."

30. Ibid.

31. Kenneth Edwards (Joshua Mkhululi) to Julius Nyerere, "Afrikans in the West," May 16, 1984, personal collection of Joshua Mkhululi, in the author's possession.

32. Ibid.

33. Ibid; emphasis added.

34. Ibid.

35. Bonacci, *Exodus!*, 139, 158.

36. Kenneth Edwards (Joshua Mkhululi) to Julius Nyerere, "Afrikans in the West."

37. Manley, "Grenada in the Context of History," 7–9, 45–47.

38. Levi, *Michael Manley*, 227.

39. The United States had been highly suspicious of Manley's government due in large part to his nonalignment and his friendship with Fidel Castro.

40. Edwards to Nyerere, "Afrikans in the West."

41. Ibid.

42. Ibid.

43. "Crowd, Colour Greet Nyerere," *Jamaica Daily News*, September 15, 1974.

44. Edwards to Nyerere, "Afrikans in the West."

45. M. K. Pinda to Ras Bupe Karudi, "Africans in the West," December 12, 1985, personal collection of Ras Bupe Karudi, in the author's possession.

46. Mizengo Kayanza Peter Pinda, interview with the author, Dar es Salaam, October 5, 2007.

47. Jah Bupe Akiiki Karudi, "Repatriation of Africans from Jamaica to Africa," January 30, 1986, box 7, folder 192, C. L. R. James Papers, Special Collections, Alma Jordan Library.

48. Ibid.

49. See Homiak, "'Ancients of Days' Seated Black."

50. Iman Mani, interview with the author, October 11, 2007.

51. Iman L. Mani, to the regional commissioner, "Afrikans from the West," September 1, 1994, in the author's possession; Iman Mani, interview with the author, October 11, 2007.

52. Iman Mani, interview with the author, October 11, 2007.

53. Yawney, "Exodus," 171.

54. Sangi Davis, interview with the author, June 1, 2015.

55. Jah Bupe Akiiki Karudi to C. L. R. James, September 6, 1986, box 7, folder 192, C. L. R. James Papers, Special Collections, Alma Jordan Library.

56. Ama, "From Mythologies to Realities," 3.
57. Ras Ato Kidani, interview with the author, May 2, 2013.
58. Ato Kidani Roberts, interview with the author, July 28, 2015.
59. Young, *African Colonial State*, 280.
60. Julius K. Nyerere, "The Race Problem in East Africa," in *Freedom and Unity*, 26.
61. Iliffe, *Modern History of Tanganyika*, 521.
62. Nyerere, "The Principles of Citizenship," in *Freedom and Unity*, 126, 128.
63. Ibid., 128.
64. Julius K. Nyerere, "President Nyerere's Speech to the Jamaican Parliament," September 17, 1974, Speeches and Statements, Mwalimu Nyerere Foundation.
65. To Nyerere's credit, lively discussions over creolisation had long been a part of Caribbean discourse and even leading pan-Africanists such as C. L. R. James presented the Caribbean in such terms. The prevalence of this discourse had even made for a more elastic notion of blackness among certain of the region's proponents of black power. Walter Rodney had included Indians in his definition of blackness and Eusi Kwayana, also Guyanese, was particularly concerned with how to make pan-Africanism work in a society as diverse as his. More on James's position in chapter 6. For a pioneering work on creolization in the Caribbean, see Edward Brathwaite, *Development of Creole Society in Jamaica 1770–1820*. For an overview of competing notions of creolization, which range from Brathwaite's conception of Afrogenesis to definitions that completely destabilize Africa in the creation of a Caribbean identity, see Verene A. Shepherd and Glen L. Richards, *Questioning Creole*. Walter Rodney, *Groundings with My Brothers*, 16; Kwayana's brand of pan-Africanism was shaped by his concerns over "how to share power in multi-ethnic societies." Nigel Westmaas, "An Organic Activist," 161.
66. Brennan, *Taifa*, 156. By contrast, in a speech Michael Manley made at the University of Dar es Salaam in 1973, he explained that "as a country," Jamaica "springs originally from Africa" and that, for his delegation, traveling to Tanzania brought about a "very real feeling of returning home . . . a sense of spiritual and historical homecoming." He added that as "an African people in the Caribbean we are not only concerned ideologically but we are concerned in a deeper *racial* sense." Manley, "The Prime Minister Addresses Members of the University Community."
67. Nettleford, *Identity, Race and Protest in Jamaica*, 41, 14.
68. Ibid., 14.
69. Owens, *Dread*, 57.
70. Nettleford, "Foreword," xii.
71. "Racism: White Supremacy," *URIA Voice* 2 (1984): 2, National Anthropological Archives, Smithsonian Institute.
72. Mkhululi, "Closing the Dispensation"; Roberts, interview with the author.
73. This point is made in Owens, *Dread*, 232.
74. The immigration department held files for each Rastafarian family, which were consulted each time the Rastafarians sought renewal.

75. MacLeod, *Visions of Zion*, 194.
76. Bonacci, *Exodus!*, 389.
77. Nyerere, "The Dilemma of the Pan-Africanist," *Freedom and Socialism*. London: Oxford University Press, 1968.

Chapter Five

1. Jah Bupe Akiiki Karudi, "Support for On-Going Mission of Repatriation and All Related," November 12, 1986, box 7, folder 192, C. L. R. James Papers, Special Collections, Alma Jordan Library.
2. Jah Bupe Akiiki Karudi to C. L. R. James, March 12, 1987, box 7, folder 192, C. L. R. James Papers, Special Collections, Alma Jordan Library.
3. Kisembo Karudi, interview with the author, July 16, 2016.
4. For a discussion of black men who talked about "manly sacrifice for a higher political cause," see Matera, *Black London*, chap. 5.
5. Ras Bupe Karudi, personal correspondence with the author, August 14, 2014.
6. Nkrumah, *Ghana*, 42.
7. Ras Bupe Karudi, personal correspondence with the author, August 14, 2014.
8. Kisembo Karudi, interview with the author, July 16, 2016.
9. Ato Kidani Roberts, interview with the author July 28, 2015; Kisembo Karudi, interview with the author, July 16, 2016; Joshua Mkhululi, "Closing the Dispensation: A Rastafari Cultural Representation," personal journal, in the author's possession.
10. Kisembo Karudi, interview with the author, July 16, 2016.
11. Bonacci, *Exodus!*, 192–93.
12. Jah Bupe Akiiki Karudi, "Repatriation of Africans from Jamaica to Africa," box 7, folder 192, C. L. R. James Papers, Special Collections, Alma Jordan Library.
13. Ibid.
14. Joseph R. Mack to Jah Bupe Akiiki Karudi, December 12, 1986, box 7, folder 192, C. L. R. James Papers, Special Collections, Alma Jordan Library.
15. Conrad W. Worrill to Jah Bupe Akiiki Karudi, November 12, 1986, box 7, folder 192, C. L. R. James Papers, Special Collections, Alma Jordan Library.
16. Al Hajj Anas M. Luqman to Jah Bupe Akiiki Karudi, November 25, 1986, box 7, folder 192, C. L. R. James Papers, Special Collections, Alma Jordan Library.
17. Jacob Carruthers to Jah Bupe Akiiki Karudi, November 25, 1986, box 7, folder 192, C. L. R. James Papers, Special Collections, Alma Jordan Library.
18. John Henrik Clarke to Jah Bupe Akiiki Karudi, October 4, 1986, box 7, folder 192, C. L. R. James Papers, Special Collections, Alma Jordan Library; L. E. Mitchell Jr. to Jah Bupe Akiiki Karudi, November 1, 1986, box 7, folder 192, C. L. R. James Papers, Special Collections, Alma Jordan Library.
19. Jamaican reggae star Jimmy Cliff pledged support. Jah Bupe Akiiki Karudi to C. L. R. James, April 24, 1986, box 7, folder 192, C. L. R. James Papers, Special Collections, Alma Jordan Library.
20. Karudi to James, March 12, 1987.

21. Ras Bupe Karudi, personal correspondence with the author, August 4, 2014.

22. Ras Bupe Karudi to C. L. R. James, August 15, 1986, box 7, folder 192, C. L. R. James Papers, Special Collections, Alma Jordan Library.

23. Ras Bupe Karudi to C. L. R. James, August 19, 1986, box 7, folder 192, C. L. R. James Papers, Special Collections, Alma Jordan Library.

24. Joshua Mkhululi, interview with the author, February 10, 2008.

25. Bonacci, *Exodus!*, 154–55.

26. Mkhululi, "Closing the Dispensation." For a discussion of various responses to polygyny by women within Rasta, see Yawney, "Moving with the Dawtas of Rastafari," 67–68.

27. Mair, *Historical Study of Women*, 43, 44. For evidence of nuclear families during the period of enslavement, see Higman, "Household Structure and Fertility"; and Higman, "The Slave Populations of the British Caribbean."

28. Beckles, *Natural Rebels*, 118.

29. Burrill, *States of Marriage*, 9.

30. Moore and Johnson, *Neither Led nor Driven*, 96, 97.

31. Ibid., 98; emphasis in the original.

32. Karudi to James, March 12, 1987.

33. Jah Bupe Akiiki Karudi to C. L. R. James, April 4, 1986, box 7, folder 192, C. L. R. James Papers, Special Collections, Alma Jordan Library.

34. "URIA Doctrine & Principles," *URIA Voice* 4 (1984): 38. National Anthropological Archives, Smithsonian Institute.

35. Clegg, *Price of Liberty*, 90.

36. M. Y. C. Lumbanga, Ministry of Lands, Natural Resources and Tourism, to Joshua Mkhululi, "Repatriation of Africans from Jamaica to Africa—Land for Resettlement," September, 15, 1989, in the author's possession.

37. Ibid.

38. Ofisi Ya Waziri Mkuu Na Makamu wa Kwanza wa Rais, Barua Nd. J. K. Kileo, "Wajamaika Weusi Kuruhusiwa Kuishi Tanzania (Bwana Ras Bupe Akuki Karudi)," February 18, 1991, in the author's possession.

39. Ibid.; my translation.

40. Ibid.

41. Ofisi ya Mkuu Mkoa, Barua, Mkuu wa Wilaya, "Wajamaica Weusi Walioruhusiwa Kuishu Tanzania Kama 'Special Case,'" July 19, 1992, in the author's possession. The letter did not provide details as to exactly what type of assistance the district commissioner should provide beyond the title deed, but mentioned that he had received some funds from the prime minister's office.

42. Coldham, "Land Tenure and Reform in Tanzania," 227.

43. Manji, "Gender and the Politics of the Land Reform Process," 647.

44. Tanzania had been a one-party state since independence, but in 1990 Nyerere opened multiparty debate in the country. In 1991 the Nyalali Commission was appointed to examine the multiparty issue, and by May 1992 the National Assembly passed legislation to initiate a multiparty system.

45. Ministry of Lands, *Report of the Presidential Commission of Inquiry*, 94.
46. Ibid., 21.
47. Schneider, "Developmentalism and Its Failings," 236.
48. Coldham, "Land Tenure and Reform in Tanzania," 242.
49. Campbell, "Land Issues and the Democratisation Process in Tanzania," 78.
50. Geiger, *TANU Women*, 1.
51. Askew, "Sung and Unsung," 19.
52. Ministry of Lands, *Report of the Presidential Commission of Inquiry*.
53. Ibid., 94.
54. Ibid., 8.
55. Campbell, "Land Issues and the Democratisation Process in Tanzania," 75.
56. Shivji, *Not Yet Democracy*, 2.
57. Ministry of Lands, *Report of the Presidential Commission of Inquiry*, 12.
58. Shivji, *Not Yet Democracy*, 3.
59. Ministry of Lands, *Report of the Presidential Commission of Inquiry*, 16.
60. Ibid., 114.
61. Shivji, *Not Yet Democracy*, 8.
62. Iman Mani, interview with the author, August 25, 2009.
63. Mizengo Kayanza Peter Pinda, interview with the author, Dar es Salaam, October 5, 2007.
64. Julius Nyerere, "*Ujamaa*-The basis of African Socialism," in *Ujamaa: Essays on Socialism*, 4.
65. Ibid., 5.
66. Kisembo Karudi, interview with the author, July 16, 2016
67. Ibid.
68. Ibid.
69. Ibid. Carole Yawney also found this to be true for some Rasta women. See Yawney, "Moving with the Dawtas of Rastafari," 72. For a discussion of how Rasta women have defined and redefined themselves, see Tafari-Ama, "Rastawoman as Rebel."
70. Ibid.
71. Ibid.
72. Homiak, "Never Trade a Continent for an Island," 206.
73. Mkhululi, "Closing the Dispensation."
74. Yawney, "Exodus," 134.
75. Thobile Gola to Jah Bupe Karudi, July 9, 1985, box 7, folder 192, C. L. R. James Papers, Special Collections, Alma Jordan Library.
76. Karudi did not provide an explanation as to why he chose to align with the PAC as opposed to the African National Congress. It is not likely that he was oblivious to the ideological differences between both groups, or to the problems the PAC faced as a group in Tanzania.
77. Karudi, "Support for On-going Mission of Repatriation."

78. Ibid.

79. "Mozambique," *URIA Voice* 2 (1984): 10, 12, 13, 19, 20. National Anthropological Archives, Smithsonian Institute.

80. Mkhululi, "Closing the Dispensation."

81. Horace Campbell, "Long Live the Spirit of Joshua Mkhululi: A Tribute to a Tireless Defender of Freedom and Justice," *Swahili Times*, March 29, 2009.

82. "Message by Hon. C. D. Msuya, MP, Minister for Finance, Economic Affairs and Planning," *Tanzania Daily News*, March 26, 1988.

83. "Inauguration of the Institute of Accountancy Arusha," *Tanzania Daily News*, March 26, 1988.

84. "Message by Hon. C. D. Msuya."

85. Mkhululi, "Closing the Dispensation."

86. Ras Bupe Karudi, "Every Story Has an Ending," unpublished autobiographical manuscript, in the author's possession, 2002, 32.

87. Ras Bupe Karudi, "Distribution of Black Books in Mother Afrika," proposal on URIA stationery, n.d., box 7, folder 192, C. L. R. James Papers, Special Collections, Alma Jordan Library.

88. Bgoya, "From Tanzania to Kansas and Back Again," 105.

89. Markle, "'Book Publishers for a Pan-African World,'" 16.

90. Nyerere, "The Importance and Pleasure of Reading," in *Freedom and Socialism*, 107–8.

91. Karudi to James, March 12, 1987.

92. Moyer, "Street-Corner Justice in the Name of Jah," 32, 34, 35, 48.

93. Rajabu, "Rastafari in Tanzanian Cultural Context."

94. Ishii, *African Rastafari*.

95. Ato Kidani Roberts, interview with the author, July 28, 2015; Ishii, *African Rastafari*, 270.

96. Ato Kidani Roberts, interview with the author, July 28, 2015.

97. Ishii, *African Rastafari*, 271.

98. Ato Kidani Roberts, interview with the author, July 28, 2015.

99. Ras Mabondo (Mekonnen) to Carole Yawney, n.d. Carole Yawney Papers, correspondence file, box 9, National Anthropological Archives, Smithsonian Institution.

100. Ibid. The word "churchical" is a part of the Rastafarian lexicon and refers to a focus on the religious aspect of Rastafari.

101. Ras Mabondo (Mekonnen) to Carole Yawney

102. Ato Kidani Roberts, interview with the author, July 28, 2015.

103. Moyer, "Street-Corner Justice in the Name of Jah," 48.

104. Ishii, *African Rastafari*, 273.

105. Robinson, *Black Marxism*, 262, 263.

106. Ras Bupe Karudi, interview with the author, August 14, 2014.

107. Tripp, *Changing the Rules*, 2.

108. Prashad, *Poorer Nations*, 5.

109. Shivji, *Where Is Uhuru?*, 156–57.

110. Z. S. H. Mwaruka to Prof. Joshua Mkhululi, September 9, 1992, in the author's possession.

111. "Ofisi Ya Waziri Mkuu Na Makamu wa Kwanza wa Rais."

112. Karudi, "Repatriation of Africans from Jamaica to Africa."

Chapter Six

1. Ras Bupe Karudi to C. L. R. James, April 4, 1986, box 7, folder 192, C. L. R. James Papers, Special Collections, Alma Jordan Library.

2. James was, by then, eighty-five years old. Ras Bupe Karudi to C. L. R. James, September 6, 1986, box 7, folder 192, C. L. R. James Papers, Special Collections, Alma Jordan Library.

3. For an excellent study, see Makalani, *In the Cause of Freedom*.

4. Putnam, *Radical Moves*, 49, 79.

5. Makalani, *In the Cause of Freedom*.

6. Sixth Pan African Congress, "Focus on the Sixth Pan African Congress: C. L. R James: an Overview," 1–2, Congress Newsletter, box 8, folder 208, C. L. R. James Papers, Special Collections, Alma Jordan Library.

7. C. L. R. James to Robert Hill, passage to be read by Hill at the TransAfrica Dinner where James was given the African Freedom Award, May 23, 1985, box 7, folder 192, C. L. R. James Papers, Special Collections, Alma Jordan Library.

8. Jah Bupe Akiiki Karudi to C. L. R. James, September 20, 1986, box 7, folder 192, C. L. R. James Papers, Special Collections, Alma Jordan Library.

9. Karudi to James, September 6, 1986.

10. Ibid.

11. C. L. R. James to Jah Bupe Akiiki Karudi, December 27, 1985, box 7, folder 192, C. L. R. James Papers, Special Collections, Alma Jordan Library.

12. Ibid.

13. Kelley, "World the Diaspora Made," 113.

14. C. L. R. James, "Rastafari at Home and Abroad," in *At the Rendezvous of Victory*, 163, 164.

15. Kelley, "World the Diaspora Made," 119.

16. C. L. R. James, speech delivered on September 7, 1969 for the African and American Teachers Association, an event hosted by John Henrik Clarke, box 20, folder 375, C. L. R. James Papers, Special Collections, Alma Jordan Library, 8. Along with a letter asking him to edit it for publication in the journal *Freedomways*, Clarke sent a typed transcript of the speech to James on April 17, 1970.

17. Ibid., 20. For more on James's praise for Tanzania and Nyerere, see James, *Nkrumah and the Ghana Revolution*, 214–23.

18. James speech, September 7, 1969, 20. Also see James, *History of Pan-African Revolt*.

19. For a detailed description of the *Arusha Declaration*, see chapter 2.

20. For examples of the literature, much of it published before James's exchanges with Rastafarians in the mid-1980s, see Hydén, *Beyond Ujamaa in Tanzania*; Coulson, *Tanzania, 1800–1980*; Shivji, *Silent Class Struggle*; Eckert, "Useful Instruments of Participation?"; Schneider, "Developmentalism and Its Failings"; Finucane, *Rural Development and Bureaucracy in Tanzania*; and Ingle, *From Village to State in Tanzania*.

21. C. L. R. James, "The 7th Pan African Congress," box 8, folder 225, C. L. R. James Papers, Special Collections, Alma Jordan Library.

22. McClendon, *C. L. R. James's Notes*, 3. For James's assessment of Nkrumah's misstep and the fall of Ghana as the beacon of black pride, see James, *Nkrumah and the Ghana Revolution*.

23. Nyerere, "Education for Self-Reliance," in *Ujamaa: Essays on Socialism*, 46.

24. I have taken the concept of "miseducation" from Carter G. Woodson's seminal work *Mis-Education of the Negro*, which was first published in 1933.

25. Rodney, "Education in Africa and Contemporary Tanzania," 84.

26. After Tanzania became the headquarters for the Organization of African Unity's Liberation Committee, it became a mecca for revolutionaries, who could gain a political education based on the revolutionary activity there. In addition, many of the liberation movements set up actual schools in Tanzania.

27. Nyerere, "Education for Liberation," 2, 3.

28. Edmonds, *Rastafari: From Outcasts to Culture Bearers*, 48.

29. Joshua Mkhululi (Ken Edwards) and Ras Bupe Karudi to the Afrikan Heads of State, "The O.A.U," July 11, 1987, personal collection of Joshua Mkhululi, in the author's possession.

30. Freire, *Pedagogy of the Oppressed*, 58.

31. Ras Bupe Akiiki Karudi, "Every Story Has an Ending," unpublished autobiographical manuscript, 2002, 16, in the author's possession.

32. Bob Marley and the Wailers, "Babylon System," on *Survival* (Kingston: Tuff Gong, 1979).

33. C. L. R. James, "The Former Colonial World," October 27, 1983, box 23, folder 456, C. L. R. James Papers, Special Collections, Alma Jordan Library.

34. C. L. R. James, untitled document, October 29, 1984, box 23, folder 456, C. L. R. James Papers, Special Collections, Alma Jordan Library.

35. Brian Hackland to C. L. R. James, February 16, 1984, box 8, folder 204, C. L. R. James Papers, Special Collections, Alma Jordan Library; C. L. R. James to Brian Hackland, February 11, 1984, box 8, folder 204, C. L. R. James Papers, Special Collections, Alma Jordan Library.

36. M. A. Shakespeare to C. L. R. James, box 8, folder 204, C. L. R. James Papers, Special Collections, Alma Jordan Library.

37. C. L. R. James, "The Former Colonial World," box 7, folder 192, C. L. R. James Papers, Special Collections, Alma Jordan Library.

38. Bogues, *Black Heretics, Black Prophets*.

39. Henry and Buhle, *C. L. R. James's Caribbean*, ix.

40. C. L. R. James, in *At the Rendezvous of Victory*, 21.

41. Bogues, "C. L. R. James, Pan-Africanism and the Black Radical Tradition," 492.

42. For a discussion of the Drum and Spear Press and Karudi's book project, see chapter 5.

43. Bogues, "C. L. R. James, Pan-Africanism and the Black Radical Tradition."

44. See Lamming, *In the Castle of My Skin*; Lamming, *Pleasures of Exile*; and Thiong'o, "Beyond Nativism."

45. Henry and Buhle, *C. L. R. James's Caribbean*, x.

Epilogue

1. For an excellent examination of the historiographical issues surrounding women and gender in the history of Pan-Africanism, see Blain, Leeds, and Taylor, "Guest Editor Introduction."

2. Joshua Mkhululi (Ken Edwards) and Ras Bupe Karudi to the Afrikan Heads of State, "The O.A.U," July 11, 1987, personal collection of Joshua Mkhululi, in the author's possession.

3. Ishii, *African Rastafari*, 261, 370, 267, 269.

4. This point was made by Tanzanian Rastafarians with whom the author spoke in Dar es Salaam in 2007.

5. Ishii, *African Rastafari*, 268; Ishii uses the newspaper *Alasiri* to make this point. I have also seen copies of this and other Kiswahili newspapers in the Tanzanian National Archives that documented the growing Rastafarian presence in the late 1990s.

6. Moyer, "Street-Corner Justice in the Name of Jah," 50–51.

7. Rastafarians who repatriated to Ghana also faced this stigma associated with Ganja. See Carmen M. White, "Living in Zion: Rastafarian Repatriates in Ghana, West Africa," 311.

8. Senior, *Dying to Better Themselves*; Watkins-Owens, *Blood Relations*; Putnam, *Radical Moves*.

9. The author witnessed this exchange (which occurred both in the morning and at the end of the school day) while in Tanzania in June 2005.

10. Joshua Mkhululi, "Closing the Dispensation: A Rastafari Cultural Presentation," in the author's possession.

11. Gray, "Predation Politics"; Meeks and Lindahl, *New Caribbean Thought*; Bogues, "Politics, Nation and PostColony." For an engagement with Afro-pessimism, see Diawara, *In Search of Africa*.

12. Patterson, *Children of Sisyphus*.

13. Achebe, *Man of the People*.

14. Julius K. Nyerere, "Speech at the Graduate Institute of International Studies, Geneva," January 18, 1990, Speeches and Statements, Mwalimu Nyerere Foundation.

15. Governor Blackburn, "The Dispatch No. 637," enclosed in P. J. Kitcatt to Colonial Office, FO 371/138109 C695658, British National Archives.

16. Glaude, *Exodus!*; Smith, *Conjuring Culture*.

Bibliography

Archives and Libraries

Atlanta, Georgia
    Robert W. Woodruff Library of the Atlanta University Center
College Park, Maryland
    National Archives of the United States
Dar es Salaam, Tanzania
    Mwalimu Nyerere Foundation
    Tanzania National Archives
    University of Dar es Salaam Library
Kingston, Jamaica
    Institute of Jamaica
    Michael Manley Foundation
    National Library of Jamaica
Port of Spain, Trinidad
    Alma Jordan Library, University of the West Indies
United Kingdom
    Black Cultural Archives, London
    National Archives, Kew, England
Washington, DC
    Smithsonian Institution, National Anthropological Archives

Private Collections

Papers of Angela "Bunny" Heron
Papers of Ras Bupe Karudi
Papers of Joshua Mkhululi

Newspapers and Periodicals

Black Man Speaks
Bongo Man
Ch'indaba
Daily Gleaner
Guardian
Jamaica Daily News
Jamaica Observer
Nationalist, Tanzania
Our Own
Public Opinion
Rastafari Speaks
Standard

Swahili Times
Tanzania Daily News
Uhuru

URIA Voice
Voice of Rasta

Interviews by the Author

Butiku, Joseph. Dar es Salaam, October 10, 2007.
Christie, Joseph. Hanover, Jamaica, July 24, 2009.
Davis, Sangi, June 1, 2015.
Karudi, Kisembo. July 16 and 23, 2016.
Karudi, Ras Bupe. Dar es Salaam, July 10, 2005.
Mani, Iman. Dar es Salaam, October 11, 2007.
Manley, Beverley. Kingston, July 2, 2012.
McDonald, Errol. Kingston, August 9, 2007.
Mkhululi, Joshua (Kenneth Edwards). Arusha, Tanzania, October 9, 2007.
Pennicott-Smith, Grace. St. James, Jamaica, July 22, 2009.
Pinda, Mizengo Kayanza Peter. Dar es Salaam, October 5, 2007.
Roberts, Ato Kidani, July 28, 2015.
Sister Angela, Kingston, July 10, 2001.
Sister Barbara, Kingston, July 9 2001.
Small, Robin "Jerry." Kingston, July 10, 2008.
Thompson, Dudley. Weston, FL, July, 2009.

Secondary Sources

Achebe, Chinua. *A Man of the People*. London: Heinemann, 1966.
Adams, Norman (Jah Blue). *The Rastafari Movement in England: A Historical Report*. London: GWA Works, 2002.
Adi, Hakim. *West Africans in Britain, 1900–1960: Nationalism, Pan-Africanism, and Communism*. London: Lawrence and Wishart, 1998.
Agyeman, Opoku. "The Osagyefo, the Mwalimu, and Pan-Africanism: A Study in the Growth of a Dynamic Concept." *Journal of Modern African Studies* 13, no. 4 (1975): 653–74.
Alleyne, Mervyn C. *Construction and Representation of Race and Ethnicity in the Caribbean and the World*. Kingston: University of the West Indies Press, 2002.
Allman, Jean. "Phantoms of the Archive: Kwame Nkrumah, a Nazi Pilot Named Hanna, and the Contingencies of Postcolonial History Writing." *American Historical Review* 118, no. 1 (2013): 104–29.
Allman, Jean Marie, and John Parker. *Tongnaab: The History of a West African God*. Bloomington: Indiana University Press, 2005.
Alpers, Edward. "The African Diaspora in the Northwestern Indian Ocean: Reconsideration of an Old Problem, New Directions for Research."

Comparative Studies of South Asia, Africa and the Middle East 17, no. 2 (1997): 62–81.

Ama [Tracey-Ann Clarke]. "From Mythologies to Realities: The Iconography of Ras Daniel Heartman." *Small Axe* 23 (11, no. 2) (2007): 66–87.

Aminzade, Ronald. *Race, Nation, and Citizenship in Post-colonial Africa: The Case of Tanzania*. New York: Cambridge University Press, 2013.

Anderson, Benedict. *Imagined Communities: Reflections on the Origin and Spread of Nationalism*. New York: Verso, 1983.

Appiah, Kwame Anthony. *In My Father's House: Africa in Philosophy and Culture*. New York: Oxford University Press, 1992.

Askew, Kelly. *Performing the Nation: Swahili Music and Cultural Politics in Tanzania*. Chicago: University of Chicago Press, 2002.

———. "Sung and Unsung: Musical Reflections on Tanzanian Postsocialism." *Africa* 76, no. 1 (2006): 15–43.

Askew, Kelly, and M. Anne Pitcher, eds. "African Socialisms and Postsocialisms." Special issue, *Africa: Journal of the International African Institute* 76, no. 1 (2006).

Austin-Broos, Diane J. *Jamaica Genesis: Religion and the Politics of Moral Orders*. Chicago: University of Chicago Press, 1997.

Baer, Hans A., and Merrill Singer. *African American Religion: Varieties of Protest and Accommodation*. Knoxville: University of Tennessee Press, 2002.

Baraka, Imamu Amiri. "Towards Pan-Africanism: Tanzania Independence Anniversary." *Black World*, March 1972, 65–67.

Barnett, Michael, ed. *Rastafari in the New Millennium: A Rastafari Reader*. Syracuse, NY: Syracuse University Press, 2012.

———. "Rastafari in the New Millennium: Rastafari at the Dawn of the Fifth Epoch." In *Rastafari in the New Millennium: A Rastafari Reader*, edited by Michael Barnett, 1–12. Syracuse, NY: Syracuse University Press, 2012.

Barrett, Leonard E. *The Rastafarians: A Study in Messianic Cultism on Jamaica*. San Juan, Puerto Rico: Institute of Caribbean Studies, 1968.

Beckles, Hilary. *Britain's Black Debt: Reparations for Caribbean Slavery and Native Genocide*. Kingston: University of the West Indies Press, 2013.

———. *Natural Rebels: A Social History of Enslaved Black Women in Barbados*. New Brunswick, NJ: Rutgers University Press, 1989.

Bedasse, Monique. "Rasta Evolution: The Theology of the Twelve Tribes of Israel." *Journal of Black Studies* 40, no. 5 (2010): 960–73.

Bender, Matthew V. "'For More and Better Water, Choose Pipes!' Building Water and Nation on Kilimanjaro, 1961–1985." *Journal of Southern African Studies* 34, no. 4 (2008): 841–59.

Bennett, J. Harry. *Bondsmen and Bishops: Slavery and Apprenticeship on the Codrington Plantations of Barbados, 1710–1838*. Berkeley: University of California Press, 1958.

Berger, Iris. "Fertility as Power: Spirit Mediums, Priestesses and the Pre-colonial State in Interlacustrine East Africa." In *Revealing Prophets: Prophecy in Eastern African History*, edited by David Anderson and Douglas H. Johnson. Athens: Ohio University Press, 1995.

Bgoya, Walter. "From Tanzania to Kansas and Back Again." In *No Easy Victories: African Liberation and American Activists over a Half Century, 1950-2000*, edited by William Minter, Gail Hovey, and Charles Cobb Jr. Trenton, NJ: Africa World Press, 2008.

Bishton, Derek. *Black Heart Man*. London: Chatto and Windus, 1986.

Blain, Keisha N., Asia Leeds, and Ula Y. Taylor, eds. "Guest Editor Introduction." *Women, Gender, and Families of Color* 4, no. 2 (2016): 139-45.

Blommaert, Jan. "Intellectual and Ideological Leadership in Ujamaa Tanzania." *African Languages and Cultures* 10, no. 2 (1997): 129-44.

Bogues, Anthony. *Black Heretics, Black Prophets: Radical Political Intellectuals*. New York: Routledge, 2003.

———. "C. L. R. James, Pan-Africanism and the Black Radical Tradition." *Critical Arts* 25, no. 4 (2011): 484-99.

———. "Michael Manley, Trade Unionism, and the Politics of Equality." In *Caribbean Labor and Politics: Legacies of Cheddi Jagan and Michael Manley*, edited by Perry Mars and Alma H. Young, 40-63. Detroit: Wayne State University Press, 2004.

———. "Politics, Nation and PostColony: Caribbean Inflections." *Small Axe* 6, no. 1 (March 2002): 1-30.

Bonacci, Giulia. *Exodus! Heirs and Pioneers, Rastafari Return to Ethiopia*. Translated by Antoinette Tidjani Alou. Kingston: University of the West Indies Press, 2015.

———. "The Return to Ethiopia of the Twelve Tribes of Israel." *New West Indian Guide* 90 (2016): 1-27.

Bones, Jah. *One Love: History, Doctrine and Livity*. London: Voice of Rasta, 1985.

Brathwaite, Edward. *The Development of Creole Society in Jamaica 1770-1820*. Oxford: Clarendon Press, 1978.

Breitman, George, ed. *Malcolm X Speaks: Selected Speeches and Statements*. New York: Grove, 1994.

Brennan, James R. "Blood Enemies: Exploitation and Urban Citizenship in the Nationalist Political Thought of Tanzania, 1958-1975." *Journal of African History* 47 (2006): 389-413.

———. *Taifa: Making Nation and Race in Urban Tanzania*. Athens: Ohio University Press, 2012.

Brown, Scot. *Fighting for Us: Maulana Karenga, the US Organization, and Black Cultural Nationalism*. New York: New York University Press, 2003.

Bryan, Patrick E. *Edward Seaga and the Challenges of Modern Jamaica*. Kingston: University of the West Indies Press, 2009.

Bryson, Sasha Turner. "The Art of Power: Poison and Obeah Accusations and the Struggle for Dominance and Survival in Jamaica's Slave Society." *Caribbean Studies* 41, no. 2 (2013): 61-90.

Burrill, Emily. *States of Marriage: Gender, Justice, and Rights in Colonial Mali*. Athens: Ohio University Press, 2015.

Buruku, Daisy Sykes. "The Townsman: Kleist Sykes." In *Modern Tanzanians*, edited by John Iliffe, 95–114. Dar es Salaam: EAPH, 1973.

Butler, Kim D. "Defining Diaspora, Refining a Discourse." *Diaspora* 10, no. 2 (2001): 189–219.

Cabral, Amilcar. *Return to the Source: Selected Speeches of Amilcar Cabral*. New York: Africa Information Service and the African Party for the Independence of Guinea and the Cape Verde Islands, 1973.

Campbell, Horace G. "Land Issues and the Democratisation Process in Tanzania: A Review of the Report of the Presidential Commission of Inquiry." *Utafiti* 3, no. 1 (1996): 67–90.

———. *Rasta and Resistance: From Marcus Garvey to Walter Rodney*. Trenton, NJ: Africa World Press, 1987.

———. "Walter Rodney: A Biography and Bibliography." *Review of African Political Economy* 18 (1980): 132–37.

———. "Walter Rodney and Pan-Africanism Today." Paper presented at the Africana Studies and Research Center, Cornell University, September 28, 2005.

Campbell, Horace G., and Howard Stein. *Tanzania and the IMF: The Dynamics of Liberalization*. Boulder, CO: Westview, 1992.

Campbell, Horace G., and Rodney Worrell. *Pan-Africanism, Pan-Africanists, and African Liberation in the 21st Century: Two Lectures*. Washington, DC: New Academic, 2006.

Campt, Tina. *Other Germans: Black Germans and the Politics of Race, Gender, and Memory in the Third Reich*. Ann Arbor: University of Michigan Press, 2005.

Cashmore, Ernest. *Rastaman: The Rastafarian Movement in England*. Boston: Allen and Unwin, 1979.

Catlin-Jairazbhoy, Amy, and Edward A. Alpers. *Sidis and Scholars: Essays on African Indians*. Trenton, NJ: Red Sea, 2004.

Center for Contemporary Cultural Studies. *The Empire Strikes Back: Race and Racism in 70s Britain*. London: Routledge, 1982.

Chater, Kathleen. *Untold Histories: Black People in England and Wales during the Period of the British Slave Trade, c. 1660–1807*. Manchester, England: Manchester University Press, 2011.

Chevannes, Barry. *Betwixt and Between: Explorations in an African-Caribbean Mindscape*. Kingston: Randle, 2006.

———. "Rastafari and the Exorcism of the Ideology of Racism and Classism in Jamaica." In *Chanting Down Babylon: The Rastafari Reader*, edited by Nathaniel Samuel Murrell, William D. Spencer, and Adrian Anthony McFarlane. Philadelphia: Temple University Press, 1998.

———. *Rastafari: Roots and Ideology*. Syracuse, NY: Syracuse University Press, 1994.

———. "Rastafari: Towards a New Approach." *New West Indian Guide* 64, nos. 3–4 (1990): 127–48.

———. "Ships That Will Never Sail: The Paradox of Rastafari Pan-Africanism." *Critical Arts* 25, no. 4 (2011): 565–75.

Christensen, Jeanne. *Rastafari Reasoning and the Rastawoman: Gender Constructions in the Shaping of Rastafari Livity.* Lanham, MD: Lexington, 2014.

Chude-Sokei, Louis. "Roots, Diaspora and Possible Africas." In *Global Reggae*, edited by Carolyn Cooper. Kingston: Canoe, 2012.

Clark, Sebastian. *Jah Music: The Evolution of Popular Jamaican Song.* London: Heinemann, 1980.

Clegg, Claude Andrew. *The Price of Liberty: African Americans and the Making of Liberia.* Chapel Hill: University of North Carolina Press, 2004.

Cliffe, Lionel, and John S. Saul. *Socialism in Tanzania: An Interdisciplinary Reader.* Nairobi, Kenya: East African Publishing House, 1972.

Cobb, Charlie. *Africa Notebook: Views on Returning "Home."* Chicago: Institute of Positive Education, 1972.

Coldham, Simon. "Land Tenure and Reform in Tanzania: Legal Problems and Perspectives." *Journal of Modern African Studies* 33, no. 2 (1995): 227–42.

Cole, Margaret. "The Fabian Society." *Political Quarterly* 15 (1944): 245–56.

———. "The Story of the Society." *Fabian Journal* 12 (1954): 4–10ff.

Cooper, Frederick. *Citizenship between Empire and Nation: Remaking France and French Africa, 1945–1960.* Princeton, NJ: Princeton University Press, 2016.

———. *Decolonization and African Society: The Labor Question in French and British Africa.* Cambridge: Cambridge University Press, 1996.

———. "Possibility and Constraint: African Independence in Historical Perspective." *Journal of African History* 49, no. 2 (2008): 167–96.

Coulson, Andrew. *African Socialism in Practice: The Tanzanian Experience.* Nottingham, England: Spokesman, 1979.

———. *Tanzania 1800–1980: A Political Economy.* Oxford: Clarendon, 1982.

Curtin, Philip. *Two Jamaicas: The Role of Ideas in a Tropical Colony, 1830–1865.* New York: Atheneum, 1955.

Dawes, Kwame. *Natural Mysticism: Towards a New Reggae Aesthetic.* Leeds, England: Peepal Tree Press, 1999.

Diawara, Manthia. *In Search of Africa.* Cambridge, MA: Harvard University Press, 1998.

Drake, St. Clair. *The Redemption of Africa and Black Religion.* Chicago: Third World, 1970.

Du Bois, David Graham. "Afro-American Militants in Africa: Problems and Responsibilities." *Black World*, February 1972, 4–11.

Duke, Eric D. *Building a Nation: Caribbean Federation in the Black Diaspora.* Gainesville: University Press of Florida, 2016.

Dupuy, Alex. "Race and Class in the Postcolonial Caribbean: The Views of Walter Rodney." *Latin American Perspectives* 23, no. 2 (1996): 107–29.

Eckert, Andreas. "Useful Instruments of Participation? Local Government and Cooperatives in Tanzania, 1940s to 1970s." *International Journal of African Historical Studies* 40 (2007): 97–118.

Edmonds, Ennis B. "Dread 'I' in-a-Babylon: Ideological Resistance and Cultural Revitalization." In *Chanting Down Babylon: The Rastafari Reader*, edited by Nathaniel Samuel Murrell, William D. Spencer, and Adrian Anthony McFarlane, 23–35. Philadelphia: Temple University Press, 1998.

———. *Rastafari: From Outcasts to Culture Bearers*. Oxford: Oxford University Press, 2003.

———. *Rastafari: A Very Short Introduction*. New York: Oxford University Press, 2013.

Edwards, Brent Hayes. *The Practice of Diaspora: Literature, Translation, and the Rise of Black Internationalism*. Cambridge, MA: Harvard University Press, 2003.

———. "The Uses of Diaspora." *Social Text* 66, no. 1 (2001): 45–73.

El Hamel, Chouki. *Black Morocco: A History of Slavery, Race and Islam*. Cambridge: Cambridge University Press, 2013.

Erskine, Noel Leo. *From Garvey to Marley: Rastafari Theology*. Gainesville: University Press of Florida, 2004.

Ewing, Adam. *The Age of Garvey: How a Jamaican Activist Created a Mass Movement and Changed Global Black Politics*. Princeton, NJ: Princeton University Press, 2014.

Falola, Toyin. *Nationalism and African Intellectuals*. Rochester, NY: University of Rochester Press, 2001.

Fanon, Frantz. *The Wretched of the Earth*. Translated by Jean-Paul Sartre. New York: Grove, 2005.

Feierman, Steven. "Colonizers, Scholars, and the Creation of Invisible Histories." In *Beyond the Cultural Turn: New Directions in the Study of Society and Culture*, edited by Victoria E. Bonnell and Lynn Hunt, 182–216. Berkeley: University of California Press, 1999.

Ferguson, James. *Global Shadows: Africa in the Neoliberal World Order*. Durham, NC: Duke University Press, 2006.

Finucane, James R. *Rural Development and Bureaucracy in Tanzania: The Case of Mwanza Region*. Uppsala: Scandinavian Institute of African Studies, 1974.

Fredrickson, George M. *Black Liberation: A Comparative History of Black Ideologies in the United States and South Africa*. New York: Oxford University Press, 1995.

Freedman, Jim. *Nyabingi: The Social History of an African Divinity*. Tervuren, Belgium: Musée Royal de L'Afrique Centrale, 1984.

Freire, Paulo. *Pedagogy of the Oppressed*. Translated by Myra Bergman Ramos. New York: Continuum, 2000.

Friedland, William, and Carl Rosberg, eds. *African Socialism*. Palo Alto, CA: Stanford University Press, 1964.

Fryer, Peter. *Staying Power: The History of Black People in Britain*. London: Pluto, 1984.

Gaines, Kevin. *American Africans in Ghana: Black Expatriates and the Civil Rights Era*. Chapel Hill: University of North Carolina Press, 2006.

Garrett, James. "A Historical Sketch: The Sixth Pan African Congress: An Overview," *Black World*, March 1974: 21–24.

Garrison, Len. *Black Youth, Rastafarianism and the Identity Crisis in Britain*. London: Acer Books, 1980.

Gebrekidan, Fikru Negash. *Bond without Blood: A History of Ethiopian and New World Black Relations, 1896–1991*. Trenton, NJ: Africa World Press, 2004.

Geiger, Susan. *TANU Women: Gender and Culture in the Making of Tanganyikan Nationalism, 1955–1965*. Portsmouth, NH: Heinemann, 1997.

Gilroy, Paul. *The Black Atlantic: Modernity and Double Consciousness*. Cambridge, MA: Harvard University Press, 1993.

———. *There Ain't No Black in the Union Jack: The Cultural Politics of Race and Nation*. Chicago: University of Chicago Press, 1991.

Girvan, Norman. "After Rodney—The Politics of Student Protest in Jamaica." *New World Quarterly* 3–4 (1967–68): 59–68.

Glassman, Jonathon. *War of Words, War of Stones: Racial Thought and Violence in Colonial Zanzibar*. Bloomington: Indiana University Press, 2011.

Glaude, Eddie S., Jr. *Exodus! Religion, Race, and Nation in Early Nineteenth-Century Black America*. Chicago: University of Chicago Press, 2000.

Glazier, Stephen D. *Encyclopedia of African and African-American Religions*. New York: Routledge, 2001.

Gomez, Michael A. *Diasporic Africa: A Reader*. New York: New York University Press, 2006.

———. *Exchanging Our Country Marks: The Transformation of African Identities in the Colonial and Antebellum South*. Chapel Hill: University of North Carolina Press, 1998.

Gonsalves, Ralph. "The Rodney Affair and Its Aftermath." *Caribbean Quarterly* 25, no. 3 (1979): 1–24.

Grant, Colin. *Negro with a Hat: The Rise and Fall of Marcus Garvey and His Dream of Mother Africa*. New York: Oxford University Press, 2008.

Gray, Obika. "Predation Politics and the Political Impasse in Jamaica." *Small Axe* 7, no. 1 (2003): 72–94.

———. *Radicalism and Social Change in Jamaica, 1960–1972*. Knoxville: University of Tennessee Press, 1991.

Hall, Douglas. *Free Jamaica, 1835–1865: An Economic History*. New Haven, CT: Yale University Press, 1959.

Hall, Stuart. "Cultural Identity and Diaspora." In *Colonial Discourse and Post-Colonial Theory: A Reader*, edited by Laura Chrisman and Patricia Williams. New York: Columbia University Press, 1994.

Hansen, Holger Bernt. "The Colonial Control of Spirit Cults in Uganda." In *Revealing Prophets: Prophecy in Eastern African History*, edited by David M. Anderson and Douglas H. Johnson. Athens: Ohio University Press, 1995.

Hansin, Katrin. *Rasta, Race and Revolution: The Emergence and Development of the Rastafari Movement in Socialist Cuba*. London: Lit Verlag, 2006.

Harris, Joseph E. *African American Reactions to War in Ethiopia: 1936–1941*. Baton Rouge: Louisiana State University Press, 1994.

———. *Global Dimensions of the African Diaspora*. 2nd ed. Washington, DC: Howard University Press, 1993.

Hartman, Saidiya V. *Lose Your Mother: A Journey along the Atlantic Slave Route*. New York: Farrar, Straus and Giroux, 2008.

Hatch, John Charles. *Two African Statesmen: Kaunda of Zambia and Nyerere of Tanzania*. Chicago: Regnery, 1976.

Hegel, G. W. F. *The Philosophy of History*. Translated by J. Sibree. New York: Dover, 2004.

Helton, Laura, ed. "The Question of Recovery: Slavery, Freedom, and the Archive." Special issue, *Social Text* 33, no. 4–125 (2015): 1–18.

Henry, Paget. *Caliban's Reason: Introducing Afro-Caribbean Philosophy*. New York: Routledge, 2000.

Henry, Paget, and Paul Buhle. *C. L. R. James's Caribbean*. Durham, NC: Duke University Press, 1992.

Heron, Taitu, and Yanique Hume. "Stepping Out: Peter Tosh and the Dynamics of Afro-Caribbean Existence." *Caribbean Quarterly* 58, no. 4 (2012): 25–49.

Higman, B. W. "Household Structure and Fertility on Jamaican Slave Plantations: A Nineteenth Century Example." *Population Studies* 27, no. 3 (1973): 527–50.

———. "The Slave Populations of the British Caribbean: Some Nineteenth Century Variations." *Social History* 9, no. 18 (1976): 237–55.

Hill, Robert A. *Dread History: Leonard P. Howell and Millenarian Visions in the Early Rastafarian Religion*. Chicago: Research Associates/School Times/Frontline, 2001.

———, ed. *The Marcus Garvey and Universal Negro Improvement Association Papers*. 9 vols. Berkeley: University of California Press, 1983.

Hintzen, Percy. "The Caribbean: Race and Creole Ethnicity." In *A Companion to Racial and Ethnic Studies*, edited by David Theo Goldberg and John Solomos, 475–94. Oxford: Blackwell, 2002.

Holt, Thomas C. *The Problem of Freedom: Race, Labor, and Politics in Jamaica and Britain, 1832–1938*. Baltimore: Johns Hopkins University Press, 1992.

Homiak, John P. "The 'Ancient of Days' Seated Black: Eldership, Oral Tradition and Ritual in Rastafari Culture." PhD diss., Brandeis University, 1985.

———. "Never Trade a Continent for an Island: Rastafari Diasporic Practice, Globalisation, and the African Renaissance." In *A United States of Africa?*, edited by Eddy Maloka. Pretoria: Africa Institute of South Africa, 2001.

———. "Rastafari." In *Encyclopedia of African and African-American Religions*, edited by Stephen D. Glazier, 257. New York: Routledge, 2001.

———. "When Goldilocks Met Dreadlocks: Reflections on the Contributions of Carole D. Yawney to Rastafari Studies." In *We Must Start with Africa: Foundations of Rastafari Scholarship*, edited by Jahlani Niaah and Erin MacLeod, 56–116. Kingston: University of the West Indies Press, 2013.

Hopkins, Elizabeth. "The Nyabingi Cult of Southwestern Uganda." In *Protest and Power in Black Africa*, edited by Robert I. Rotberg and Ali A. Mazrui. New York: Oxford University Press, 1970.

Houser, George M. *No One Can Stop the Rain: Glimpses of Africa's Liberation Struggle*. New York: Pilgrim, 1989.

Hunwick, J. O. "African Slaves in the Mediterranean World." In *Global Dimensions of the African Diaspora*, 2nd ed., edited by Joseph E. Harris, 289–324. Washington, DC: Howard University Press, 1993.

Hutton, Clinton, and Nathaniel Samuel Murrell. "Rastas' Psychology and Blackness, Resistance, and Somebodiness." In *Chanting Down Babylon: The Rastafari Reader*, edited by Nathaniel Samuel Murrell, William D. Spencer, and Adrian Anthony McFarlane, 36–54. Philadelphia: Temple University Press, 1998.

Hydén, Göran. *Beyond Ujamaa in Tanzania: Underdevelopment and an Uncaptured Peasantry*. Berkeley: University of California Press, 1980.

———. "Mao and Mwalimu: The Soldier and the Teacher as Revolutionary." *Transition* 34 (1967–68): 24–30.

———. *Political Development in Rural Tanzania*. Nairobi, Kenya: East African Publishing House, 1969.

Iliffe, John. *A Modern History of Tanganyika*. Cambridge: Cambridge University Press, 1979.

Ingle, Clyde R. *From Village to State in Tanzania: The Politics of Rural Development*. Ithaca, NY: Cornell University Press, 1972.

Ishemo, Shubi L. "A Symbol That Cannot Be Substituted: The Role of Mwalimu JK Nyerere in the Liberation of Southern Africa, 1955–1990." *Review of African Political Economy* 27, no. 83 (2000): 85–94.

Ishii, Miho. "African Rastafari: The Development of a Socio-Religious Movement in Urban Tanzania." *Japanese Journal of Cultural Anthropology* 63 (1998): 259–82.

Iton, Richard. *In Search of the Black Fantastic: Politics and Popular Culture in the Post–Civil Rights Era*. Oxford: Oxford University Press, 2008.

Ivaska, Andrew M. *Cultured States: Youth, Gender, and Modern Style in 1960s Dar es Salaam*. Durham, NC: Duke University Press, 2011.

James, C. L. R. *At the Rendezvous of Victory: Selected Writings*. London: Allison and Busby, 1984.

———. *A History of Pan-African Revolt*. Oakland, CA: PM Press, 2012.

———. *Nkrumah and the Ghana Revolution*. Westport, CT: Hill, 1977.

———. "Towards the Seventh: The Pan-African Congress—Past, Present and Future." *Ch'indaba* 1, no. 2 (1976).

Jayasuriya, Shihan de S. *The African Diaspora in Asian Trade Routes and Cultural Memories.* Lewiston, NY: Mellen, 2010.

———. *African Identity in Asia: Cultural Effects of Forced Migration.* Princeton, NJ: Wiener, 2008.

Jennings, Michael. "'Almost an Oxfam in Itself': Oxfam, Ujamaa and Development in Tanzania." *African Affairs* 101 (2002): 509-30.

———. "We Must Run While Others Walk": Popular Participation and Development Crisis in Tanzania, 1961-9." *Journal of Modern African Studies* 41, no. 2 (2003): 63-187.

Johnson, Michele A., and Brian L. Moore. *"They Do as They Please": The Jamaican Struggle for Cultural Freedom after Morant Bay.* Kingston: University of the West Indies Press, 2011.

Johnston, Harry. *A History of the Colonization of Africa by Alien Races.* New York: Cooper Square, 1966.

Karioki, James N. *Tanzania's Human Revolution.* University Park: Penn State University Press, 1979.

Kariuki, Josiah. *Mau Mau Detainee: The Account by a Kenya African of His Experiences in Detention Camps, 1953-1960.* New York: Oxford University Press, 1976.

Kelley, Robin D. G. *Freedom Dreams: The Black Radical Imagination.* Boston: Beacon Press, 2002.

———. "The World the Diaspora Made: C. L. R. James and the Politics of History." In *Rethinking C. L. R. James: A Critical Reader,* edited by Grant Farred, 103-30. Cambridge, MA: Blackwell, 1996.

Khadiagala, Gilbert M. *Allies in Adversity: The Frontline States in Southern African Security, 1975-1993.* Athens: Ohio University Press, 1994.

Kilby, Kenneth, and Elliott Leib. "Kumina, the Howellite Church and the Emergence of Rastafarian Traditional Music in Jamaica." *Jamaica Journal* 19, no. 3 (1986): 22-28.

King, Kenneth. "James E. K. Aggrey: Collaborator, Nationalist, Pan-African." *Canadian Journal of African Studies* 3, no. 3 (1969): 511-30.

King, Stephen A. *Reggae, Rastafari, and the Rhetoric of Social Control.* Jackson: University Press of Mississippi, 2002.

Lake, Obiagele. *Rastafari Women: Subordination in the Midst of Liberation Theology.* Durham, NC: Carolina Academic Press, 1998.

Lal, Priya. *African Socialism in Postcolonial Tanzania: Between the Village and the World.* New York: Cambridge University Press, 2015.

———. "Maoism in Tanzania: Material Connections and Shared Imaginaries." In *Mao's Little Red Book: A Global History,* edited by Alexander Cook. New York: Cambridge University Press, 2014.

———. "Self-Reliance and the State: The Multiple Meanings of Development in Early Post-Colonial Tanzania." *Africa: Journal of the International African Institute* 82, no. 2 (2012): 212-34.

Lamming, George. *In the Castle of My Skin.* Ann Arbor: University of Michigan Press, 1991.

———. *The Pleasures of Exile.* Ann Arbor: University of Michigan Press, 1991.

Lee, Hélène, and Stephen Davis. *The First Rasta: Leonard Howell and the Rise of Rastafarianism.* Chicago: Hill, 2003.

Levi, Darrell E. *Michael Manley: The Making of a Leader.* Kingston: University of the West Indies Press, 1997.

Lewis, Rupert Charles. "Jamaican Black Power in the 1960s." In *Black Power in the Caribbean*, edited by Kate Quinn, 53–75. Gainesville: University Press of Florida, 2014.

———. "Marcus Garvey and the Early Rastafarians: Continuity and Discontinuity." In *Chanting Down Babylon: The Rastafari Reader*, edited by Nathaniel Samuel Murrell, William D. Spencer, and Adrian Anthony McFarlane, 145–58. Philadelphia: Temple University Press, 1998.

———. *Walter Rodney: 1968 Revisited.* Kingston: University of the West Indies Press, 1994.

———. *Walter Rodney's Intellectual and Political Thought.* Detroit: Wayne State University Press, 1998.

Lofchie, Michael F. "Agrarian Socialism in the Third World: The Tanzanian Case." *Comparative Politics* 8, no. 3 (1976): 479–99.

———. *The Political Economy of Tanzania: Decline and Recovery.* Philadelphia: University of Pennsylvania Press, 2014.

MacLeod, Erin C. *Visions of Zion: Ethiopians and Rastafari in the Search for the Promised Land.* New York: New York University Press, 2014.

Maddox, Gregory, and James Giblin. *In Search of a Nation: Histories of Authority and Dissidence in Tanzania.* Oxford: Currey, 2005.

Mair, Lucille Mathurin. *A Historical Study of Women in Jamaica: 1655–1844.* Kingston: University of the West Indies Press, 2006.

Makalani, Minkah. *In the Cause of Freedom: Radical Black Internationalism from Harlem to London, 1917–1939.* Chapel Hill: University of North Carolina Press, 2011.

Maloka, Eddy, ed. *A United States of Africa?* Pretoria: Africa Institute of South Africa, 2001.

Manji, Ambreena. "Gender and the Politics of the Land Reform Process in Tanzania." *Journal of Modern African Studies* 36, no. 4 (1998): 645–67.

Manley, Beverley. *The Manley Memoirs.* Kingston: Randle, 2008.

Manley, Michael. "Grenada in the Context of History: Between Neocolonialism and Independence." *Caribbean Review* 12 (1983): 7–9, 45–47.

———. *Jamaica: Struggle in the Periphery.* London: Oxford University Press, 1982.

———. *The Politics of Change: A Jamaican Testament.* Washington, DC: Howard University Press, 1975.

———. *A Voice in the Work-Place: Reflections on Colonialism and the Jamaican Worker.* London: Deutsch, 1975.

Manley, Rachel. *Horses in Her Hair: A Granddaughter's Story.* Toronto: Key Porter, 2008.

———. *In My Father's Shade: A Daughter's Insight into the Man behind the Prime Minister's Mask.* London: Black Amber, 2004.

Markle, Seth. "'Book Publishers for a Pan-African World': Drum and Spear Press and Tanzania's Ujamaa Ideology." *Black Scholar* 37, no. 4 (2008): 16–26.

Mars, Perry, and Alma H. Young. *Caribbean Labor and Politics: Legacies of Cheddi Jagan and Michael Manley.* Detroit: Wayne State University Press, 2004.

Matera, Marc. *Black London: The Imperial Metropolis and Decolonization in the Twentieth Century.* Berkeley: University of California Press, 2015.

Mawby, Spencer. *Ordering Independence: The End of Empire in the Anglophone Caribbean, 1947–69.* London: Palgrave Macmillan, 2012.

Mazrui, Ali A. "Tanzaphilia." *Transition* No. 31 (June–July 1967): 20–26.

Mbughuni, Azaria. "Tanzania and the Pan African Quest for Unity, Freedom, and Independence in East, Central, and Southern Africa: The Case of the Pan African Freedom Movement for East and the Central Africa/Pan African Freedom Movement for East Central and South Africa," *Journal of Pan African Studies* 7, no. 4 (October 2014): 211–38.

McClendon, James H. *C. L. R. James's Notes on Dialectics.* Lanham, MD: Lexington, 2005.

Meeks, Brian, and Folke Lindahl. *New Caribbean Thought: A Reader.* Kingston: University of the West Indies Press, 2001.

Mercer, Kobena. *Welcome to the Jungle: New Positions in Black Cultural Studies.* New York: Routledge, 1994.

Meriwether, James. *Proudly We Can Be Africans: Black Americans and Africa, 1935–1961.* Chapel Hill: University of North Carolina Press, 2002.

Middleton, Darren J. N. *Rastafari and the Arts: An Introduction.* New York: Routledge, 2015.

Milburn, Josephine Fishel. "The Fabian Society and the British Labour Party." *Western Political Quarterly* 11, no. 2 (1958): 319–39.

Ministry of Lands. *Report of the Presidential Commission of Inquiry into Land Matters.* Dar es Salaam: Housing and Urban Development, Government of the United Republic of Tanzania, 1994.

Minter, William. *Apartheid's Contras: An Inquiry into the Roots of War in Angola and Mozambique.* Johannesburg: Witwatersrand University Press, 1994.

Minter, William, Gail Hovey, and Charles Cobb Jr., eds. *No Easy Victories: African Liberation and American Activists over a Half Century, 1950–2000.* Trenton, NJ: Africa World Press, 2008.

Miran-Guyon, Marie, and Jean-Louis Triaud. "Islam." In *The Oxford Handbook of Modern African History,* edited by John Parker and Richard Reid, 243–62. Oxford: Oxford University Press, 2013.

Mitchell, Michele. *Righteous Propagation: African Americans and the Politics of Racial Destiny after Reconstruction.* Chapel Hill: University of North Carolina Press, 2004.

Monson, Jamie. *Africa's Freedom Railway: How a Chinese Development Project Changed Lives and Livelihoods in Tanzania.* Bloomington: Indiana University Press, 2011.

Moore, Brian L., and Michele A. Johnson. *Neither Led nor Driven: Contesting British Cultural Imperialism in Jamaica, 1865–1920.* Kingston: University of the West Indies Press, 2004.

Morrow, Sean, Brown Maaba, and Loyiso Pulumani. *Education in Exile: SOMAFCO, the African National Congress School in Tanzania, 1978 to 1992.* Cape Town: HSRC Press, 2004.

Moyer, Eileen. "Street-Corner Justice in the Name of Jah: Imperatives for Peace among Dar es Salaam Street Youth." *Africa Today* 51, no. 3 (2005): 31–58.

Mpangala, Gaudens P. "Tanzania's Support to the Liberation Struggle in Southern Africa." In *Sites of Memory: Julius Nyerere and the Liberation Struggle of Southern Africa*, edited by Haroub Othman. Zanzibar: Zanzibar International Film Festival, 2007.

Mudimbe, V. Y. *The Invention of Africa: Gnosis, Philosophy, and the Order of Knowledge.* Bloomington: Indiana University Press, 1988.

Mwakikagile, Godfrey. *Relations between Africans and African Americans: Misconceptions, Myths and Realities.* Dar es Salaam: New Africa Press, 2007.

Naphtali, Karl Phillpotts. *The Testimony of His Imperial Majesty Emperor Haile Selassie I, Defender of the Faith.* Washington, DC: Zewd, 1999.

Nellis, John. *A Theory of Ideology: The Tanzanian Example.* London: Oxford University Press, 1972.

Nettleford, Rex. "Foreword." In *Rastafari in the New Millennium: A Rastafari Reader*, edited by Michael Barnett, x. Syracuse, NY: Syracuse University Press, 2012.

———. *Identity, Race and Protest in Jamaica.* New York: Morrow, 1972.

Niaah, Jahlani, and Erin MacLeod, eds. *Let Us Start with Africa: Foundations of Rastafari.* Kingston: University of the West Indies Press, 2013.

Nkrumah, Kwame. *Ghana: The Autobiography of Kwame Nkrumah.* New York: International Publishers, 1971.

Nye, Joseph S. *Pan-Africanism and East African Integration.* Cambridge, MA: Harvard University Press, 1965.

Nyerere, Julius K. *The Arusha Declaration Teach-In.* Dar es Salaam: Information Services, 1967.

———. *The Arusha Declaration Ten Years After.* In *African Socialism in Practice: The Tanzanian Experience*, edited by Andrew Coulson. Nottingham, England: Spokesman, 1979.

———. "Education for Liberation." Delivered at the Dag Hammarskjold Seminar, Dar es Salaam, May 20, 1974. Reprinted in *Sites of Memory: Julius Nyerere and* the Liberation Struggle of Southern Africa, edited by Haroub Othman. Zanzibar: Zanzibar International Film Festival, 2007.

———. *Freedom and Socialism/Uhuru na Ujamaa: A Selection from Writings and Speeches 1965-1967.* New York: Oxford University Press, 1968.

———. *Freedom and Unity/Uhuru na Umoja: A Selection from Writings and Speeches 1952-1965.* London: Oxford University Press, 1967.

———. "The Mwongozo—TANU Guidelines 1971." In *African Socialism in Practice: The Tanzanian Experience*, edited by Andrew Coulson. Nottingham, England: Spokesman, 1979.

———. *Ujamaa: Essays on Socialism.* Dar es Salaam: Oxford University Press, 1968.

Othman, Haroub, ed. *Sites of Memory: Julius Nyerere and the Liberation Struggle of Southern Africa.* Zanzibar: Zanzibar International Film Festival, 2007.

Owens, Joseph. *Dread: The Rastafarians of Jamaica.* Kingston: Sangster's, 1976.

Padmore, George. *Pan-Africanism or Communism?* New York: Roy, 1956.

Palmer, Colin A. "The African Diaspora." *Black Scholar* 30, nos. 3-4 (2001): 56-59.

———. *Eric Williams and the Making of the Modern Caribbean.* Chapel Hill: University of North Carolina Press, 2006.

Pankhurst, Richard. *The Ethiopians: A History.* Malden, MA: Blackwell, 1998.

Parsons, Timothy. *The 1964 Army Mutinies and the Making of Modern East Africa.* Westport, CT: Praeger, 2003.

———. *The Second British Empire: In the Crucible of the Twentieth Century.* Lanham, MD: Rowman and Littlefield, 2014.

Paton, Diana. *The Cultural Politics of Obeah: Religion, Colonialism and Modernity in the Caribbean World.* Cambridge: Cambridge University Press, 2015.

Patterson, Orlando. *The Children of Sisyphus.* New York: Houghton Mifflin, 1965.

Payne, Anthony. *Politics in Jamaica.* London: Hurst, 1988.

Pease, Edward R. *The History of the Fabian Society.* London: Cass, 1963.

Perry, Kennetta Hammond. *London Is the Place for Me: Black Britons, Citizenship, and the Politics of Race.* New York: Oxford University Press, 2015.

Pierre, Jemima. *The Predicament of Blackness: Postcolonial Ghana and the Politics of Race.* Chicago: University of Chicago Press, 2013.

Plummer, Brenda Gayle. *In Search of Power: African Americans in the Era of Decolonization, 1956-1974.* Cambridge: Cambridge University Press, 2013.

Pollard, Velma. *Dread Talk: The Language of Rastafari.* Kingston: Canoe, 2000.

Post, Ken. *Arise Ye Starvelings: The Jamaican Labour Rebellion of 1938 and Its Aftermath.* The Hague: Nijhoff, 1978.

Powell, Eve Troutt. *A Different Shade of Colonialism: Egypt, Great Britain, and the Mastery of the Sudan.* Berkeley: University of California Press, 2003.

Prashad, Vijay. *The Poorer Nations: A Possible History of the Global South.* London: Verso, 2012.

Pratt, Cranford. *The Critical Phase in Tanzania, 1945-1968: Nyerere and the Emergence of a Socialist Strategy.* Cambridge: Cambridge University Press, 1976.

———. "Julius Nyerere: Reflections on the Legacy of Socialism." *Canadian Journal of African Studies* 33, no. 1 (1999): 137–52.

Price, Charles. "The Cultural Production of a Black Messiah: Ethiopianism and the Rastafari." *Journal of Africana Religions* 2, no. 3 (2014): 418–33.

Putnam, Lara. *Radical Moves: Caribbean Migrants and the Politics of Race in the Jazz Age*. Chapel Hill: University of North Carolina Press, 2013.

Quinn, Kate, ed. *Black Power in the Caribbean*. Gainesville: University Press of Florida, 2014.

Rajabu, John. "Rastafari in Tanzanian Cultural Context." Master's thesis, University of Dar es Salaam, 1998.

Rickford, Russell. *We Are an African People: Independent Education, Black Power, and the Radical Imagination*. Oxford: Oxford University Press, 2016.

Robinson, Cedric. *Black Marxism: The Making of the Black Radical Tradition*. Chapel Hill: University of North Carolina Press, 2000.

Robinson, Randall. *Defending the Spirit: A Black Life in America*. New York: Dutton, 1998.

Rodney, Walter. "The Black Scholar Interviews: Walter Rodney." *Black Scholar* 6, no. 3 (November 1974): 38–47.

———. "Contemporary Political Trends in the English Speaking Caribbean." *Black Scholar* 7, no. 1 (1975): 15–21.

———. "Education in Africa and Contemporary Tanzania." *Education and Black Struggle—Notes from the Colonized World*, edited by the Institute of the Black World, Harvard Education Review (monograph no. 2): 82–99.

———. *The Groundings with My Brothers*. London: Bogle-L'Ouverture, 1969.

———. *Walter Rodney Speaks: The Making of an African Intellectual*. Trenton, NJ: Africa World Press, 1990.

Roper, Hugh Trevor. *The Rise of Christian Europe*. London: Thames and Hudson, 1966.

Rowe, Maureen. "The Woman in Rastafari." *Caribbean Quarterly* 26, no. 4 (1980): 13–21.

Salim, Salim Ahmed. "Mwalimu Julius K. Nyerere and African Unity." In *The Commemorations of Mwalimu Julius K. Nyerere's 79th and 80th Birth Dates*, edited by Gaudens P. Mpangala, Bismarck U. Mwansasu, and Mohammed Omar Maundi. Dar es Salaam: Mwalimu Nyerere Foundation, 2004.

Savishinsky, Neil. "The Baye Faal of Senegambia: Muslim Rastas in the Promised Land?" *Africa* 64, no. 2 (1994): 211–19.

———. "Rastafari in the Promised Land: The Spread of a Jamaican Socioreligious Movement among the Youth of West Africa." *African Studies Review* 37 (1994): 19–50.

Schneider, Leander. "Developmentalism and Its Failings: Why Rural Development Went Wrong in 1960s and 1970s Tanzania." PhD diss., Columbia University, 2003.

———. "'High on Modernity'? Explaining the Failings of Tanzanian Villagization." *African Studies* 66, no. 1 (2007): 9-38.

———. "The Tanzania National Archives." *History in Africa* 30 (2003): 447-54.

Schroeder, Richard A. *Africa after Apartheid: South Africa, Race, and Nation in Tanzania*. Bloomington: Indiana University Press, 2012.

Schuler, Monica. *Alas, Alas, Kongo: A Social History of Indentured African Immigration into Jamaica, 1841-1865*. Baltimore: Johns Hopkins University Press, 1980.

Scobie, Edward. *Black Britannia: A History of Blacks in Britain*. Chicago: Johnson, 1972.

Scott, David. "The Dialectic of Defeat: An Interview with Rupert Lewis." *Small Axe* 5, no. 2 (September 2001): 85-177.

Scott, James C. *Seeing like a State: How Certain Schemes to Improve the Human Condition Have Failed*. New Haven, CT: Yale University Press, 1998.

Scott, William R. "Black Nationalism and the Italo-Ethiopian Conflict 1934-1936." *Journal of Negro History* 63, no. 2 (1978): 118-34.

———. *Sons of Sheba's Race: African-Americans and the Italo-Ethiopian War, 1935-1941*. Bloomington: Indiana University Press, 1993.

Senior, Olive. *Dying to Better Themselves: West Indians and the Building of the Panama Canal*. Kingston: University of the West Indies Press, 2014.

Shack, William A. "Ethiopia and Afro-Americans: Some Historical Notes, 1920-1970." *Phylon* 35, no. 2 (1974): 142-55.

Shaw, George Bernard. *The Fabian Society: Its Early History*. London: Fabian Society, 1892.

Sheller, Mimi. *Citizenship from Below: Erotic Agency and Caribbean Freedom*. Durham, NC: Duke University Press, 2012.

Shepherd, Verene, and Bridget Brereton. *Engendering History: Caribbean Women in Historical Perspective*. New York: St. Martin's, 1995.

Shepherd, Verene A. and Glen L. Richards. *Questioning Creole: Creolisation Discourses in Caribbean Culture*. Kingston: Ian Randle Publishers, 2002.

Shivji, Issa G. *Class Struggles in Tanzania*. New York: Monthly Review Press, 1976.

———. *Not Yet Democracy: Reforming Land Tenure in Tanzania*. Dar es Salaam: IIED/HAKIARDHI/Faculty of Law, University of Dar es Salaam, 1998.

———. *Pan-Africanism or Pragmatism? Lessons of the Tanganyika-Zanzibar Union*. Dar es Salaam: Mkuki Na Nyota, 2008.

———. "Rodney and Radicalism on the Hill, 1966-1974." *Maji Maji* 43 (1974): 29-39.

———. *The Silent Class Struggle*. Dar es Salaam: Tanzania Publishing House, 1973.

———. *Where Is Uhuru? Reflections on the Struggle for Democracy in Africa*. Oxford: Pambazuka, 2009.

Simpson, George E. "The Rastafarian Movement in Jamaica: A Study of Race and Class Conflict." *Social Forces* 34, no. 2 (1955): 167-70.

Smith, Edwin William. *Aggrey of Africa: A Study in Black and White*. New York: Smith, 1930.

Smith, M. G., Roy Augier, and Rex Nettleford. *The Ras Tafari Movement in Kingston, Jamaica*. Kingston: Institute of Social and Economic Research, University of the West Indies, 1960.

Smith, Theophus Harold. *Conjuring Culture: Biblical Formations of Black America*. New York: Oxford University Press, 1994.

Sorenson, John. *Imagining Ethiopia: Struggles for History and Identity in the Horn of Africa*. New Brunswick, NJ: Rutgers University Press, 1993.

Spencer, William David. *Dread Jesus*. London: Society for Promoting Christian Knowledge, 1999.

———. "The First Chant: Leonard Howell's The Promised Key." In *Chanting Down Babylon: The Rastafari Reader*, edited by Nathaniel Samuel Murrell, William D. Spencer, and Adrian Anthony McFarlane, 361–89. Philadelphia: Temple University Press, 1998.

Sterling, Marvin. *Babylon East: Performing Dancehall, Roots Reggae and Rastafari in Japan*. Durham, NC: Duke University Press, 2010.

Stewart, Robert J. *Religion and Society in Post-Emancipation Jamaica*. Knoxville: University of Tennessee Press, 1992.

Stoger-Eising, Viktoria. "Ujamaa Revisited: Indigenous and European Influences in Nyerere's Social and Political Thought." *Africa* 70, no. 1 (2000): 118–43.

Stolberg, Claus, and Swithin R. Wilmot. *Plantation Economy, Land Reform and the Peasantry in a Historical Perspective: Jamaica, 1838–1980*. Kingston: Ebert, 1992.

Sutherland, Bill, and Matt Meyer. *Guns and Gandhi in Africa: Pan-African Insights on Nonviolence, Armed Struggle and Liberation in Africa*. Trenton, NJ: Africa World Press, 2000.

Tafari-Ama, Imani M. "Rastawoman as Rebel: Case Studies in Jamaica," chapter 7 in *Chanting Down Babylon: A Rastafari Reader*, edited by Nathaniel Samuel Murrell, William D. Spencer, and Adrian Anthony McFarlane. Philadelphia, PA: Temple University Press, 1998.

———. "Resistance Without and Within: Reasonings on Gender Relations in Rastafari." In *Rastafari in the New Millennium*, edited by Michael Barnett, 190–21. Syracuse, NY: Syracuse University Press, 2012.

Tate, Lessie. "The Power of Pan Africanism: Tanzanian/African American Linkages, 1947–1997." PhD diss., University of Illinois at Urbana-Champaign, 2015.

Thiong'o, Ngugi wa. "Beyond Nativism: An Interview with Ngugi wa Thiong'o," by Angela Lamas Rodriguez. *Research in African Literatures* 35, no. 3 (2004): 161–67.

Thomas, Deborah A. *Exceptional Violence: Embodied Citizenship in Transnational Jamaica*. Durham, NC: Duke University Press, 2011.

Thomas, Deborah, John L. Jackson Jr. and Junior "Gabu" Wedderburn. *Bad Friday: Rastafari after Coral Gardens*. Documentary. Distributed by Third World Newsreel, 2011.

Thompson, Dudley. *From Kingston to Kenya: The Making of a Pan-Africanist Lawyer.* Dover, MA: Majority Press, 1993.

Thompson, Vincent Bakpetu. *Africa and Unity: The Evolution of Pan-Africanism.* Harlow, UK: Longmans, 1969.

Tripp, Aili Mari. *Changing the Rules: The Politics of Liberalization and the Urban Informal Economy in Tanzania.* Berkeley: University of California Press, 1997.

Turner, Mary. *Slaves and Missionaries: The Disintegration of Jamaican Slave Society, 1787–1834.* Urbana: University of Illinois Press, 1982.

Turner, Terisa, and Bryan J. Ferguson, eds. *Arise Ye Mighty People! Gender, Class, and Race in Popular Struggles.* Trenton, NJ: Africa World Press, 1994.

Van Dijk, Frank Jan. "Sociological Means: Colonial Reactions to the Radicalization of Rastafari in Jamaica, 1956–1959." *NWIG: New West Indian Guide/Nieuwe West Indische Gids* 69, no. 1/2 (1995): 67–101.

———. "The Twelve Tribes of Israel: Rasta and the Middle Class." *New West Indian Guide* 62, nos. 1–2 (1988): 1–26.

Walters, Ronald W. *Pan Africanism in the African Diaspora: An Analysis of Modern Afrocentric Political Movements.* Detroit: Wayne State University Press, 1993.

Warner-Lewis, Maureen. "African Continuities in the Rastafari Belief System." *Caribbean Quarterly* 39, nos. 3–4 (1993): 108–23.

———. *Central Africa in the Caribbean: Transcending Time, Transforming Cultures.* Kingston: University of West Indies Press, 2003.

———. *Guinea's Other Suns: The African Dynamic in Trinidad Culture.* Dover, MA: Majority Press, 1991.

Waters, Anita M. *Race, Class, and Political Symbols: Rastafari and Reggae in Jamaican Politics.* New Brunswick, NJ: Transaction, 1985.

Watkins-Owens, Irma. *Blood Relations: Caribbean Immigrants and the Harlem Community, 1900–1930.* Bloomington: Indiana University Press, 1996.

West, Michael O. "The Seeds Are Sown: The Impact of Garveyism in Zimbabwe in the Interwar Years." *International Journal of African Historical Studies* 35, nos. 2–3 (2002): 335–62

Westcott, N. J. "An East African Radical: The Life of Erica Fiah." *Journal of African History* 22, no. 1 (1981): 85–101.

Westmaas, Nigel. "An Organic Activist: Eusi Kwayana, Guyana, and Global Pan-Africanism." In *Black Power in the Caribbean*, edited by Kate Quinn, 159–80. Gainesville: University Press of Florida, 2014.

White, Carmen. "Living in Zion: Rastafarian Repatriates in Ghana, West Africa," *Journal of Black Studies* 37, no.5 (May 2007): 677–709.

White, Timothy. *Catch a Fire: The Life of Bob Marley.* New York: Holt, 2006.

Wilkins, Fanon Che. "In the Belly of the Beast: Black Power, Anti-Imperialism, and the African Liberation Solidarity Movement 1968–1975." PhD diss., New York University, 2001.

Williams, K. M. *The Rastafarians.* London: Ward Lock Educational, 1981.

Williams, Patrick, and Laura Chrisman, eds. *Colonial Discourse and Post-Colonial Theory: A Reader*. New York: Columbia University Press, 1994.

Williams, Prince, and Michael Kuelker. *Book of Memory: A Rastafari Testimony*. Kingston: Caribsound, 2004.

Wilmot, Swithin. "Black Space/Room to Manoeuvre: Land and Politics in Trelawny in the Immediate Post-Emancipation Period." In *Plantation Economy, Land Reform, and the Peasantry in a Historical Perspective: Jamaica 1830–1890*, edited by Claus Stolberg and Swithin Wilmot. Kingston: Ebert, 1992.

Woodard, Komozi. *A Nation within a Nation: Amiri Baraka (LeRoi Jones) and Black Power Politics*. Chapel Hill: University of North Carolina Press, 1999.

Woodson, Carter G. *The Mis-Education of the Negro*. Trenton, NJ: Africa World Press, 1990.

Yawney, Carole D. "Exodus: Rastafari, Repatriation, and the African Renaissance." In *A United States of Africa?*, edited by Eddy Maloka. Pretoria: Africa Institute of South Africa, 2001.

——. "Moving with the Dawtas of Rastafari: From Myth to Reality." In *Arise Ye Mighty People! Gender, Class and Race in Popular Struggles*, edited by Terisa E. Turner with Bryan J. Ferguson. Trenton, NJ: Africa World Press, 1994.

——. "Rastafarian Sistren by the Rivers of Babylon." *Canadian Woman Studies* 5, no. 2 (1983): 73–75.

Yawney, Carole D., and John P. Homiak. "Rastafari." In *Encyclopedia of African and African-American Religions*, edited by Stephen D. Glazier, 263. New York: Routledge, 2001.

Young, Crawford. *The African Colonial State in Comparative Perspective*. New Haven, CT: Yale University Press, 1994.

Index

Note: page numbers in italics refer to figures.

Aesthetics, of dreadlocks, 29
Africa: in Caribbean identity, 180–81; cultural identity and, 171–72; "forgetting" of, 65; polygyny in, 142; repatriation to, 1–2, 4–5, 184–85; slavery and, 4; spelling of, 6; utopian promise of, 72. *See also* Precolonial Africa
African Americans: for African liberation, 67; citizenship of, 69; Pan African Skills Project for, 67–68; Tanzania travel by, 67; *warejeaji* 67
African Commercial Association, 53–54
African identity, 1
African liberation: African Americans for, 67; education for, 177; James for, 178; Lusaka Manifesto of 1969 influence on, 71–72; Michael Manley, for, 94; monetary contribution for, 75; of Mozambique, 102; Julius Nyerere for, 61–63; race in, 94; repatriation for, 136, 154, 185; Tanzania and, 61–63, 65–67, 174
African National Congress (ANC): multiracialism and, 126; in Tanzania, 76
African Reform Church: by Claudius Henry, 44, 200n116; socialism and, 44–45
African Society for Cultural Relations with Independent Africa (ASCRIA), 70
Afrikan nation, 20–21, 36–37
"Afro-pessimism," 186–87

Aggrey, James, 53
Agrarian reform, 96
Antiapartheid activism: by Iman Mani, 121; by Michael Manley, 93
Anticolonial activism: education for, 176, 221n24; pan-Africanism and, 13–14, 20–22, 79–80, 180–81, 193n42; by Walter Rodney, 83
Archive: code of silence influence on, 10; of repatriation, 8, 193n30; transnational human networks as, 7; trodding diaspora and, 6–7, 184
Art: by Ras Daniel Heartman, 122–23; by Edna Manley, 103
Arusha Declaration (Julius Nyerere): government push for, 147–48; on human equality, 60; self-reliance in, 60–61, 155–56
Attitude of mind, 92

Babylon: capitalism and, 40–41, 43; Jamaica as, 1–2, 7, 12–13, 20, 22; slavery and, 27–28
Bangi, 29–30, 86–87, 183–84
Baraka, Amiri, 48
Battle of Adwa, 49–50
Beyen, Melaku E., 30–31
Bingi: language of, 160; by Nyabingi, 35–36
Black intellectuals, 171
Black Jacobins, The (C. L. R. James), 178–79
Black Man Speaks (Small), 45–46

Black power movement: Jamaican diversity of, 81–82; Julius Nyerere and, 101; Tanzania influence on, 5–6, 48

Black radicalism: black intellectuals and, 171; independence resonating with, 171–72; Jamaica Labour Party against, 81, 207nn9–10; by C. L. R. James, 168, 179–80; by Michael Manley, 79; metropole in, 166; pan-Africanism and, 12–13, 92–93, 184; by Rastafarians, 18–19; religion and, 170; Walter Rodney on, 45–46, 201n122

Black theology, 25–26

Blyden, Edward Wilmot, 26

Bobo Shanti: communal living by, 44; as mansions, 10–11, 193n33

Bones, Jah: on England, 111; on Rastafari, 13

Book project, 157–58

Brooks, Fred, 73

Cacoon Castle, 97–98

Capitalism: Babylon and, 40–41, 43; from colonialism, 64–65, 187–88; Great Depression from, 40–41; racism from, 21–22, 40–41, 188; Universal Rastafari Improvement Association against, 40–41

Caribbean: Creole nationalism of, 80–81; Tanzania and, 69–71

Caribbean identity: Africa in, 180–81; by C. L. R. James, 178–81; language and, 179

Carrington, Vernon, 30

Carruthers, Jacob: Ras Bupe Karudi and, 15; for repatriation, 140

Catholicism, 27

Christianity: in colonialism, 22–23, 143, 195n8; C. L. R James against, 172–73; Myalism from, 23–24, 195nn15–16; Pukumina and, 24; Rastafari incorporation of, 15–16; Twelve Tribes of Israel for, 31–32, 198n52; Zion adoption of, 24

Christie, Joseph, 97

Citizenship: of African Americans, 69; Jamaica and, 18, 109, 194n54; of Ras Bupe Karudi, 114; race influence on, 125; for Tanzania, 107, 115–16, 119, 132–33

Clarke, John Henrik, 15

Class dynamics: in Jamaica, 92; by Twelve Tribes of Israel, 34–35; in *Ujamaa* pamphlet, 92

Clothing, *164*

Code of silence, 10

Cold War, 72–73

Colonial education, 177–78

Colonialism: capitalism from, 64–65, 187–88; Christianity in, 22–23, 143, 195n8; cultural identity after, 188; dread talk against, 27–28; "forgetting" Africa by, 65; Leonard Howell against, 42–43; marriage and, 142–43; reggae music and, 86; in Tanzania, 161–62

Commission of Inquiry into Land Matters, 146–47, 217n44

Communal living: by Bobo Shanti, 44; Ras Bupe Karudi, for, 150–51; of Mbigiri commune, 183, 222n5; radical Left and, 43; for Tanzania, 96, 120

Communism: Rastafarians and, 43; *ujamaa* influenced by, 57–58, 203n51

Consciousness, 64–65

Creole nationalism, 80–81

Cultural identity: of Africa, 171–72; after colonialism, 188

Dar es Salaam: Liberation Committee in, 62–63, 75–76, 192n18; Solomon Mahlangu Freedom College in, 76

Decolonization: nation-state influenced by, 106–7, 213n3; political independence and, 13; race and, 131; by repatriation, 16; transnational

approaches for, 56–57; by trodding diaspora, 3; in West Indies, 172
Democratic Socialism: The Jamaican Model: on ideology, 89; by People's National Party, 87–88
Diet, 29–30
Doctrinal diversity, 32
Dreadlocks, 29
Dread talk, 27–28

East African federation, 54–55
Education: for African liberation, 177; for anticolonial activism, 176, 221n24; Ras Bupe Karudi, and, 153, 157, 185–86, 222n9; Kisembo Karudi and, 153; in Tanzania, 155–56, 175–76
"Education for Self-Liberation" (Julius Nyerere), 176–77, 221n26
"Education for Self-Reliance" (Julius Nyerere), 175–76
Emperor Haile Selassie I Rainbow Circle Throne Ancient Mystical Order of Nyabingi: clothing of, *164*; members of, 160–61, *162–63*; "upside-down trinity" symbol by, *163*
England: Bones on, 111; Paul Gilroy on, 10–11; Ras Daniel Heartman in, 124–25; Jamaican immigration to, 109; Ras Bupe Karudi from, 108; Kisembo Karudi in, 113–14, 182; land tenure by, 148–49; Norman Manley in, 109–10; Portugal against, 72; Rastafari in, 11–12, 110; Second World War influence on, 108–9; Twelve Tribes of Israel in, 111–12; Universal Rastafari Improvement Association in, 10–11, 110–11, 193n34; women conference in, 112
Ethiopia: Battle of Adwa and, 49–50; Italian invasion of, 154, 179–80; pan-Africanism of, 50; Tanzania replacement of, 17, 49
Ethiopianism: black theology from, 25–26; Edward Wilmot Blyden for, 26; Garveyism influenced by, 26; in Jamaica, 26
Ethiopian World Federation (EWF): by Melaku Beyen, 30–31, 197n44; Twelve Tribes of Israel from, 30–31, 197nn46–47

Fabian socialism: by Fabian Society, 89–90, 209n52, 209n54; Harold Laski for, 90; Michael Manley for, 89–90, 209n56, 209n58; morality of, 91; Julius Nyerere for, 89–91, 209n62
Fabian Society, 89–90, 209n52, 209n54
Family dynamics: of Kisembo Karudi, 152–53; in repatriation, 143–44; of Ras Kwetenge Sokoni, 143–44
Fiah, Erica: African Commercial Association by, 53–54; for Garveyism, 53–54; *Kwetu* by, 54; Tanganyika African Welfare and Commercial Association by, 53–54
Fighting: by Liberation Committee, 61–62; Universal Rastafari Improvement Association for, 62
Finances: by C. L. R. James, 173; by Ras Bupe Karudi, 120–21; by Kisembo Karudi, 138, 151–52, 182; of Tanzania, 141, 166–67
Foreign policy, 92, 94, 186
"Forgetting" Africa, 65
Freedom fighters, 94–95
Free Villages, 41–42, 200n105
Frente de Libertação de Moçambique (FRELIMO): on Mozambique, 75–76, 95–96; Universal Rastafari Improvement Association on, 155
Fund-raising: by Ras Bupe Karudi, 138–42; by Joshua Mkhululi, 141–42

Ganja: Gun Court laws influence on, 86–87, 208n40; Michael Manley against, 86–87; in ritual practice, 29–30, 183–84

Garvey, Marcus: Ethiopianism and, 26; as prophet, 27
Garveyism: for Catholicism, 27; Ethiopianism influence on, 26; Fiah for, 53–54; miscegenation and, 37–38; Rastafarians celebration of, 26–27, 196n28, 196n30; against Revivalism, 27
Gender identities: nationalism and, 10; in Universal Rastafari Improvement Association, 21, 36–37
Gender inequality: trodding diaspora and, 135–36, 167–68; Twelve Tribes of Israel and, 39; of women, 38–40
Germans, 148
Ghana, 48–49
Gilroy, Paul, 11–12
Global South, 187
God: of Rastafarians, 1; Haile Selassie I as, 1–2, 32, 160–61, 173–74, 188–89, 198n56
Great Depression, 40–41
Great Revival of 1860, 24
Grenada, invasion of, 116
Groundings with My Brothers, The (Walter Rodney), 82–83
"Grow a daughter," 152
Gun Court laws, 86–87, 208n40

Hasfal, Frank, 45
Heartman, Ras Daniel: art by, 122–23; in England, 124–25; immunization of, 125; Joshua Mkhululi and, 123–24, 124; *Not Far Away* by, 123; passport of, 106, 123–24; in Tanzania, 123–24
Henry, Claudius: African Reform Church by, 44, 200n116; People's National Party association with, 85
History: from Ras Bupe Karudi, 7; from Joshua Mkhululi, 7; written sources for, 8, 193n30
Howell, Leonard: against colonialism, 42–43; Pinnacle by, 41–42, 200n105

Human equality: *Arusha Declaration* on, 60; in socialism, 59–60

Ideology, 89
Immigration, 121–22
Immunization, 125
Independence: black radicalism and, 171–72; of Jamaica, 80–81; nationalism for, 186–87
"I-n-I," 28–29, 32–33
Institute of Accountancy Arusha (IAA), 156
International Monetary Fund, 16–17
Italian invasion, 154, 179–80
Ital lifestyle, 30

Jamaica: agrarian reform in, 96; as Babylon, 1–2, 7, 12–13, 20, 22; Black power movement diversity in, 81–82; citizenship and, 18, 109, 194n54; class dynamics in, 92; England immigration and, 109; Ethiopianism in, 26; independence of, 80–81; liberation fund by, 93–94; Joshua Mkhululi on, 116; multiracialism of, 102–3, 129–30; Julius Nyerere, visiting of, 98–100; passport for, 133; race in, 128–29, 215n65; Rastafari emergence in, 20; Walter Rodney in, 82; Haile Selassie I in, 102; Tanzania and, 15, 17, 76–77, 79–80, 96, 186; women of, 38–39, 199n80
Jamaica Labour Party (JLP): against Black radicalism, 81, 207nn9–10; boycott by, 99, 101; neocolonialism by, 83–84, 117, 214n39; Mortimo Planno against, 101
Jamaican identity, 1
James, C. L. R.: for African liberation, 178; *The Black Jacobins* by, 178–79; black radicalism by, 168, 179–80; for book project, 158; Caribbean identity by, 178–81; against Chris-

tianity, 172–73; colonial education of, 177–78; finances by, 173; Ras Bupe Karudi and, 18, 140–41, 169, 172–73, 181; Julius Nyerere supported by, 174–75; on Pan African Congress, 14, 171; precolonial Africa and, 169; religion and, 173–74; for repatriation, 174, 220n16; for Tanzania, 49, 174–75

Karudi, Kisembo: education and, 153; in England, 113–14, 182; family dynamics of, 152–53; finances by, 138, 151–52, 182; Ras Bupe Karudi and, 1, 112–13, 191n1; marriage of, 152–53; pan-Africanism by, 182–83; repatriation by, 9–10, 182

Karudi, Ras Bupe: book project by, 157–58; Jacob Carruthers and, 15; citizenship of, 114; John Henrik Clarke and, 15; for communal living, 150–51; death of, 184; education and, 153, 157, 185–86, 222n9; from England, 108; finances by, 120–21; fund-raising by, 138–42; "grow a daughta" by, 152; history from, 7; C. L. R. James and, 18, 140–41, 169, 172–73, 181; Kisembo Karudi, K and, 1, 112–13, 191n1; land grant for, 146, 217n41; malaria of, 144–45; masculinity of, 137–38; Pan African Congress and, 154–55, 218n76; passport of, 20, 106; private information of, 138–39; repatriation and, 9–10, 17, 32–34, 112–13, 135, 214n25; in Tanzania, 114; women view by, 136–37

Kelley, Robin, 12–13

Kwayana, Eusi: African Society for Cultural Relations with Independent Africa by, 70; against Pan African Congress, 14

Kwetu, 54

Land grant: belonging from, 18; Commission of Inquiry into Land Matters for, 146–47, 217n44; for Ras Bupe Karudi, 146, 217n41; local people against, 150; for Iman Mani, 150; repatriation legitimized by, 146; by Tanzania, 135, 145, 167; for women, 147–48

Land Lease Project, 96–97

Land Ordinance of 1923, 148–49

Land tenure, 148–49

Language: of bingi, 160; Caribbean identity and, 179

Laski, Harold, 90

Lewis, Rupert, 83

Liberation and Support Committee, 154

Liberation Committee: in Dar es Salaam, 62–63, 75–76, 192n18; fighting by, 61–62; of Organization of African Unity, 5, 49, 61–63, 75–76, 192n18

Liberation fund, 93–94

Luqman, Al Hajj Anas M., 139–40

Lusaka Manifesto of 1969, 71–72

Makonnen, Tafari, 1–2

Malaria, 144–45

Mani, Iman: antiapartheid activism by, 121; immigration by, 121–22; as journalist, 185; land grant for, 150

Manley, Beverley, 103–4, 212n118

Manley, Edna, 103

Manley, Michael: for African liberation, 94; antiapartheid activism by, 93; black radicalism by, 79; for Fabian Socialism, 89–90, 209n56, 209n58; foreign policy of, 92, 94, 186; freedom fighters relationship with, 94–95; against ganja, 86–87; Beverley Manley, marriage with, 103–4, 212n118; New Left courting by, 84; Joshua Nkomo and, 94–95, 211n85; Julius Nyerere and, 15, 17–18, 79–80, 87–92, 102; of People's National

Manley, Michael (cont.)
Party, 83–84, 207n23; *The Politics of Change* by, 87–89; as prime minister, 78–79; race of, 78; on reggae music, 78, 86; Tanzania visit by, 74–75, 79, 206n127

Manley, Norman: in England, 109–10; for multiracialism, 102–3

Mansions: Bobo Shanti as, 10–11, 193n33; Nyabingi as, 10–11, 193n33; of Rastafarian movement, 10–11; Twelve Tribes of Israel as, 10–11, 30, 111–12, 193n33; Universal Rastafari Improvement Association and, 21

Marley, Bob: Eileen Moyer on, 158–59; for People's National Party, 85–86; reggae music of, 12, 158–59

Marriage: colonialism and, 142–43; of Kisembo Karudi, 152–53

Marxism: Pinnacle and, 43; religion and, 170

Masculinity, 137–38

Mbigiri commune, 183, 222n5

Mekonnen, Ras Mabondo, 160–61, 219n100

Men: repatriation by, 9–10, 135–36; of Universal Rastafari Improvement Association, 21, 36–38

Middle class: Joshua Mkhululi as, 34; women of, 39

Miscegenation, 37–38

Mkhululi, Joshua: for cooperative village, 117–18; death of, 184; fundraising by, 141–42; Ras Daniel Heartman and, 123–24, *124*; history from, 7; Institute of Accountancy Arusha by, 156; on Jamaica, 116; Liberation and Support Committee by, 154; as middle class, 34; Julius Nyerere and, 108, 115–16; pan-Africanism by, 14–15; repatriation and, 17, 32–33, 80; Shiloah and, 33; for Tanzania, 51–52, 108, 115; for *ujamaa*, 156

Mogadishu Declaration, 72

Morality, 91

Moyer, Eileen, 158–59

Mozambique: African liberation of, 102; Frente de Libertação de Moçambique report on, 75–76, 95–96

Multiracialism: African National Congress and, 126; of Jamaica, 102–3, 129–30; Norman Manley for, 102–3; of Tanganyika Citizenship Bill, 129

Myalism: from Christianity, 23–24, 195nn15–16; Great Revival of 1860 and, 24; Revivalism and, 24–25

National Black United Front (NBUF), 139

National culture, 68

Nationalism: gender identities and, 10; for independence, 186–87; nation-state and, 51–52, 120;

Nation-state: decolonization influence on, 106–7, 213n3; ideological debates of, 73; nationalism and, 51–52, 120; of Tanzania, 18, 76, 107, 117–19; *ujamaa* framework from, 52

Neocolonialism: by Jamaica Labour Party, 83–84, 117, 214n39; Walter Rodney and, 83

Neoliberalism: "Afro-pessimism" and, 186–87

Neto, Agostinho, 71–72

New Left, 84

Nkomo, Joshua, 94–95, 211n85

Not Far Away, 123

Nyabingi: bingi by, 35–36; drumming session of, *165*; as mansions, 10–11, 193n33; origins of, 35, 198nn69–70; by Ato Kidani Roberts, 159–60; women of, 40; from Youth Black Faith, 35–36

Nyerere, Julius: for African liberation, 61–63; *Arusha Declaration* by, 60; Black power and, 101; Cold War addressed by, 72–73; for East African federation, 54–55; "Education for

Self-Liberation" by, 176–77, 221n26; "Education for Self-Reliance" by, 175–76; for Fabian socialism, 89–91, 209n62; of Global South, 187; Jamaica visit by, 98–100; C. L. R. James hope for, 174–75; Michael Manley and, 15, 17–18, 79–80, 87–92, 102; Joshua Mkhululi and, 108, 115–16; for one-party system, 88, 102; Pan-African Freedom Movement of East, Central and Southern Africa by, 57; for pan-Africanism, 119, 127–28; People's National Party and, 98–99; *The Politics of Change* influenced by, 87–88; for precolonial Africa, 64; president step down by, 16–17; religion and, 170; against *Review and Land Tenure Policy*, 149; of Tanzania, 5, 65–66, 192n16; Dudley Thompson and, 55–56, 99–100, 211n104; tribute for, 100; *ujamaa* by, 52–55, 57–59, 74, 202nn33–34

"Nyerere Farm," 97–98

Obeah, 23–24
One-party system, 88, 102
Operation Vijiji, 6
Organization of African Unity (OAU): Liberation Committee of, 5, 49, 61–63, 75–76, 192n18; from Haile Selassie I, 50–51
Origins discourses, in trodding diaspora, 4
Our Own (Hasfal), 45

Padmore, George, 56
Pan African Congress (PAC): C. L. R. James on, 14, 171; Ras Bupe Karudi and, 154–55, 218n76; Eusi Kwayana against, 14
Pan-African Freedom Movement of East, Central and Southern Africa (PAFMECSA), 57

Pan-Africanism: anticolonial activism and, 13–14, 20–22, 79–80, 180–81, 193n42; black radicalism and, 12–13, 92–93, 184; of Ethiopia, 50; of Ghana, 48–49; ideological positions of, 14, 194n47; by Kisembo Karudi, 182–83; Robin Kelley on, 12–13; Al Hajj Anas M. Luqman for, 139–40; by Joshua Mkhululi, 14–15; for nationalism, 187–88; Julius Nyerere for, 119, 127–28; race and, 104–5, 125; repatriation and, 189; Haile Selassie I and, 46–47, 50; in Tanganyika, 54; Tanzania and, 52, 66–67, 74–76, 107–8, 133–34, 213n8; by Dudley Thompson, 55–56; trodding diaspora and, 76; from *ujamaa*, 52–53; by women, 182

Pan African Skills Project (PASP): for African Americans, 67–68; Walter Rodney for, 69–70

Passport: of Ras Daniel Heartman, 106, 123–24; for Jamaica, 133; of Ras Bupe Karudi, 20, 106

People's National Party (PNP): *Democratic Socialism: The Jamaican Model* by, 87–88; Claudius Henry association with, 85; Land Lease Project by, 96–97; Michael Manley and, 83–84, 207n23; Bob Marley and, 85–86; Julius Nyerere and, 98–99; Rastafarian culture appropriated by, 79, 84–85, 208n26; Hugh Shearer against, 98–99; socialism by, 83–84, 87–88; Dudley Thompson and, 55–56

Pinnacle: as Free Villages, 41–42, 200n105; by Leonard Howell, 41–42, 200n105; Marxism and, 43; socialism of, 41–43

Planno, Mortimo: against Jamaica Labour Party, 101; Dudley Thompson mission with, 86

Policy making, 74

Political independence, 13
Politics of Change, The (Michael Manley): Julius Nyerere influence on, 87–88; on two-party system, 88–89
Polygyny, 142
Portugal, 72
Precolonial Africa: C. L. R. James and, 169; Julius Nyerere for, 64; socialism and, 58–59
Prime minister, 78–79
Prophet Gad, 30–32, 198n52
Pukumina, 24
Putnam, Lara, 170

Race: in African liberation, 94; citizenship influenced by, 125; decolonization and, 131; in Jamaica, 128–29, 215n65; of Michael Manley, 78; pan-Africanism and, 104–5, 125; Rastafarian philosophy of, 130–31; by Tanganyika African National Union, 125–27; in Tanzania, 125–27; Universal Rastafari Improvement Association and, 131–32
Racism, 21–22, 40–41, 188
Radical Left, 43
Rastafarians. See C. L. R. James; Ras Bupe Karudi; Kisembo Karudi; Michael Manley; Joshua Mkhululi; Julius Nyerere; Haile Selassie I.
Reggae music: colonialism and, 86; Michael Manley on, 78, 86; of Bob Marley, 12, 158–59
Religion: black radicalism and, 170; C. L. R. James and, 173–74; Marxism and, 170; Julius Nyerere and, 170; obeah and, 23–24; Lara Putnam on, 170; repatriation and, 189; slavery and, 23, 195n11, 195n13
Repatriation: to Africa, 1–2, 4–5, 184–85; for African liberation, 136, 154, 185; archive of, 8, 193n30; Jacob Carruthers for, 140; decolonization and, 16; family dynamics in, 143–44; C. L. R. James for, 174, 220n16; Ras Bupe Karudi and, 9–10, 17, 32–34, 112–13, 135, 214n25; by Kisembo Karudi, 9–10, 182; land grant legitimizing of, 146; by men, 9–10, 135–36; Joshua Mkhululi and, 17, 32–33, 80; National Black United Front for, 139; pan-Africanism and, 189; religion and, 189; by Ato Kidani Roberts, 123–25, 124; for Tanzania, 107, 120, 141–42, 167, 183; Twelve Tribes of Israel for, 31, 122; by Universal Rastafari Improvement Association, 11–12, 21, 194n5; women and, 136–38, 167–68
Residency, 125, 132, 215n74
Review and Land Tenure Policy, 149
Revivalism: Garveyism against, 27; Myalism and, 24–25; Twelve Tribes of Israel and, 24–25; Youth Black Faith against, 25, 196n20, 196n23
Roberts, Ato Kidani: Nyabingi practice by, 159–60; repatriation by, 123–25, 124; as *wajamaika weusi*, 163–64
Rodney, Walter: anticolonial activism by, 83; banning of, 81–83, 207n15; *Black Man Speaks* and, 46; on black radicalism, 45–46, 201n122; Fred Brooks correspondence with, 73; *The Groundings with My Brothers* by, 82–83; in Jamaica, 82; Rupert Lewis on, 83; neocolonialism and, 83; for Pan African Skills Project, 69–70; on Rastafarians, 17; Rodney Affair of 1968 and, 81–82, 207n15; on Tanzania, 69
Rodney Affair of 1968, 81–82, 207n15
Rod of correction, 103–4

Second World War, 108–9
Selassie I, Haile: as God, 1–2, 32, 160–61, 173–74, 188–89, 198n56; in Jamaica, 102; loyalty to, 22–23; Ras Mabondo Mekonnen worship of, 160–61, 219n100; Organization of

African Unity from, 50–51; ousting of, 51; pan-Africanism and, 46–47, 50; as Shiloah, 33; teachings of, 50–51; veneration of, 12–13, 50
Self-reliance: in *Arusha Declaration*, 60–61, 155–56; "Education for Self-Reliance" on, 175–76
Sexual deviance, 37
Shamba, 183
Shearer, Hugh, 98–99
Shiloah, 33
Sister May, 30, 40
Slavery: Africa and, 4; Babylon and, 27–28; religion and, 23, 195n11, 195n13; women influenced by, 36–37
Small, Robin "Jerry," 45–46
Socialism: African Reform Church and, 44–45; as attitude of mind, 92; human equality in, 59–60; by People's National Party, 83–84, 87–88; of Pinnacle, 41–43; precolonial Africa and, 58–59; theology of, 58–59
Sokoni, Ras Kwetenge: family dynamics of, 143–44; polygyny by, 142
Solomon Mahlangu Freedom College (SOMAFCO), 76
State building, 15–16
State documents, 8–9
Swahili, 66

Tanganyika: James Aggrey in, 53; Germans acquisition of, 148; Land Ordinance of 1923 for, 148–49; pan-Africanism in, 54
Tanganyika African National Union (TANU), 125–27
Tanganyika African Welfare and Commercial Association (TAWCA), 53–54
Tanganyika Citizenship Bill, 129
Tanganyika Education Trust, 91
Tanzania: African Americans travel to, 67; African liberation and, 61–63, 65–67, 174; African National Congress in, 76; Amiri Baraka on, 48; black power movement influenced by, 5–6, 48; Caribbean and, 69–71; citizenship for, 107, 115–16, 119, 132–33; colonialism of, 161–62; communal living for, 96, 120; education in, 155–56, 175–76; Ethiopia replaced by, 17, 49; finances of, 141, 166–67; Ghana and, 48–49; Ras Daniel Heartman in, 123–24; Jamaica and, 15, 17, 76–77, 79–80, 96, 186; C. L. R. James for, 49, 174–75; Ras Bupe Karudi, in, 114; land grant by, 135, 145, 167; Michael Manley visit to, 74–75, 79, 206n127; Joshua Mkhululi for, 51–52, 108, 115; national culture of, 68; nation-state of, 18, 76, 107, 117–19; Julius Nyerere of, 5, 65–66, 192n16; Pan-African Freedom Movement of East, Central and Southern Africa for, 57; pan-Africanism and, 52, 66–67, 74–76, 107–8, 133–34, 213n8; race in, 125–27; Rastafarian philosophy for, 161–62, 183–84, 188–89; repatriation for, 107, 120, 141–42, 167, 183; Walter Rodney on, 69; romanticized notions dispelled by, 73; trodding diaspora in, 136; *ujamaa* of, 5, 46–47, 49, 58, 117–18, 203n55; *Utamaduni wa kitaifa* of, 63; war involvement of, 71; Zion and, 2–3, 47, 201n125
Tanzania National Archive (TNA), 8–9
Theology, 25–26, 58–59
Thomaz, Americo, 71
Thompson, Dudley: Julius Nyerere and, 55–56, 99–100, 211n104; George Padmore influence on, 56; pan-Africanism by, 55–56; People's National Party and, 55–56; Mortimo Planno mission with, 86
Transnational human networks, 7

Transnationalism: for decolonization, 56–57; of trodding diaspora, 3, 132–33, 191n8

Tripartite election, 126–27

Trodding diaspora: archive and, 6–7, 184; Continental Africans traveling for, 73–74, 206n123; decolonization by, 3; gender inequality and, 135–36, 167–68; origins discourses in, 4; pan-Africanism and, 76; "roots" of, 1, 4, 191n9; in Tanzania, 136; transnationalism of, 3, 132–33, 191n8

Twelve Tribes of Israel: by Vernon Carrington, 30; for Christianity, 31–32, 198n52; class dynamics by, 34–35; doctrinal diversity by, 32; in England, 111–12; from Ethiopian World Federation, 30–31, 197nn46–47; gender inequality and, 39; as mansions, 10–11, 30, 111–12, 193n33; Prophet Gad reverence by, 30–32, 198n52; for repatriation, 31, 122; Revivalism and, 24–25; Sister May of, 30, 40

Two-party system, 88–89

Ujamaa: for consciousness, 64–65; against "forgetting" Africa, 65; ideal citizen and, 63; Joshua Mkhululi for, 156; nation-state framework for, 52; by Julius Nyerere, 52–55, 57–59, 74, 202nn33–34; pamphlet on, 59–61, 92; pan-Africanism from, 52–53; policy making for, 74; *shamba* and, 183; of Tanzania, 5, 46–47, 49, 58, 117–18, 203n55; against white supremacy, 63–64

Ujamaa pamphlet, 59–61, 92

Unity, 21

Universal Rastafari Improvement Association (URIA): Afrikan nation by, 36–37; against capitalism, 40–41; in England, 10–11, 110–11, 193n34; for fighting, 62; on Frente de Libertação de Moçambique, 155; gender identities in, 21, 36–37; mansions and, 21; men of, 21, 36–38; race and, 131–32; repatriation by, 11–12, 21, 194n5; against sexual deviance, 37

University of the West Indies, 34, 45–46, 69–70, 74, 82, 98, 100

"Upside-down trinity" symbol, *163*

Utamaduni wa kitaifa, 63

Utopia, 72

Villagization, 6

Wajamaika weusi: residency for, 125, 132, 215n74; Roberts as, 163–64

War, 71–72

Warejeaji, 67

Wealth, 164–65

West Indies, 50, 54–55, 86, 115–16, 129, 172

White supremacy: by tripartite election, 126–27; *ujamaa* against, 63–64

Wicken, Joan, 91

Women: England conference on, 112; gender inequality of, 38–40; of Jamaica, 38–39, 199n80; Ras Bupe Karudi's views on, 136–37; land grant for, 147–48; of middle class, 39; of Nyabingi, 40; pan-Africanism by, 182; repatriation and, 136–38, 167–68; slavery influence on, 36–37

Youth Black Faith: Nyabingi from, 35–36; against Revivalism, 25, 196n20, 196n23

Zion: as home, 28; Tanzania and, 2–3, 47, 201n125

www.ingramcontent.com/pod-product-compliance
Lightning Source LLC
Chambersburg PA
CBHW022208221125
35799CB00025B/862